AF449218

D. H. Lawrence's "Lady"

D. H. Lawrence's "Lady"

A NEW LOOK AT
LADY CHATTERLEY'S LOVER

EDITED BY MICHAEL SQUIRES
AND DENNIS JACKSON

THE UNIVERSITY OF GEORGIA PRESS   ATHENS

© 1985 by the University of Georgia Press
Athens, Georgia 30602
All rights reserved

Wood engraving by Michael McCurdy
Text design by Sandra Strother Hudson
Set in 11 on 13 Goudy Old Style

The paper in this book meets the guidelines for
permanence and durability of the Committee on
Production Guidelines for Book Longevity of the
Council on Library Resources.

Printed in the United States of America
89 88 87 86 85   5 4 3 2 1

Library of Congress Cataloging in Publication Data
Main entry under title:

D. H. Lawrence's "Lady".

Includes index.
1. Lawrence, D. H. (David Herbert), 1885–1930. Lady
Chatterley's lover—Addresses, essays, lectures.
I. Squires, Michael. II. Jackson, Dennis, 1945–   .
PR6023.A93L313   1985   823'.912   84-181
ISBN 0-8203-0724-6

For permission to quote from an unpublished letter by D. H.
Lawrence, the editors thank Laurence Pollinger Limited and the
Estate of Frieda Lawrence Ravagli.

Contents

A Note on Citations

All current editions of *Lady Chatterley's Lover* are textually corrupt, and since the definitive text is not yet complete, we quote from the Florence edition of 1928, which Lawrence supervised. For the convenience of readers, however, we cite page numbers of the Grove Press "Black Cat" edition, widely available in America.

The following abbreviations of frequently cited sources are used throughout the book:

CL	*The Collected Letters of D. H. Lawrence.* Edited by Harry T. Moore. 2 vols. New York: Viking, 1962.
FLC	Version 1 of *Lady Chatterley's Lover,* published as *The First Lady Chatterley.* New York: Dial, 1944. Reprint. London: Heinemann, 1972.
JTLJ	Version 2 of *Lady Chatterley's Lover,* published as *John Thomas and Lady Jane.* London: Heinemann, 1972; New York: Viking, 1972.
LCL	Version 3 of *Lady Chatterley's Lover.* Florence: Orioli, 1928. Reprint. New York: Grove, Revised Black Cat Edition, 1982.
Phoenix	*Phoenix: The Posthumous Papers of D. H. Lawrence.* Edited by Edward D. McDonald. 1936. Reprint. New York: Viking, 1972.
Phoenix II	*Phoenix II: Uncollected, Unpublished, and Other Prose Works by D. H. Lawrence.* Edited by Warren Roberts and Harry T. Moore. New York: Viking, 1970.

Introduction

Although D. H. Lawrence's last novel appeared over fifty years ago, its literary reputation is not yet secure; the scent of pornography clings. Too, a novelist's early work often seems more accessible to readers than does the late work, which is typically darker, more complex, more deeply shaded with ideology. Hence the frequent preference for *Pride and Prejudice* over *Mansfield Park*, for *David Copperfield* over *Our Mutual Friend*, for *The Mill on the Floss* over *Middlemarch*, for *Far from the Madding Crowd* over *Jude the Obscure*, for *A Portrait of the Artist as a Young Man* over *Ulysses*, for *Sons and Lovers* over *Lady Chatterley's Lover*. But the twelve essays collected here demonstrate that *Lady Chatterley*, while not perhaps Lawrence's masterpiece, is indeed a major work whose artistic strength and intellectual vitality amply justify serious criticism.

Lawrence's novel evolved curiously. When he began drafting it about 22 October 1926, in the pine woods near Florence, Italy, he apparently thought it would be a novella like *The Virgin and the Gipsy*. Dissatisfied by the episodic thinness of his first draft, Lawrence began a second version about December first, patiently developing his themes and characters, but later deciding that the novel lacked force and concentration. In November 1927, though increasingly ill, he began the third and final version—which most of these essays assess— finishing it on 8 January 1928. Because his regular publishers, Secker and Knopf, would consider only an emasculated edition, Lawrence was left to do his own copy editing, designing, and proofreading. In the summer of 1928 he published the novel privately, helped only by his friend "Pino" Orioli, a Florentine bookseller. With uncommon skill and persistence, Lawrence and Orioli distributed hundreds of copies by mail—some to England, some to America, many of them confiscated by customs authorities. Unable to obtain a copyright, Lawrence watched, helpless at first, as pirated editions appeared—and profits disappeared. Not until May 1929 did he combat the pirates with his inexpensive Paris edition of the novel.

In the decades that followed, *Lady Chatterley* ignited controversy the world over. *The First Lady Chatterley*, published by the Dial Press in 1944, was found obscene in a magistrate's court on Staten Island, though the decision was later overturned. In Japan *Lady Chatterley's Lover* prompted three major court trials between 1950 and 1957, the Japanese Supreme Court eventually branding the book obscene. Both in America and in England, where the unexpurgated text had never been legally published, *Lady Chatterley* inspired landmark judicial decisions. In 1959 Judge Frederick vanPelt Bryan ruled that the U.S. postmaster had no legal right to ban the Grove Press unexpurgated edition from the mails; and in 1960 a similar proceeding against the Penguin edition took place in London, where thirty-five distinguished witnesses, testifying for the book, helped to secure a favorable verdict. These decisions empowered legislators to reform the obscenity laws of both countries and to win greater freedom for the printed word.

The initial reaction of critics was also extreme, ranging from a rhapsody on the novel's "magnificent" achievement (*New York Sun*) to a venomous assault on its "depravity" (*John Bull*)—and that division of response, though more moderate, has persisted through the Lawrence revival of the fifties into our own time. Important books by F. R. Leavis (1956), Eliseo Vivas (1960), and George Ford (1965) either ignore or seriously fault the novel. At the same time, solid critical assessments by Mark Spilka (1955), Mark Schorer (1957), Graham Hough (1957), Julian Moynahan (1963), H. M. Daleski (1965), and Scott Sanders (1974) eloquently defend the novel's intelligence, artistry, and humanity. In the past decade many specialized studies have also appeared—of Lawrence's treatment of women, of myth and romance, of Lawrence's biography, of symbolism, and of the composition of the three versions.

The attraction of the twelve essays collected here is not only that they offer perceptive and original readings, but that they view the novel as it could not have been viewed fifty years ago, freshly assessing its links to modernist ideas, to the novels of other writers, to Lawrence's *ouevre* and literary heritage, and to history.

Opening the collection are three essays that examine the social or intellectual significance of Lawrence's ideas in *Lady Chatterley's Lover*. Scott Sanders explores their meaning for our contemporary world, threatened anew by imminent catastrophe. Lydia Blanchard, using Foucault's *History of Sexuality* as her frame, evaluates the novel's language as it both expresses and questions sexual experience. T. H. Adamowski probes the intellectual continuities between Lawrence and Sartre, discovering unexpected affinities.

The three essays that follow widen our critical perspective by connecting Lawrence's novel to the fiction of other writers. Whereas Frederick P. W. McDowell dissects the concerns of art and life that Lawrence shares with Forster, James C. Cowan examines Lawrence's surprising use of Joycean epiphanies, and Zack Bowen sets forth the striking parallels between *Lady Chatterley* and *Ulysses*.

Two essayists explore *Lady Chatterley* in the light of Lawrence's other work. Gavriel Ben-Ephraim considers the union of Connie and Mellors as a culmination of Lawrence's earlier efforts to balance male and female polarities. Focusing on *The Virgin and the Gipsy*, Keith Cushman analyzes the ways in which this novella, completed early in 1926, is a precursor of the third version.

The novel's allusive and mythical texture is examined in two essays. Dennis Jackson identifies and explicates a central strand of the novel's literary allusions; and Evelyn J. Hinz and John J. Teunissen discuss the novel's subtle uses of the Ares/Aphrodite/Hephaestus mythical complex.

Finally, two authors reexamine the novel's historical context. Craig Munro provides a critical account of a 1930 edition of *Lady Chatterley's Lover*, which Lawrence appears to have authorized. And from his unique perspective as Lawrence's literary executor, Gerald J. Pollinger describes the novel's fortunes in the commercial world.

In his lifetime Lawrence fought courageously for his novel, stressing its regenerative phallic qualities—the things "which will save us from horrors," he says in a letter (*CL* 1047). And that, we believe, is what these dozen essays accomplish: they defend the claim that *Lady Chatterley's Lover* is a work of major social, intellectual, and literary importance—a work that has centrally shaped our culture.

D. H. Lawrence's "Lady"

SCOTT R. SANDERS

Lady Chatterley's Loving
and the Annihilation Impulse

While a thunderstorm crashes outside, stirring the remnant trees of Sherwood Forest, the game-keeper shelters in his hut with Constance Chatterley. Secure amidst the deluge ("It was like being in a little ark in the Flood"), he ruminates about doomsday: "Quite nice! To contemplate the extermination of the human species and the long pause that follows before some other species crops up, it calms you more than anything else. And if we go on in this way, with everybody, intellectuals, artists, governments, industrialists and workers all frantically killing off the last human feeling, the last bit of their intuition, the last healthy instinct; if it goes on in algebraical progression, as it is going on: then ta-tah! to the human species!" (*LCL* 279). Is that warning, or is that yearning? The gamekeeper seems half to dread the prospect of extermination, half to relish it. A similar ambivalence runs through most of Lawrence's doomsday visions, which appear with impressive frequency in his writings from the war years onward, beginning with *The Rainbow* and *Women in Love*; continuing in essays and letters during the 1920s; extending into all three versions of his last novel, *Lady Chatterley's Lover*;[1] and occupying the center of his last book, appropriately entitled *Apocalypse*.

In works written during and immediately after the Great War, the yearning for annihilation frequently predominates, as when Rupert Birkin in *Women in Love* declares, "I abhor humanity, I wish it was swept away. It could go, and there would be no *absolute* loss, if every human being perished to-morrow."[2] Lawrence himself seemed at times during the war to feel that the only hope for the renewal of the world was a holocaust, a violent collapse of industrial civilization. Yet even in those years of bitterness, his visions of doom were most often warnings; in a letter of 1915 he wrote, "The disintegrating process of the war has become an internal evil, so vast as to be almost unthinkable, so nearly overwhelming us, that we stand on the very brink of oblivion" (*CL* 375). By the time he came to write the three versions of *Lady Chatterley's Lover,* there remained only the slightest trace of his earlier ambivalence regarding the prospect of annihilation, as the lines from the gamekeeper quoted above would suggest. Instead, those last novels provide wholehearted warnings about what Constance Chatterley, in *John Thomas and Lady Jane,* foresees as "the suicide of the human race" (*JTLJ* 288).

When I began reading Lawrence in the late 1960s, I discounted such visions of annihilation as the hyperbole of a writer who had spent too many childhood days listening to readings from the Old Testament, or as the mild hysteria of a man who was convinced humanity had taken a wrong turn, or as the occasional misanthropy of someone who had been sorely used by his contemporaries. I now take these visions much more seriously, for reasons that have less to do with Lawrence's history than with our own.

During the First World War, the latest devices of annihilation, including aerial bombardment and poison gas, were used to kill ten million people. During the Second World War, "improved" weapons led to the annihilation of entire cities, such as Dresden and Hiroshima, and to the death of more than fifty million people. Operating on Jews and Gypsies and Slavs, the Nazis pioneered scientific methods for exterminating races. Since 1945 there have been more than 150 civil and regional wars, each one fought with the newest available weaponry, all of them combined slaughtering a greater number of people than the first two world wars. Most nations on earth continue to devote a large proportion of their wealth, resources, and talent to preparations for war. In the United States during the mid-1980s, for example, roughly half of all federal taxes go to the military, and fully half of all the scientists and technicians in the country are engaged in military research.

An all-out nuclear exchange between the United States and the Soviet Union could kill three hundred million people outright and sentence millions more to lingering death by hunger and disease. The long-term effects of radiation and ecological disruption would extermi-nate many species—perhaps including, within a generation or two, our own. After a million-year struggle to escape the assaults of nature we have constructed machineries of destruction that make plagues and earthquakes seem mild by comparison. The suicide of the human race, of which Lawrence so often warned, is now *literally* possible. How has this come to pass? Why have we pushed ourselves and our planet to this brink of annihilation? There is no deeper mystery, nor any we need more urgently to solve.

Lawrence died in 1930, fifteen years before the first atomic bombs were exploded. Yet he would certainly have recognized the impulse that led to the building of these weapons and to their use on Hiro-shima and Nagasaki. There is nothing new about the human compul-sion to obliterate whatever stands in the way of personal or tribal or national will. Our tools for *acting* on that compulsion are constantly being strengthened, however, and are now commensurate with our most gargantuan jealousies, our most ambitious schemes. Weary of sharing daylight and pasture and praise with his brother, Cain slew Abel, but could use only his bare hands, or perhaps a club or stone, to perform the deed. We are not so limited. Today, a nation possessing nuclear weapons can treat any brother or sister nation as a collective Abel, a rival to be erased. Genocide is only an enlargement, a perfect-ing, of fratricide.

So Lawrence would not have been surprised, although he would doubtless have been dismayed, by the development of tools for exter-mination. In novel after novel, essay after essay, for more than two decades, he traced the origins of human destructiveness to the *desire for mastery*—over nature, over the body, over one's mate, over servant classes and rival nations and whatever appears to resist the personal or collective will. If the mountain blocks your highway, blast a tunnel through it. If the river floods your fields, dam it up. When people of a color or creed different from your own occupy the land you covet, then butcher them, make them gifts of blankets infected with small-pox, tear up their crops and slaughter their game. If a rival nation defies your wishes, point missiles at its cities. The evil effects of the desire for domination were painfully evident to Lawrence in the war, and in the brutalized people and devastated landscape of his native industrial Midlands.

This quest for mastery is founded, according to Lawrence, upon the *illusion of separation:* the illusion that mind can be divorced from body, self from other, humanity from nature. The attitude of domination presupposes a master and something *else* to be mastered. Before "conquering" the flesh or the forest or the enemy, we must first create barriers, imagine distance. We can only bring ourselves to devastate what we have first defined as radically alien. A part of creation—another country, another class, another person, a parcel of forest—is imagined as a *thing,* reduced to the status of an object, and then subjected to our violent will. One can readily think of examples: whales, redwoods, Indians, communists, capitalists, the visiting football team, worshippers of another god; imagined as prey or resources or enemy, each is annihilated first in thought, and then in fact.

We enter a universe that is all of a piece, and with our minds and machines we slice it full of rents—this is Lawrence's persistent message, repeated with increasing urgency toward the end of his life, as in this passage from *Apocalypse:* "We are unnaturally resisting our connection with the cosmos, with the world, with mankind, with the nation, with the family. . . . We *cannot bear connection.* That is our malady. We *must* break away, and be isolate. We call that being free, being individual. Beyond a certain point, which we have reached, it is suicide. Perhaps we have chosen suicide."[3] The most elementary form of this malady is the illusion of the isolated ego, self-sufficient and all-powerful, distinct from flesh and from nature, in competition with other egos. In its epidemic forms the malady spreads to entire tribes and nations, transforming the group into a collective ego. The remedy clearly lies in erasing the illusory barriers we have erected—between mind and body, self and other, humanity and nature.

In tracing the sources of human violence to the desire for mastery and the illusion of separateness, Lawrence was echoing a view common to many of the world's religions. What did Adam and Eve hope to gain from biting the apple, after all, if not godlike power over creation? Lawrence was original, not in his analysis of human destructiveness, but in the psychological acuity and stylistic power with which he rendered both the malady and its remedy. Consider as an illustration that last, gentle novel he wrote three times, about the lady and her gamekeeper.

All three versions of *Lady Chatterley's Lover* open with the same arresting phrase: "Ours is essentially a tragic age." Tragic how? one wonders. Lawrence immediately goes on to explain, with different phrasing in each version, that the age is tragic because "the cataclysm has fallen," the terrible war has occurred, and yet people go on living among the ruins as if nothing has been changed by the half decade of bloodshed. In Lawrence's eyes, the paroxysm of violence that gripped Europe between 1914 and 1918 called into question the most fundamental assumptions of industrial civilization.

Instead of tracing the origins of war to the quest for domination—over nature, over subject classes and colonial peoples, over rival nations—the leaders and ideologists for all sides in the conflict blamed the cataclysm on the "enemy," thus reinforcing the psychology of domination and preparing the way for the Second World War. After that later war, with its vast escalation of violence, Albert Einstein warned: "The unleashed power of the atom has changed everything save our modes of thinking, and thus we drift toward unparalleled catastrophe."[4] The First World War had persuaded Lawrence of the same truth. Long before the unleashing of the atom, he was warning us that we must transform our ways of thinking and feeling if we are to avoid being annihilated by our own murderous inventions.

Clifford Chatterley epitomized for Lawrence those who, resuming power after the Armistice, set about intensifying the very processes that had led to the war. As a member of the ruling class, Clifford insists upon his right to dominate the working class. "What the mass of people want is *masters*," he tells Connie (*JTLJ* 200). Like that earlier industrial magnate in *Women in Love*, Gerald Crich, whom he resembles in so many other respects, Clifford regards his employees as tools, extensions of his will: "The miners were, in a sense, his own men; but he saw them as objects rather than men, parts of the pit rather than parts of life, crude raw phenomena rather than human beings along with him" (*LCL* 50). Here we see the gesture of estrangement which accompanies every gesture of domination and destruction. Those whom you would manipulate or murder, you must first dehumanize.

As an owner of mines, Clifford hurls himself into a mechanized war against nature, succumbing to "the long-enduring ecstasy of the struggle with uncanny Matter. It was as if he fused himself into the very existence of coal and sulphur and petroleum and rock, and lost his humanity, as the trolls have lost theirs, in iron" (*JTLJ* 335). The very earth becomes his antagonist. Just as he refuses to acknowledge the independent life of the miners, so he refuses to acknowledge the life of nature itself. Pheasants exist to be shot, trees to be felled, coal to be mined: objects awaiting the exercise of his sovereign will. He takes on the shape of his imagined opponent, becomes matter wrestling with matter, robot man confronting inanimate nature.

As a husband, Clifford expresses the same desire for mastery over Connie, leading her to fear that "she would become just a half-animate automaton worked entirely from Clifford's will, coming as he willed, going as he willed, thinking only the thoughts he released in her mind, feeling only the feelings he allowed to come forth" (*FLC* 51–52). Although he is more courtly in his dealings with her than in his dealings with the colliers and the coal, he is no less insistent in the exercise of his will. He is emotionally dependent on Connie, to be sure, yet he dominates her in intellectual matters and in the affairs of daily life.

His craving for mastery feeds upon his sense of isolation: "he was finally limited entirely to himself. No breath entered him from any other living being or creature or thing. He was as it were cut off from the breathing contact of the living universe" (*FLC* 37). Here we behold the illusion of separation in its purest form. As his continual reading of the famous idealists—from Plato and Plotinus through Hegel and Rilke—would suggest, Clifford perceives the material universe as an inferior imitation of some higher spiritual realm. His own ego figures prominently in that empyrean. At one point, quoting an idealist philosopher, he proclaims to Connie: "The universe shows us two aspects: on one side it is physically wasting, on the other it is spiritually ascending" (*LCL* 296). Once again, nature takes on the guise of enemy. Clifford fondly dreams of erasing everything that resists the touch, everything that breathes—everything, that is, except himself.

Locked within the fortress of his ego, Clifford regards the rest of the cosmos as an infringement on his bloated self: "He felt that, in the universe, he was a thing apart, and that all the other things in the universe were probably taking away a portion of life he himself might have had. The expansive yellow face of the dandelion irritated him, with its crude yellowness and its exposed foolishness. He preferred the nipped bud, in the rain" (*JTLJ* 246). It would be hard to imagine any attitude more repellent to Lawrence than this jealousy of dandelions, this grotesque inflation of the ego to such proportions that it squeezes out every other creature.

Clifford is a monster of self-importance. But he is also a cripple, and this makes it difficult to judge clearly the role he plays in the symbolic landscape of *Lady Chatterley's Lover*. The war has left him paralyzed from the waist down, forever excluded from any pleasures of the flesh, including sexual intercourse. Is it so shocking that such a man would despise fleshly existence? Lawrence himself conceded, in a later remark on the novel, that it was perhaps clumsy of him to have made Clifford a physical as well as a psychological cripple: "As to whether the 'symbolism' is intentional—I don't know. Certainly not in the beginning, when Clifford was created. When I created Clifford and Connie, I had no idea what they were or why they were. They just came, pretty much as they are. . . . And when I read the first version, I recognized that the lameness of Clifford was symbolic of the paralysis, the deeper emotional or passional paralysis, of most men of his sort and class today" (*Phoenix II* 514). In the novel itself Lawrence takes pains to show, through Connie's recollections and perceptions, that Clifford's contempt for the body and hostility toward the physical universe preceded the war. His paralysis is an outward symptom of an inward condition, just as the war itself was a terrible symptom of the profound disorder at the heart of industrial civilization. As member of the ruling class, as mine owner, husband, ego, Clifford is *a thing apart*. Other people and nature itself only exist as objects of his power. Whatever resists his power he will annihilate, in desire if not in fact. Thus when Connie names the gamekeeper as her lover, Clifford responds by shouting, "[Y]ou ought to be wiped off the face of the earth!" (*LCL* 367). In this bullying owner of mines, Lawrence depicted the psychopathology of the unbridled desire for domination.

Terrified of becoming an "automaton worked entirely from Clifford's will," Connie struggles to free herself from his domineering influence. She struggles, not into the splendid isolation of her own ego, there to become a wielder of power to rival Clifford, but into communion with nature, with the gamekeeper, and, through him, into fitful contact with the local working people. In all her motions of thought and feeling, she moves in a direction contrary to Clifford. He yearns for separation, she for connection. He longs to enslave the colliers, she to understand them. He sets himself up as master of the countryside; she enters sympathetically into the life of the forest, almost as a beast among the trees. He strives to hammer the imprint of his being onto the world, she to decipher the being of the world itself. Whereas Clifford demonstrates those attitudes which had produced the First World War, the deep hatred between classes and the industrial blight, Connie demonstrates those attitudes which, in Lawrence's eyes, might heal the blight and overcome the hatred and prevent future wars.

She does not arrive all at once, or easily, at her new vision of things. Life with Clifford has reduced her to a state of nervous exhaustion: "Connie was aware . . . of a growing restlessness. Out of her disconnection, a restlessness was taking possession of her like madness. . . . Vaguely she knew herself that she was going to pieces in some way. Vaguely she knew she was out of connection: she had lost touch with the substantial and vital world" (*LCL* 54–55). Clifford seems to be reconciled to this state of "disconnection," but Connie suffers from it. Her story in all three versions of the novel is one of painfully restoring connections. The notorious lovemaking with the gamekeeper puts her back in touch with her own body. But even before she lies down for the first time in the keeper's hut, she enters into communion with the forest itself; and this connection, we realize by the end of the novel, is more fundamental and comprehensive than the sexual one: "Constance sat down with her back to a young pinetree, that swayed against her like an animate creature, so subtly rubbing itself against her, the great, alive thing with its top in the wind! And she watched the daffodils sparkle in a burst of sun, that was warm on her face; and she caught the faint tarry scent of the flowers; and gradually everything went still in her, so still, so still and disentangled!" (*JTLJ* 84). Here is the antidote for the frenzy into which life with Clifford has driven her. Instead of feeling diminished by the life of other things (as does Clifford, jealous of the dandelion's glow), Connie feels comforted by this brush with a life greater than her own.

The language in this description of communion with nature, like that in many such descriptions throughout Lawrence's works, is strongly sexual. That "great, alive thing" "so subtly rubbing itself against her" is clearly phallic. And yet—which is primary, the tree or the phallus? Should we read Connie's communion with the forest as a sublimation of her sexual yearning, or should we regard her later sexual enlightenment as a deepening and confirmation of her contact with the animate universe? I hold with the latter view. Consider this description of Connie's reaction to a bout of lovemaking:

> She felt herself filled with new blood, as if the blood of the man had swept into her veins like a strong, fresh, rousing wind, changing her whole self. All her self felt alive, and in motion, like the woods in spring. She could not but feel that a new breath had swept into her body from the man, and that she was like a forest soughing with a new, soft wind, soughing and moving unspoken into bud. All her body felt like the dark interlacing of the boughs of an oak wood, softly humming in a wind, and humming inaudibly with the myriad, myriad unfolding of buds. Meanwhile the birds had their heads laid on their shoulders and slept with delight in the vast interlaced intricacy of the forest of her body. [*FLC* 36]

Here the metaphorical exchange is reversed: instead of the forest taking on the overtones of sexuality, sex takes on the shapes of the forest. Sex powerfully reveals the true ground of her existence; but she has been connected to that ground, unknowing, since birth and through all the celibate months of her marriage to Clifford. In Lawrence's world, one might be barred from lovemaking by youth or age, by distance or—as Lawrence himself was during his last years—by illness; yet one can still maintain one's "touch with the substantial and vital world."

Connie discovers *through* sex her rootedness in nature, and she is alerted to the awesome power of life in nature itself. After another bout of lovemaking, she sees the world in this light:

> The trees seemed to be bulging and surging, at anchor on a tide, and the heave of the slope of the park was alive. She herself was a different creature, sensitive and alert, quietly slipping among the live presences of trees and hills and a far-off star.
>
> . . . Time was a full soft urge, with no minutes to it. And the universe ceased to be the vast clock-work of circling planets and pivotal suns, which she had known. The stars opened like eyes, with a consciousness in them, and the sky was filled with a soft, yearning stress of consolation. It was not mere atmosphere. It had its own feeling, its own anima. Everything had its own anima.
>
> The quick of the universe is in our own bodies, deep in us. [*JTLJ* 170]

This is the central moment of discovery in one after another of Lawrence's works, this perception of the world's vast inhuman aliveness, and of one's participation in it. Having seen this, Connie recognizes that Clifford's view of nature as inert matter is monstrous. His pretense of "owning" the woods or the neighboring coal mines is grotesque. "Cut off from the breathing contact of the living universe," he is very dangerous, and grows more dangerous as machines multiply the destructive power of his will. Others embracing Clifford's outlook have produced the gruesome villages and devastated landscapes of industrial England, villages like Tevershall and Stacks Gate whose ugliness wrings Connie's heart, landscapes such as the mining country around Nottingham where Lawrence grew up and which he visited again in 1926 just before starting the first version of *Lady Chatterley's Lover*. His letters of the time show that Lawrence felt, like Connie, "a tenderness . . . , a wistfulness, for this disfigured countryside, and the disfigured, strange, almost wraithlike populace" (*FLC* 45). Clifford's central fault is that of all industrial magnates, seeing the earth as a warehouse of "resources," treating workers as "hands" for harvesting wealth, regarding the material universe as a playground for his desires.

Connie's view points toward affirmation of nature, Clifford's toward exploitation—or, when his will is obstructed, toward annihilation.

What Connie has learned about her own body and about nature she also learns, through her lover, about the working class. At the outset of each version of the novel, she is acutely aware of the seemingly un-bridgeable distance between herself and the "common people." She feels trapped on one side of an incipient class war: "It was something she dreaded coldly and fatally, the working-out of this new, unconscious, cold, reptilian sort of hate that was rising between the colliers of the under-earth, the iron-workers of the great furnaces, and the educated, owning class to which she belonged, by the accident of destiny" (*JTLJ* 106). This is more than a theoretical concern about the possibility of class war, as the repeated references to the Bolshevik revolution and to socialism would suggest. ("She knew a good deal about the terrible revolution in Russia, and the convulsive class hatred which had wreaked itself without expending itself there" [*FLC* 74].) England itself had teetered on the brink of revolution in 1919, when the disgruntled troops returned from the war to find the same old arrangements of wealth and power; and it was teetering again in 1926, during the months in which Lawrence made his visit to the strikebound Midlands and began writing *The First Lady Chatterley*.

Of all the "disconnections" explored in the novel, this gulf be-tween classes poses the most immediate threat of cataclysm. Just as Clifford, on the one side, strives for "mastery" and yearns to enslave the workers, so workers on the opposing side exhibit "a capacity for a ruthless destruction" (*JTLJ* 150). The two classes gaze at one another as into a mirror, hatred matched by hatred, every gesture of violence answered by violence. While justice clearly stands on the side of those who have been oppressed, both sides are equally vulnerable to the annihilation impulse. The very willingness to destroy the "enemy" poisons the heart of worker and owner alike. Imagine the rival classes as nations, and one sees the confrontation between Britain and Ger-many which led to the First World War, or the long-standing duel between the United States and the Soviet Union, which might lead to the Last World War.

How to break out of the vicious circle? How to abolish the walls between classes? Politicians, theologians, and revolutionaries would all proffer their own—generally sweeping—solutions. Being a novelist, a fabricator of characters instead of laws, Lawrence offers a remedy centered in personal relations rather than politics. Connie seeks "the clue to this gruesome business of class war. . . . But . . . she could only sympathise with a particular man, not with a whole villageful or a whole class" (*FLC* 88). If the "clue" to this "business of class war" is the imagined *division* of humanity into groups of masters and servants, the solution is a discovery of the *connection* between person and person, a connection more fundamental than any seeming divisions. This recovery of human connections is a matter not of theory but of direct experience: "It was touch that one needed: some sort of touch between her class and the under class" (*JTLJ* 106). Even while Lady Chatterley persists in thinking in class terms, her experience with the gamekeeper erases all such categories: "Parkin was beyond class in passion" (*FLC* 120). In passion, Connie escapes not only the illusions of class, but also the illusions of human separation from nature: "passion overcame her, and the body of the man seemed silken and powerful and pure god-stuff, and the thrusting of the haunches the splendid, flamboyant, urgent god-rhythm, the same that made the stars swing round and the sea heave over, and all the leaves turn and the light stream out from heaven" (*JTLJ* 167). Thus Connie recovers all her "connections" at once, with her body and with the "common people" and with the "quick of the universe."

Her liaison with the gamekeeper will not reconcile her class with his, will not unseat the rulers or liberate the workers, any more than her revery in the forest will halt the woodcutters' blades. However close the two lovers feel personally, they are still divided socially, by differences of wealth and education and privilege. That Lawrence felt compelled, in writing each successive version of the novel, to reduce the social distance between the lady and the gamekeeper is a measure of how seriously he regarded divisions of class as impediments to love.[5] Lawrence himself yearned to escape from society into a territory of freedom, of pure passionate relationships with other people and with nature. He searched in vain—and so do Connie and the gamekeeper. The lovers shelter in their hut in the woods, secure for a time against the crippling influences of the human world. But poachers lurk in the shadows, nearby smokestacks vent noxious fumes, Clifford puffs along through the wildflowers in his motorized chair, and acre-by-acre the woods are chopped down. Many of the oldest trees were felled during the war to supply props for mineshafts and trenches. A neighboring estate has already been razed. The lovers' sanctuary, like their passion, is besieged and vulnerable.

The contrast between Clifford and Connie sums up the choice Lawrence saw before us, the choice between two opposed ways of relating to one another, to other social groups and nations, and to the earth. As usual in Lawrence, the choice is presented as a series of variations on one fundamental dichotomy: at one extreme, the isolation and exaltation of the ego (or collective ego of class, race, nation), coupled with a desire to dominate or annihilate whatever stands outside the ego; at the other extreme, a discarding of all barriers dividing person from person or humankind from nature, a respect for the ways of living things and for the needs of all people, a reverence for the "quick of the universe" that is present in all creation.

One characteristic formulation of this dichotomy appears in *John Thomas and Lady Jane,* when Connie remarks to her sister, "It's so different . . . *knowing* life, and *being* it" (*JTLJ* 304). Scholars in particular will find this opposition a disturbing one. Clifford is in fact very much the scholar, locked away with his books, trying to seize the world through ideas while avoiding direct contact. Knowledge is for him a mode of power—power over the mines and the miners, over Connie, over the material universe. Once he "knows" a thing, he can control it, and the thing itself is evacuated of all meaning. Of course, "*knowing* life, and *being* it" need not be so radically opposed as they are in Clifford's case. Connie learns a great deal through her loving, but the knowledge she gains is connecting rather than severing. When she learns "to see the trees bulging and urging like ships at anchor on a tide: to feel the world full of its own strange, ceaseless life" (*FLC* 67), she begins to participate in the larger being of nature.

Lawrence also poses the choice between Clifford's way and Connie's way in terms of the opposition between industry and forest, the familiar romantic dichotomy between mechanical and organic: "there were two main sorts of energy, the frictional, seething, resistant, explosive, blind sort, like that of steam-engines and motor-cars and electricity, and of people such as Clifford and Bill Tewson and modern, insistent women, and these queer vacuous miners: then there was the other, forest energy, that was still and softly powerful, with tender, frail bud-tips and gentle finger-ends full of awareness" (*JTLJ* 367). Connie herself is divided between these two kinds of energy, as we all must be, since human life would be impossible without our exerting *some* control over the environment. Simply building a fire is an exercise in manipulation. The light by which I see to write these lines depends upon the harnessing of electricity. Lawrence does not confront either Connie or us with the absurd alternative between fully embracing and fully repudiating technology. Rather, he forces us to decide whether we owe our deepest respect to the energy of machines or to the energy of the forest, whether our highest purpose is to control or to participate in nature. We are left in no doubt as to which allegiance Connie chooses, or which one Lawrence would have us choose:

> Life is so soft and quiet, and cannot be seized. It will not be raped. Try to rape it, and it disappears. Try to seize it, and you have dust. Try to master it, and you see your own image grinning at you with the grin of an idiot.
>
> Whoever wants life must go softly towards life, softly as one would go towards a deer and a fawn that was nestling under a tree. One gesture of violence, one violent assertion of self-will, and life is gone. You must seek again. And softly, gently, with infinitely sensitive hands and feet, and a heart that is full and free from self-will, you must approach life again, and come at last into touch. . . .
>
> But with quietness, with an abandon of self-assertion and a fulness of the deep, true self one can approach another human being, and know the delicate best of life, the touch. The touch of the feet on the earth, the touch of the fingers on a tree, on a creature, the touch of hands and breasts, the touch of the whole body to body, and the interpenetration of passionate love. [*JTLJ* 107–8]

Stated simply, in the traditional terms that Lawrence himself employed, this is the choice between the way of power and the way of love. The most highly industrialized and militarized nations have chosen the way of power. By means of weapons and machines, we try constantly to impose our will upon the land, upon "enemies," upon those who are weaker or poorer than we, upon the chemistry of our own bodies. If we look honestly at our situation, we should agree with Connie that "the individual, the company, the nation, they are alike all possessed with one insanity, the insanity of conceit, the mania of the swollen ego" (*JTLJ* 99).

That way lies doom, said Lawrence, and I think he was right. The planet is too small to sustain for very long so many gluttonous egos, so many—even two—tyrannical nuclear governments. The assault upon nature and the assault upon rival nations are both expressions of the drive for total security, the craving for unchallenged supremacy. With the First World War so recently behind her, the prospects for class war immediately in front of her, and the devastating effects of rampant industrialism visible on all sides, Connie has good reason to feel "a terror of the incipient insanity of the whole civilised species" (*LCL* 156). We have even more reason to feel that terror now. In the letter he writes to Connie at the close of *Lady Chatterley's Lover*, the game-keeper grimly predicts, "there's a bad time coming! If things go on as they are, there's nothing lies in the future but death and destruction, for these industrial masses" (*LCL* 373). We have all become members of the "industrial masses," depending for our survival on a biosphere that is under daily assault from human greed. We are hostages to rival political systems that operate in the nuclear age with a bullying ideol-ogy more appropriate to the stone age. "If man could will it," Lawrence warned in *Apocalypse*, "it would be cosmic suicide. But the cosmos is not at man's mercy, and the sun will not perish to please us."[6] The sun remains immune to us; but the earth, at least, is now at our mercy, and our relentless accumulation of bombs and poisons suggests that we are quite capable of willing its destruction.

What we are shown in the history of Lady Chatterley's loving is the education of one woman's consciousness. That seems a humble spectacle in the face of the enormous horror that Lawrence con-fronted, and the even greater catastrophe that we now face. And yet, in proportion as we are drawn into her loving and altered by it, we are forced to realize along with her that there is no ultimate basis for distinctions between classes, between races, between nations, or between humankind and the rest of nature. Like Connie, "We are clothed with a new awareness" (*JTLJ* 171). Out of that awareness may arise new ways of living, new ways of loving one another and the earth. The reading of novels, even such generous-hearted novels as those of Lawrence, will not save us from our violence. But they may keep alive in us the vision of a gentler existence.

NOTES

1. I am well aware that the three published versions of *Lady Chatterley's Lover* differ significantly, one from another. For the purposes of certain arguments, these differences are more important than the similarities, as I have suggested in my treatment of the variations in political themes among the three versions. For a discussion, see the fifth chapter of my *D. H. Lawrence: The World of the Five Major Novels* (New York: Viking, 1974). For the purposes of the present essay, I have treated *The First Lady Chatterley, John Thomas and Lady Jane,* and *Lady Chatterley's Lover* as constituting variations on a common text, and therefore as being structurally interchangeable.

2. D. H. Lawrence, *Women in Love*, ed. Charles L. Ross (Harmondsworth, Middlesex: Penguin, 1982), p. 187.

3. D. H. Lawrence, *Apocalypse* (New York: Viking, 1966), p. 198.

4. From a telegram sent out in May 1946 inviting others to join him in the Emergency Committee of Atomic Scientists. Quoted in *Einstein on Peace*, ed. Otto Nathan and Heinz Norden (New York: Simon and Schuster, 1960), p. 376.

5. See Sanders, *The World of the Five Major Novels*, pp. 172–205.

6. Lawrence, *Apocalypse*, p. 198.

LYDIA BLANCHARD

Lawrence, Foucault, and the Language of Sexuality

And I, who loathe sexuality so deeply,
am considered a lurid sexuality specialist.
—D. H. Lawrence to Dr. Trigant Burrow, 1926

Near the end of "A Propos of *Lady Chatterley's Lover*," D. H. Lawrence recounts the story of the timid Florentine critic who cautioned him about the novel, "I don't know— I don't know—if it's not a bit too strong. . . . Listen, Signor Lawrence, you find it really necessary to *say* it?" Lawrence records his characteristically testy response, "I told him I did," and the Florentine's reaction, "he pondered" (*Phoenix II* 515).

Ponder he should. If more than fifty years after the publication of *Lady Chatterley* the critic's question no longer interests us, if it appears not only timid but ingenuous, the reason is that we rest in a false complacency, assuming that we have been freed from the repression felt by the Florentine. Fearing neither pornography nor censorship, we discount the question's obvious concern with both, cheer Lawrence for helping us overcome the "censor-morons," and look no further. But in the first volume of *The History of Sexuality* (1978), French philosopher Michel Foucault has also quoted from "A Propos"—Lawrence's argument that it is "now our business . . . to realize sex. Today the full conscious realization of sex is even more important than the act itself"—and Foucault has pondered, like the Florentine critic, the significance of Lawrence's decision. For Foucault the necessity that Lawrence found to *say* it is central to a preoccupation of the modern world which, Foucault predicts, will surely puzzle future generations.

> Perhaps one day people will wonder at [Lawrence's concern]. They
> will not be able to understand how a civilization so intent on devel-

oping enormous instruments of production and destruction found the time and the infinite patience to inquire so anxiously concerning the actual state of sex; people will smile perhaps when they recall that here were men—meaning ourselves—who believed that therein resided a truth every bit as precious as the one they had already demanded from the earth, the stars, and the pure forms of their thought; people will be surprised at the eagerness with which we went about pretending to rouse from its slumber a sexuality which everything—our discourses, our customs, our institutions, our regulations, our knowledges—was busy producing in the light of day and broadcasting to noisy accompaniment. And people will ask themselves why we were so bent on ending the rule of silence regarding what was the noisiest of our preoccupations.[1]

For Foucault, Lawrence is an example, perhaps the paradigmatic example, of those who have misunderstood the nature of discourse, of those who have misunderstood the relationship between the language in which we talk about sex and the repression of sexuality. In the essay "A Preface to Transgression," which first appeared in 1963, Foucault challenges the modern wisdom that by bringing sexuality into discourse we have regained for it "full truth as a process of nature, a truth which has long been lingering in the shadows and hiding under various disguises—until now, that is, when our positive awareness allows us to decipher it so that it may at last emerge in the clear light of language."[2] By bringing sexuality into the clear light of language, Foucault argues, we have succeeded only in controlling and thus repressing it. Like the inspector in one of Foucault's favorite images, the Panoptican of Jeremy Bentham, we have been made prisoner by what we bring under our gaze; our sexuality is trapped by the language meant to free it; rather than liberating sexuality we have "carried it to its limits: the limit of consciousness, because it ultimately dictates the only possible reading of our unconscious; . . . the limit of language, since it traces that line of foam showing just how far speech may advance upon the sands of silence."[3] Repression created our modern understanding of sexuality, and without repression sexuality loses rather than gains power.

And yet Foucault underestimates Lawrence—if not Lawrence's readers. It is true that *Lady Chatterley's Lover* remains fixed in the public mind with the battle against prudery and censorship, with the fight both to destroy the sexual restrictions of the Victorian age and to affirm the phallic reality of the body—readings of the novel certainly strengthened by the recent film *Priest of Love*. But for a novel associated in the public mind almost exclusively with sexuality, *Lady Chatterley's Lover* has also seemed, for many of its critics, curiously unsatisfactory on the subject of sex. If this dissatisfaction has manifested itself in different ways, underlying them all is uncertainty about how to read the work as a *whole*—about how to integrate the passages describing intercourse into the rest of the novel. As Scott Sanders has argued, "The insistent realism of the sexual descriptions prevents us from reading *Lady Chatterley* simply as a fable. Yet read as realism the novel appears either trivial or simply wrong-headed."[4]

Trivial, wrongheaded, quaint, silly, embarrassing—the negative litany voiced by the novel's critics is long. Certainly the passages descriptive of intercourse must be confusing, or why else the critical debates about what Lawrence is describing, much less advocating? The best-known criticism of the novel is still the attempt to determine the exact positions of the lady and her lover in the dark mysteries of the novel's final night of lovemaking. Although engaging some of our most astute critics in not one but three of our finest journals, the question of what the lady was up to remains unanswered—a failure of criticism that must come as a surprise to a general public who, even if they do not approve of the novel, certainly think they know what it is about.[5]

If the intensity of the critical debate on what is happening has led to some quite uncollegial name-calling, how much more angry we have become with each other about what we think Lawrence (or at least the novel) is advocating about sex. Is the emphasis on the importance of male sexuality, "those modes of belief and manners of sex which men display in their various ways of 'loving' "? Or is Lawrence rather interested in "the imaginative rendering of a woman's sexual experience"? Does the novel advocate a passive woman or mutual orgasm? the "apocalyptic possibility of conception" or the Italian way?[6]

Such difficulties with understanding and explaining the passages of intercourse are so great, in fact, that many readers have chosen to ignore the novel's treatment of sex altogether, a critical evasion that would surely have puzzled the novel's early censors. Numerous studies of the work either do not discuss or else minimize the importance of the sections that describe intercourse, instead treating *Lady Chatterley's Lover* as a version of the utopian or the pastoral, as a retelling of myth or medieval romance, as a philosophical tract concerned with epistemology—treating the novel, in other words, as if it were a discourse on anything but sexuality, as if (reversing the nineteenth-century convention) sexuality were itself metaphor.[7] Given the general success of these readings—they are for the most part lucid, convincing, internally consistent, compatible—even Lawrence's most sympathetic critics have concluded that *Lady Chatterley's Lover* as a whole is a failure; that because its passages of sexuality are not integrated into the rest of the novel, it falls short of the earlier works, in particular *The Rainbow* and *Women in Love*; that these passages can most generally be explained as Lawrence's attempt to reconcile himself with Frieda and to deal with his own impotence; that Lawrence fails in his attempt, however admirable, to create a language of the feelings, to achieve the full conscious realization of sex.

In fact, many critics argue that Lawrence would have done well to listen to himself, to his own bitter indictment of a sterile Wragby that destroyed sex by talking about it; that he should have heeded his own indictments about the life of the mind, surely some of the most bitter in his canon: "don't, with the nasty, prying mind, drag [sex] out from its deeps / and finger it and force it, and shatter the rhythm it keeps / when it's left alone, as it stirs and rouses and sleeps"—or more briefly, "sex, alas, gets dirtier and dirtier, worked from the mind."[8] These critics see the failure of the novel, as Sanders argues, in the fundamental contradiction implicit in Lawrence's use of "tools of consciousness to define and defend the unconscious."[9] Given Lawrence's attitude about the mental life, how could the novel be a "declaration of the phallic reality"? (*CL* 1028). How indeed can one declare that which loses force as it is declared?

How much better, these critics seem to say, if Lawrence had restricted himself to the conventions of his earlier works in which, operating in the tradition of the romantic novel, he drew on metaphor, imagery, even apparently asexual dialogue and plot to suggest both the experience of and the response to sex, the artistic decision informing such scenes as Miriam on the swing, the flowers crushed in Paul's meeting with Clara, the sheaf-gathering of *The Rainbow,* and the brutal passion of horse and rabbit in *Women in Love*—brilliant passages affirming Lawrence's ability to re-create the power of sexuality without submitting it to the cold light of explicit description.

Such reactions to those very passages that have brought *Lady Chatterley* much of its fame and many of its readers might well be attributed to the general perversity of critics. But as attractive as such an explanation might be (what adolescent ever had trouble with *Lady Chatterley?*), it does little to solve the very real tensions involved in the novel and, in fact, in all of Lawrence's work. Even the most casual readers of Lawrence, even careful readers of only this last novel, are aware that Lawrence has a fundamental interest in the relationship between language and sexuality that goes far beyond fighting the "censor-morons." Indeed, Lawrence would have condemned readers like Gay Talese who praise the novel for freeing us from our Victorian repression to enjoy the world of *Thy Neighbor's Wife.* Lawrence lashed out at the censors, but he did not write *Lady Chatterley's Lover* to open literature to Erica Jong and *The Executioner's Song.* Many readers, including Foucault, underestimate Lawrence's interest in the relationship between language and sexuality.

Lawrence was certainly interested in the full conscious realization of sex, but that interest was, for him as for Foucault, part of a broader concern with what it means to bring sexuality into discourse, part of a broader interest in the relation between language, sexuality, power, and knowledge. If Lawrence's thinking on these subjects is presented in a way less systematic than that of French critics like Foucault and Roland Barthes, Lawrence's work, in particular *Lady Chatterley's Lover,* not only addresses the same concerns but also clarifies much of what we now understand about language and its peculiar relation to sexuality.

Recent French criticism has argued the centrality of language to human communication, maintaining "that no other meaning-system can manage without its aid" and "that human beings organize virtually all their experiences along linguistic lines," but the work of Barthes and Foucault in particular has suggested a more complex relationship of language to sexuality.[10] If, as in other meaning systems, the experience of sexuality must be understood through language structures, the rhythm of sexuality itself also underlies these structures—as the rhythm of life underlies Lawrence's argument in "A Propos." Robert Scholes has maintained, "It is in . . . the various periodicities of sperm production, menstruation, courtship, and coitus, that our sense of narrative structure is itself generated."[11]

In his recent writing, therefore, Foucault has shifted from a vocabulary centering on the *episteme,* a discursive concept, to an approach centering on the *apparatus,* a concept both discursive and nondiscursive, a system of relations that Foucault maintains goes beyond discourse and that reflects a new recognition of structures that are outside of language.[12] Arguing that "*I-love-you* belongs neither in the realm of linguistics nor in that of semiology," Barthes has suggested music as its occasion ("the point of departure for speaking it"),[13] and both he and Foucault echo Lawrence's warnings of the dangers of bringing sexuality into language. "To try to write love is to confront the *muck* of language: that region of hysteria where language is both *too much* and *too little,* excessive . . . and impoverished," Barthes writes, and if he can regard the situation with some good humor (in intercourse "the Image-repertoire goes to the devil"),[14] Foucault in his word choice more closely approaches the frequent bitterness of Lawrence: for Foucault, language has "absorbed" our sexuality, "denatured" it, "cast [it] into an empty zone."[15]

Lawrence's understanding of the relationship between sexuality and language is complex. Often he simply rejects the structuralist emphasis on language (as, for example, in the late poem "If ever there was a beginning / there was no god in it / there was no Verb / no Voice / no Word").[16] On occasion he also considers how the loss of language is related to the loss of emotion. In the short story "The Man Who Loved Islands," for example, Lawrence portrays a hero who increasingly withdraws from language and thus from his humanity. Because Cathcart is unable to register his own feelings, his feelings cease to exist: "He looked stupidly over the whiteness of his foreign island, over the waste of the lifeless sea."[17] Most frequently, however, Lawrence recognizes that the sexual rhythms of the body underlie language; these rhythms, when they are brought into discourse, are controlled rather than freed.

Indeed, part of Lawrence's increased absorption in painting in the last years of his life may stem from the terrible risks he saw in bringing sexuality into discourse, risks made clear in the sterile intellectual discussions at Wragby. His letters about the progress of *Lady Chatterley* are filled with references to his simultaneous attempts to capture the phallic self on canvas. "It is fun to paint," he affirms, even though in their portrayal of sexuality his paintings are "worse" (more shocking to the public) than his writing (*CL* 959, 1037). In May 1928, while working on the last proofs of *Lady Chatterley*, he told Mark Gertler, "One's got to get back to the live, really lovely phallic self, and phallic consciousness. I think I get a certain phallic beauty in my pictures too. I know they're rolling with faults. . . . But there's something *there*" (*CL* 1062).

Why then, we must surely ask (but not as timidly as the Florentine critic), why *did* Lawrence say it in *Lady Chatterley*? Or, of more recent writers, why did Barthes write *A Lover's Discourse*? And Foucault enter into a six-volume *History of Sexuality*? Why bring into discourse an experience that will presumably lose from its expression in language? Why study the effects of such a discourse? "O know yourself, O know your sex!" Lawrence affirmed. "You must know sex in order to save it, your deepest self, from the rape / of the itching mind and the mental self, with its pruriency always agape."[18] As Barthes uses the language of eroticism to describe the pleasure of the text, and Foucault traces the history of sexuality to rescue it from its history, so Lawrence exhausts the language of sexuality to return that language to the area where he had always argued it belonged—to the darkness, to silence, to oblivion. "Man knows nothing / till he knows how not-to-know. / . . . The end of all knowledge is oblivion / sweet, dark oblivion, when I cease / even from myself, and am consummated."[19] And so Mellors writes in his final letter to Lady Chatterley, in the ignored last pages of the novel, "So many words, because I can't touch you. If I could sleep with my arms round you, the ink could stay in the bottle" (*LCL* 374).

Lawrence then is as interested as Foucault in the question of why sexuality has been brought into discourse, and the effect that such bringing of sexuality into the language has on its control; and like Foucault he has traced—though not so extensively—the cultural reasons that underlie this change in Western consciousness. Arguing that ideas of sexuality and sex are historically recent (before the eighteenth century flesh alone mattered), Foucault poses the question, "What had to happen in the history of the West for the question of truth to be posed in regard to sexual pleasure?"[20] Cultural institutions themselves created the need for the discourse, developing a vocabulary by which sexuality could be controlled. For Foucault the emphasis—at least in the work to date—is on the role of the confessional ("all those procedures by which the subject is incited to produce a discourse of truth about his sexuality which is capable of having effects on the subject himself");[21] for Lawrence the emphasis is on medicine, and he argues in "Introduction to These Paintings" that the growth of the spiritual-mental consciousness of sexuality came through fear of syphilis, which entered the blood and then the consciousness during the Renaissance, hitting the vital imagination and turning man into an "ideal being" (*Phoenix* 551–59).

Both Lawrence and Foucault see the bringing of sexuality into discourse as contemporaneous with the death of the religious feeling: "The language of sexuality has lifted us into the night where God is absent," Foucault writes. "On the day that sexuality began to speak and to be spoken, language no longer served as a veil for the infinite; and in the thickness it acquired on that day, we now experience finitude and being."[22] Sexuality is one of the areas of darkness that the Enlightenment brought into the light; to do so meant not only to create a language through which a variety of institutions—for example, the church (through the confessional), medicine (through textbook descriptions of treatment), the law (through a definition of the illegal)—could control sexuality, but also to create, through that repression, a recognition of sexuality itself, giving to sexuality a power that it did not have before the discourse of repression. "Sexuality, through thus becoming an object of analysis and concern, surveillance and control, engenders at the same time an intensification of each individual's desire, for, in and over his body."[23] We have failed to see the positive effects of repression, Foucault argues; just as madness must exist for reason to exist, so repression must exist for sexuality to have power. And so Lawrence writes that one result of freeing sexuality from repression is chastity: "Great is my need to be chaste / and apart, in this cerebral age."[24]

Lady Chatterley's Lover thus becomes an important fictional treatment—perhaps our most important fictional treatment—of the relationship between power, language, and sexuality. To deal with this relationship Lawrence had to develop formal innovations in *Lady Chatterley* as significant as those in *The Rainbow* and *Women in Love,* innovations that make special demands on the reader who tries to naturalize the text (that is, to bring it within conventions which, as Jonathan Culler has explained, enable the writing "to speak to us").[25] Striving for *vraisemblance,* the "principle of integration between one discourse and another or several others,"[26] we are constantly dislocated by *Lady Chatterley,* in particular by the passages of explicit sex. But this is because we are reading the novel within the wrong conventions, trying to naturalize it in relation to Lawrence's earlier fiction as well as to what we understand as the mimetic quality of the novel of realism. To naturalize *Lady Chatterley* as a text, however—"to bring it into relation with a type of discourse or model which is already, in some sense, natural and legible"[27]—is to see the novel as drawing simultaneously on a variety of genres.

A choice of genre is, of course, one way to naturalize the text, establishing a tacit contract between writer and reader "to make certain relevant expectations operative and thus to permit both compliance with and deviation from accepted modes of intelligibility."[28] Nearly all criticism that has found *Lady Chatterley's Lover* flawed as a novel has argued the lack of *vraisemblance* on the level of genre, but Culler points out that generic *vraisemblance* is only one way to naturalize a text; a text may also be read as an exposing of "the artifice of generic conventions and expectations."[29] On such a level the text finds "its coherence by being interpreted as a narrator's exercise of language and production of meaning. To naturalize it at this level is to read it as a statement about the writing of novels, a critique of mimetic fiction, an illustration of the production of a world by language." To introduce opposing conventions of genre is to bring about "a change in the mode of reading" and to look for a synthesis at a higher level. "It is a process of naturalization in that what seemed difficult or strange is made natural (a blur so natural as to pass unnoticed) by locating a proper level of *vraisemblance.* And this level is a repertoire of projects. Even the most radical readings of literary works propose a project from whose vantage point the blur becomes clear or natural: the project of illustrating or enacting the practice of writing."[30] It is to this project—the illustration and enactment of the practice of writing—that Lawrence addresses himself in *Lady Chatterley's Lover,* in particular to the practice of writing about sexuality, and in the process he makes extraordinary demands on the reader.

In part, Lawrence makes these demands through his use of language play and parody, perhaps most noticeably in the extensive allusions in dialogue to a variety of writers (Whitman and Shakespeare, for example) and forms of writing (for example, poetry, the Bible, hymns, and other novels). If *Lady Chatterley* in its close attention to detail often is within the tradition of the nineteenth-century novel, its traditional passages are also interspersed, unpredictably, with parody of the literary tradition. We are reminded of the courtly tradition through references to Sir Malcolm's knighthood when Sir Malcolm is at his lewdest, talking about his daughter with Mellors. We are reminded of the limits of modern theater through Michaelis and of modern fiction through Clifford Chatterley himself. Mellors is equated in village gossip to the Marquis de Sade, undermining the significance of both men; Clifford writes letters that Lady Chatterley finds uninteresting because they are good, thus questioning the value of the epistolary tradition. The examples abound, as George Levine has argued, calling *Lady Chatterley's Lover,* not surprisingly, a novel that is "importantly about novel writing": "In *Lady Chatterley's Lover,* [Lawrence] creates a work that resonates parodically with the now dead traditions of realism. . . . It stands in parodic relation to the tradition of moral-aesthetic realism, while itself (good parody that it is) belonging to that tradition."[31] But there is more. For while Lawrence was creating a language for the feelings through the passages of lovemaking, he was also using those passages to parody not only traditional forms but also his own earlier works—to question through imitation (so that he can later reaffirm) the power of those works.

Read within the context of Lawrence's earlier fiction, for example, the first passage in which Lady Chatterley and Mellors have intercourse suggests a novel like *Women in Love* in which Lawrence creates the experience of sexuality through animal imagery: as horse and rabbit suggest the brutality and cruelty of the love that Gerald and Gudrun will experience with each other, so the newborn chick suggests the tenderness of the love that will be manifested between Lady Chatterley and Mellors. But in *Women in Love* Lawrence separated the animal scenes from the lovemaking of Gerald and Gudrun, and the different scenes gain power from the suggestions that they carry back and forth. In *Lady Chatterley* Lawrence brings the two together and the power of both is significantly different. While the chick retains its brilliance as an image of the new birth that will come through love, the language through which Lady Chatterley's "tormented modern-woman's brain" tries to understand the significance of the experience is lugubrious and ponderous: "Why was this necessary? Why had it lifted a great cloud from her and given her peace? Was it real? Was it real? . . . Was it real?" (*LCL* 164). Similarly, on their second occasion of intercourse, Lady Chatterley's will keeps her detached from Mellors, and she articulates the experience for herself as "a little ridiculous . . . supremely ridiculous . . . intensely ridiculous" (*LCL* 174–75).

As the first two occasions of intercourse are set within the context of the young chicks but question their meaning, so the third is occasioned by Lady Chatterley's holding of the young Flint child and is the time she first feels the possibility of conception. After the experience "it feels like a child, . . . it feels like a child in me" (*LCL* 185). Again, however, there is the sense of the ridiculous, Mellors being likened, after all, to Balaam's ass, although the parody, the imitation, does not recall Lawrence's earlier work so much as it comments on *Lady Chatterley* itself. While the passage contains one of the lines often quoted to praise Lawrence's ability to capture the experience of a woman's orgasm (the sentence that begins "She clung to him unconscious in passion, and he never quite slipped from her," a sentence which re-creates the rhythms of intercourse in a truly brilliant way), within the same paragraph are parodies of that sentence: "Rippling, rippling, rippling, like a flapping overlapping of soft flames, soft as feathers, . . . melting her all molten inside" (*LCL* 183). Not only does the passage parody itself, it challenges the convention of narrative structure, for this is the conclusion toward which the sense of the novel has been leading. It is the experience of sexuality that Mellors recommends ("It's good when it's like that"—coming off together), and it is the experience that Lady Chatterley believes may lead to pregnancy; the narrative structure suggests that it is here the novel should end. But, of course, it does not. The novel is concerned not only with a realization of the phallic reality but with the way in which that realization is re-created in language, and Lawrence has not yet exhausted the possibilities.

In the next passage the word "ridiculous" reappears, but here in connection with the many literary allusions that fill the work: Lady Chatterley thinks of the poets who have said that "the God who created man must have had a sinister sense of humour, creating him a reasonable being, yet forcing him to take this ridiculous posture" (*LCL* 227). Caught in language that describes love in terms of the ridiculous, Lady Chatterley is divorced from the act and calls Mellors, to herself, a clown, but having done so, she is also able to lose herself, forgetting Maupassant and creating a woman's language for the description of female orgasm: "And it seemed she was like the sea" (*LCL* 228–29).

Even here, however, the language draws on the imagery of the popular sex manuals of the period, manuals that Lawrence objected to (for example in "Pornography and Obscenity"). Arguing the necessity for doing away with the secrecy surrounding sex, Lawrence also criticized the work of "idealists" like Marie Stopes, a pioneer in the study of female sexuality and an advocate of birth control ("How to get out of the dirty little secret! . . . You can't do it by being wise and scientific about it, like Dr. Marie Stopes" [*Phoenix* 182]), but in fact the language with which Stopes describes female sexuality, drawing on "the tides of the sea" and its "ebb and flow," contains imagery not significantly different from Lawrence's to describe orgasm from the point of view of the woman. Indeed, the Stopes program for married love, stressing the importance of the woman and her satisfaction, is re-created, often ironically, by the lady and the gamekeeper, Stopes even referring in her 1918 work, *Married Love,* to "flower-wreathed love-making."[32]

Having drawn on language similar to that of *Married Love*—language still used by women to describe the experience of orgasm (for example in the Hite report)—Lawrence returns to his argument that the experience exists beyond language, in touch: "What a mystery! . . . such as no consciousness could seize. Her whole self quivered unconscious and alive, like plasm. She could not know what it was. She could not remember what it had been. Only that it had been more lovely than anything ever could be. Only that. And afterwards she was utterly still, utterly unknowing, she was not aware for how long. And he was still with her, in an unfathomable silence along with her. And of this, they would never speak" (*LCL* 230–31). But the novel moves forward, in an even more dramatic way, to do precisely that, to speak of the experience of love—when it has not been satisfactory.

The next episode, in fact, is preceded by the novel's most detailed talk about intercourse. Of all the passages dealing with lovemaking, Mellors's discussion here of his previous unsatisfactory experiences presents the most extensive preliminary dialogue and the briefest description of the act itself. "He lay with her and went into her there on the hearthrug, and so they gained a measure of equanimity," as if the talk about intercourse eliminated the need for the experience of it. "And then they went quickly to bed, for it was growing chill, and they had tired each other out" (*LCL* 268).

In still another pattern, using language in still another way, on the next morning Mellors expands the use of dialect to introduce John Thomas and Lady Jane, but the allusions parody: "Say: Lift up your heads o' ye gates, that the king of glory may come in. . . . Blest be the tie that binds our hearts in kindred love" (*LCL* 270–71). Similarly, much talk precedes the scene of the dance in the rain, talk about the condition of England that makes Lady Chatterley uneasy, for as Mellors talks, "despair seemed to come down on him completely" (*LCL* 282). In the weaving of flowers that follows, again there is a parody not only of Stopes but also of the earlier Lawrence, for the significance of the bouquets that Lady Chatterley and Mellors bring to each other to accompany their love is essentially different from the significance of flowers in, for example, *Sons and Lovers*, a significance shattered by Mellors's sneeze which causes him to forget what he started to say: " 'Ay, what *was* I going to say?' He had forgotten. And it was one of the disappointments of her life, that he never finished" (*LCL* 290–91).

And so, after drawing on a variety of earlier conventions for the description, frequently to parody them, Lawrence abandons language as a tool to re-create the experience of intercourse, abandons dialect, abandons talk about sex and use of imagery to suggest the experience itself, and turns instead to the emphasis of most of his earlier work, shifting from what happened to its effect. If the experience on the night before Lady Chatterley leaves for Italy is unclear, if the "sensuality sharp and searing as fire" is not described clinically, the effect on Lady Chatterley, her rejection of the pleasure of the mind, *is* clear (*LCL* 312). Similarly, the reader is also led to understand the importance of touch—no new idea in Lawrence—and also to a recognition that one can best approach true touch through rejection of the ways in which language may be used in making love. When Lady Chatterley and Mellors are together for the last time, in Mellors's room in London, the act itself is only briefly described, accompanied by the realization that "this was the thing he had to do, to come into tender touch" (*LCL* 348).

Clifford Chatterley clings to the power of language—it is his wife's going back on her word that most incenses him, and he insists that she fulfill her commitment in language, her promise that she return to Wragby, before he will divorce her. But both Mellors and Lady Chatterley understand the life that underlies the language in which they have tried to speak, and in his final letter to her, Mellors writes that he does not "like to think too much about you, in my head, that only makes a mess of us both" (*LCL* 373). That Lawrence is using the novel to investigate the relation between language and sexuality is made clear in this final letter, a recapitulation of the novel's concerns with novel-writing that serves as the epilogue Victor Shklovsky suggests we need to show us how to read the strange and unfamiliar.[33]

As the story of two lovers, *Lady Chatterley's Lover* is curiously unfinished. The future of Mellors and Lady Chatterley is unresolved, and in "A Propos" Lawrence makes clear the uncertainty that the two will ever be freed from their previous marriages to come together again. But as a novel about the relation between language and sexuality, Mellors's final statement is clear. Like the novel as a whole, the letter moves through a variety of approaches to novel-writing—opening with a gossipy realism concerned with money and the precise details of Mellors's job; moving into a middle section that recalls the didactic preaching of Lawrence as Victorian sage, here arguing for an approach to life that Mellors believes will bring renewed spirit to the colliers; shifting from realism and didacticism to the importance of symbol and image (the forked flame, the crocus, the great grasping white hands), as Lawrence was so effectively to use image and symbol himself in his own greatest novels; re-creating in words the act of love itself, the great attempt of *Lady Chatterley's Lover*; finally recognizing that such re-creation is inadequate, for if Lady Chatterley and Mellors were together, the ink could stay in the bottle: "So many words, because I can't touch you." It is to a different system of signs, to the forked flame, to a world in which there is no need for a mediating language that Mellors and Lady Chatterley move, and it is small wonder that Lawrence's letters and discursive prose during this period also show much interest in the story of Adam and Eve, before the fall, in a time before consciousness and language.

Readers have tended to ignore this concern with the limits of language, unless to criticize or to see it as paradoxical, perhaps from fear that it will somehow lessen the significance of Lawrence's role as priest of love. But to see that Lawrence is both creating a language of the feelings and simultaneously calling into question the adequacy of that language is to see the very brilliance of the novel. Lawrence has not only created a language of love, a lover's discourse, but has also shown the limits of such a discourse, even at its most eloquent and persuasive. In addition to freeing us from the repression of sexuality, *Lady Chatterley's Lover* also frees us from the constraints of language itself. The novel achieves its brilliance through the tension it creates by drawing on traditional genres at the same time it calls those forms into question; the novel builds on the tension created by the simultaneous use of a variety of conventions.

Lawrence's use of four-letter words in a dialect his early audiences found uncomfortable, his explicit description of the body and its use in intercourse, were shocking to readers who assumed such material belonged only within the conventions of the pornographic, and in the subsequent dislocation readers attempted to naturalize the novel in its entirety within the conventions of earlier fiction, conventions used by Lawrence and in the tradition of the realistic novel; such readings, as they became acceptable, were initially freeing for many who saw the novel as a way to escape the repression of sexuality. Only recently have we begun to see how much more sophisticated and profound is the novel's treatment of sexuality and its relation to language. To understand a text, as Barthes has pointed out, "is not only to pass from one word to another, it is also to pass from one level to another"; to do so with *Lady Chatterley* is to experience *jouissance,* the "rapture of dislocation produced by ruptures or violations of intelligibility."[34] While *Lady Chatterley's Lover* utilizes parody, it is not itself parody; it is in the tradition of realism but does not take realism too seriously—it cannot, after all, adequately convey the experience of sexuality, which underlies the rhythms of language itself.

Alan Sheridan has pointed out, in considering Foucault, that when one can "*say* things in a new way," one can "*see* things in a new way."[35] It is this attempt to see sex in a new way that underlies Lawrence's desire to *say* it in a new way—but not because one must or should talk about sex. Lawrence knew, as Foucault has argued, that sex loses its power in language—even though we must use language to explain that loss. Jacques Derrida has written: "We must . . . try to free ourselves from . . . language. Not actually *attempt* to free ourselves from it, for that is impossible without denying our own historic situation. But rather, to imagine doing so. Not actually *free* ourselves from it, for that would make no sense and would deprive us of the light that meaning can provide. But rather, resist it as far as possible."[36] Mellors attempted to be silent, by withdrawing from the world of men, but without touch he was drawn back into the world, into language. At the same time, in the most simple and direct way, his final letter affirms that he and Lady Chatterley cannot truly be together as long as they are dependent solely on language. Like the novel itself they must both resist the historic situation which makes them dependent on language and simultaneously imagine what they might be without language. "Books are not life. They are only tremulations on the ether," Lawrence wrote, but we *can* listen to the "low, calling cries of the characters, as they wander in the dark woods of their destiny" (*Phoenix* 535, 760). When we are truly together, the ink *can* stay in the bottle.

Foucault is right, of course, that Lawrence did want to realize sex;

Lawrence, after all, maintained that the point of *Lady Chatterley's Lover* was "to think sex, fully, completely, honestly, and cleanly" (*Phoenix II* 489). But Lawrence also argued that "in [man's] adventure of self-consciousness [he] must come to the limits of himself and become aware of something beyond him. A man must be self-conscious enough to know his own limits, and to be aware of that which surpasses him" (*Phoenix* 185). *Lady Chatterley's Lover* is a study of the tension between these two ideas, between the need to rescue sexuality from secrecy, to bring it into discourse, and the simultaneous recognition that the re-creation of sexuality in language must always, at the same time, resist language.

NOTES

1. Michel Foucault, *The History of Sexuality*, vol. 1, trans. Robert Hurley (New York: Pantheon Books, 1978), pp. 157–58.

2. Michel Foucault, "A Preface to Transgression," in *Language, Counter-Memory, Practice: Selected Essays and Interviews*, ed. Donald F. Bouchard, trans. Bouchard and Sherry Simon (Ithaca: Cornell University Press, 1977), p. 29.

3. Ibid., p. 30.

4. Scott Sanders, *D. H. Lawrence: The World of the Five Major Novels* (New York: Viking, 1974), p. 195. Sanders is only one of a number of critics who have found Lawrence's treatment of sex in some way inadequate. See, for example, Julian Moynahan, *The Deed of Life: The Novels and Tales of D. H. Lawrence* (Princeton, N.J.: Princeton University Press, 1963), pp. 140–72; David Parker, "Lawrence and Lady Chatterley: The Teller and the Tale," *Critical Review* 20 (1978): 31–41; and Kingsley Widmer, "The Pertinence of Modern Pastoral: The Three Versions of *Lady Chatterley's Lover*," *Studies in the Novel* 5 (Fall 1973): 298–313. Moynahan, although admiring Lawrence, argues that the reader of *Lady Chatterley* "fails to achieve any deep realization of the sexual mystery" (163); Parker faults the third version of the novel for its "narrow didactic preoccupation with sex" (34); Widmer maintains that the novel's "reduction of erotic fulfillment and conversion to a highly specific, and quite likely idiosyncratic, sexuality may weaken the larger theme and exemplary role of the lovers" (300).

5. See, for example, G. Wilson Knight, "Lawrence, Joyce and Powys," *Essays in Criticism* 11, no. 4 (October 1956): 403–17, and the subsequent debate in the same journal, 12, nos. 2 and 4; 13, nos. 1–3; Mark Spilka's review of Colin Clarke's *River of Dissolution* in "Lawrence Up-Tight, or the Anal Phase Once Over," *Novel* 4, no. 3 (Spring 1971): 252–67, and the subsequent replies by George Ford, Frank Kermode, and Colin Clarke in *Novel* 5, no. 1; and John Sparrow, "Regina v. Penguin Books Ltd.," *Encounter* 13, no. 2 (February 1962): 35–43.

6. For two different emphases on the novel's treatment of sexuality, representative of the divided approaches, see the recent collection *D. H. Lawrence: The Man Who Lived,* ed. Robert B. Partlow, Jr., and Harry T. Moore (Carbondale: Southern Illinois University Press, 1980): Mark Spilka, "Lawrence Versus Peeperkorn on Abdication; or *What Happens to a Pagan Vitalist When the Juice Runs Out?*" and Peter H. Balbert, "The Loving of Lady Chatterley: D. H. Lawrence and the Phallic Imagination," in particular pp. 143, 116, and 156.

7. Readings of the novel which are not centrally concerned with its language of sexuality include but are certainly not restricted to the following: Joseph C. Voelker, "The Spirit of No-Place: Elements of the Classical Ironic Utopia in D. H. Lawrence's *Lady Chatterley's Lover,*" *Modern Fiction Studies* 25, no. 2 (Summer 1979): 223–39; Michael Squires, *The Pastoral Novel: Studies in George Eliot, Thomas Hardy, and D. H. Lawrence* (Charlottesville: University Press of Virginia, 1974), pp. 196–212; Dennis Jackson, "The 'Old Pagan Vision': Myth and Ritual in *Lady Chatterley's Lover,*" *D. H. Lawrence Review* 11, no. 3 (Fall 1978): 260–71; Jerome Mandel, "Medieval Romance and *Lady Chatterley's Lover,*" *D. H. Lawrence Review* 10, no. 1 (Spring 1977): 20–33.

8. D. H. Lawrence, "Sex Isn't Sin," in *The Complete Poems of D. H. Lawrence,* ed. Vivian de Sola Pinto and F. Warren Roberts (New York: Viking, 1971), p. 464.

9. Sanders, *The World of the Five Major Novels,* p. 182.

10. Robert Scholes, *Structuralism in Literature: An Introduction* (New Haven: Yale University Press, 1974), pp. 16 and 150.

11. Ibid., p. 197.

12. See, for example, the discussion in "The Confession of the Flesh," in Michel Foucault, *Power/Knowledge: Selected Interviews and Other Writings, 1972–1977,* ed. Colin Gordon, trans. Gordon et al. (New York: Pantheon Books, 1980).

13. Roland Barthes, *A Lover's Discourse,* trans. Richard Howard (New York: Hill and Wang, 1978), p. 149.

14. Ibid., p. 99 and p. 104.

15. Foucault, "A Preface to Transgression," p. 50 and pp. 29–30.

16. "Let There be Light!" in *The Complete Poems of D. H. Lawrence,* p. 681.

17. D. H. Lawrence, *The Complete Short Stories,* vol. 3 (New York: Viking, 1961), p. 746.

18. "Sex Isn't Sin," in *The Complete Poems of D. H. Lawrence,* p. 465.

19. "Know-All," in *The Complete Poems of D. H. Lawrence,* p. 726.

20. Foucault, "The Confession of the Flesh," p. 209.

21. Ibid., pp. 215–16.

22. Foucault, "A Preface to Transgression," p. 31 and p. 51.

23. Foucault, "Body/Power," in *Power/Knowledge,* pp. 56–57.

24. "Noli me Tangere," in *The Complete Poems of D. H. Lawrence,* p. 469.

25. Jonathan Culler, *Structuralist Poetics: Structuralism, Linguistics and the Study of Literature* (Ithaca: Cornell University Press, 1975), p. 134.

26. G. Genot, quoted in Culler, *Structuralist Poetics,* p. 139.

27. Culler, *Structuralist Poetics,* p. 138. Culler writes, "Actions are plausible or

implausible with respect to the norms of a group of works, and reactions which would be thoroughly intelligible in a Proustian novel would be extremely bizarre and inexplicable in Balzac" (145).

28. Ibid., p. 147.

29. Ibid., p. 148.

30. Ibid., pp. 150–52.

31. George Levine, *The Realistic Imagination: English Fiction from Frankenstein to Lady Chatterley* (Chicago: University of Chicago Press, 1981), pp. 323–24. In a related argument, Evelyn J. Hinz writes, "Lawrence's own criticisms of various types of fictional practices and attitudes in the final version of the work and in 'A Propos of *Lady Chatterley's Lover*' are as much directed against his own practice in the first two versions as they are against any other examples." See "Pornography, Novel, Mythic Narrative: The Three Versions of *Lady Chatterley's Lover*," *Modernist Studies* 3, no. 1 (1979): 36.

32. Marie Carmichael Stopes, *Married Love: A New Contribution to the Solution of Sex Difficulties* (London: A. C. Fifield, 1918), pp. 19–20.

33. Culler, *Structuralist Poetics*, p. 223.

34. Quoted in Culler, *Structuralist Poetics*, p. 192.

35. Alan Sheridan, *Michel Foucault: The Will to Truth* (London: Tavistock Publications, 1980), p. 58.

36. Quoted in Culler, *Structuralist Poetics*, p. 252.

T. H. ADAMOWSKI

The Natural Flowering of Life: The Ego, Sex, and Existentialism

The natural flowering of life! It is not so easy for human beings as it sounds.
—Lawrence, *Etruscan Places*

*God is dead. And the moment in which one feels this death with the greatest
despair is the same in which Divine cried: "Behold the God,"
the moment of orgasm.*
—Sartre, *Saint Genet*

In 1971, in *The Prisoner of Sex*, Norman Mailer engaged in a debate with a secular view of sexual life. In this case secularism had incarnated itself in feminism, and it operated by reference to a logic very different from the one an undergraduate Mailer had found in *Lady Chatterley's Lover:* "I read *Lady Chatterley's Lover* in college. The unabridged edition. In the Treasure Room at Widener. It changed my life. It was the first thing I'd ever read that gave me the idea sex could have beauty. I learned from Lawrence that the way to write about sex was not to strike poses, but be true to the logic of each moment. There's a subtle logic to love."[1] Secular logic proceeds, however, along those lines of "rationalization" and "disenchantment of the world" that Max Weber saw comprising the Western destiny. Under the aspect of this logic, an enterprise like Lawrence's (or Mailer's) could only seem mystification.

Nevertheless, Mailer accepted secularism's challenge, and in an astonishing act of empathy with Lawrence's novelistic project (and, perhaps, the finest essay on Lawrence of the decade), he cast himself as the "Advocate" of his predecessor in a tradition that views sexual life as the Royal Road to Being. But for Mailer any journey along that road has always committed one to another tradition: existentialism. And here also, if only implicitly, Lawrence is, for Mailer, a predecessor. According to the Advocate, Lawrence tells us "again and again" that "people can win at love only when they are ready to lose everything they bring to it of ego, position, or identity—love is more stern than war—and men and women survive only if they reach the depths of their own sex down within themselves. They have to deliver themselves 'over to the unknown.' *No more existential statement of love exists,* for it is a way of saying we do not know how the love will turn out."[2] We do not know the outcome because the "subtle logic of love" rules out the "poses" by which we protect ourselves against surprise. It demands that we lose our compass-bearings of "ego, position, or identity" and that we return to what Lawrence called the *terra incognita* of the bodily life of spontaneity and natural freedom. It is, of course, our freedom—lying as it does at the heart of all risk-taking—that will be tested by the ambiguities of love; and the risks are great because we engage in this return to bodily life with another self that has also accepted its birthright of freedom.[3] Thus is a sexual act an existential act, and, Mailer has argued, we are in an "existential situation" when "something important and/or unfamiliar is taking place, and . . . [we] do not know how it is going to turn out."[4]

Strange tangle of ideas. Mailer, the existentialist Advocate of a profoundly existential Lawrence, is arguing against a secularist ideology that insists men and women are not doomed by differences of gender to differences of Spirit. The secularist Prosecutor, Kate Millett, has learned this creed from Simone de Beauvoir, whose chapter in *The Second Sex* on Lawrence's "phallic pride" says what Millett's chapter says—but says it better. And shorter. However, Simone de Beauvoir's challenge to biological determinism owes its conceptual premises to what she learned from Jean-Paul Sartre. Sartre: existentialist. And yet Mailer's point about Lawrencean sexual love is that "no more existential statement of love exists." Can this Advocate, whose protagonist in *An American Dream* is a professor of "existential psychology," be in error about Lawrence? After all, the Advocate is not a scholar but merely a "poet." Poets are notorious for turning concepts into conceits.

However, as long ago as 1934, a great *scholar* of existentialism, Jean Wahl, had pointed to affinities between Lawrence's work and "cette philosophie existentielle dont plusieurs penseurs aujourd'hui en France et en Allemagne, Gabriel Marcel, Martin Heidegger, Karl Jaspers, nous donnent l'idée."[5] And one of those philosophers, Marcel, responded with sympathy to something we know Lawrence sought to achieve in his work: "Le monde de Lawrence n'est point . . . avant tout un monde de personnes; c'est un monde de températures, de pressions, de tensions, de fulgurations; et son oeuvre me fait l'effet d'une météorologie lyrique de la nature humaine."[6] In 1930, without the benefit of Lawrence's letter to Garnett on that "which is physic— non-human in humanity," Marcel sensed Lawrence's effort to go beyond, or beneath, the "ego," the "personality," to some more basic level of the self.[7]

If there is something "existential" in Lawrence's work, we must look for it in his objection to all that is suggested by such parallel terms as *ego, character,* and *personality.*[8] What remains after the ego has been discarded is what was always already there. Before the ego comes to be, the bodily self, the "unconscious" self, *is.* It is in his conception of an impersonal self that Lawrence comes closest to the religious existentialist of Manhattan and to the secular existentialist of Paris.

Moreover, this conception of a self-of-the-body entails that sense of "otherness" that also allies Lawrence with existentialism. As Others, sealed within our bodies—or as Others because we *are* bodies—we exist as incommensurable perspectives on the world. And we feel the distance between us as something to be overcome—but overcome, Lawrence insists, without denying the body. Thus in the work of Lawrence—as in that of the existentialist Sartre, who will be my point of reference here—sexual experience comes to play an important role. What it *appears* to offer is a *way out* of the isolation of otherness while, paradoxically, respecting the corporeal precondition of otherness. And yet in this matter of sex Lawrence (and his Advocate) parts company with Sartre. For this most secular of existentialist thinkers, the word *existential* is not talismanic, and sex offers no means to reenchant the world.

To the extent that Lawrence is concerned with the pre-personal self he is not a "psychological" novelist. We must reserve this description for the work of another writer, Sir Clifford Chatterley: "The observa-

38

tion [in his stories] was extraordinary and peculiar. But there was no touch, no actual contact. It was as if the whole thing took place in a vacuum. And since the field of life is largely an artificially-lighted stage today, the stories were curiously true to modern life, to the modern psychology, that is" (*LCL* 50). The reference to the "lighted stage" of modern life makes clear that Lawrence has in mind the personal self. For him this is a self of "poses" and "masks": "*Persona*, in Latin, is a player's mask, or a character in a play" (*Phoenix* 710). Now there is only a finite number of these masks, for psychology depends on the possibility of taxonomy: the psychological writer is the classifier of masked selves. Furthermore, these masks are forms of predictability that represent the mechanization of the self and its subjection to determinism: "personalities and *egos* . . . are quite *reasonable*, which means, they are subject to the laws of cause-and-effect; they are safe and calculable: materialists, units of the material world of Force and Matter" (*Phoenix* 711). Finally, such predictability is boring. As boring as Connie comes to find her husband's conversation (it is at one with his fiction): "But when he was not 'working,' and she was there, he talked, always talked; infinite small analysis of people and motives, and results, characters and personalities, till now she had had enough" (*LCL* 126).

Until this boredom set in, however, Connie had thrilled to the revelations of "mind" offered to her, in Clifford's drawing room, by her husband and his "cronies." They thrived on her presence, for, Lawrence warns, the personal self must know itself *known*. In short, the ego is an object of *reflection*: "the self-conscious ego, the entity of fixed ideas and ideals, prancing and displaying itself like an actor" (*Phoenix* 711). It is by reference to this phenomenon of "reflection" that Lawrence indicts what Tommy Dukes calls the "mental life," with its tendency to "flourish with its roots in spite, ineffable and fathomless spite" (*LCL* 73). Indeed, insofar as the personal self *is* the mind's view of itself, and insofar as this mirrored self is a self-beyond-the-body (over there, in the mirror), friction is inevitable; for the ego is the condition of what Sartre calls our "distinction." And psychological fiction is the calculus of the small differences (within and among types of personality) that constitute distinction and that cause friction.[9] The body, however, is the place of indistinction, of that which we share, of the Similar. But, paradoxically, it is also the source of otherness—no two bodies may occupy the same space at the same time—and if otherness itself accounts for much of the tension apparent in Lawrence's accounts of relationships among selves, then in the ego we find the *surplus-anxiety* of otherness.[10]

Eventually the circle closes, and the "ideal" life of the personal self becomes the cause of bodily malaise—as in Connie's feeling that Clifford's spirit-self is a vampiric force that aims at "sucking all the life-sap out of living things" (*LCL* 137). Bodily malaise is, of course, a major concern of *Lady Chatterley's Lover*. It is there in the dreary singing of the Standard Five girls in Tevershall, in the paralysis of Clifford, in the impotence of Dukes and the premature ejaculations of Michaelis, in the distorted bodies of the colliers, and in the bodily decline of Lady Chatterley herself: "a restlessness was taking possession of her like madness. It twitched her limbs when she didn't want to twitch them, it jerked her spine when she didn't want to jerk upright but preferred to rest comfortably. It thrilled inside her body, in her womb, somewhere . . ." (*LCL* 54). Live long enough by the Spirit and you waste away—as Connie realizes, appropriately, before her mirror. But it is a sign of her Election that she recognizes the cause of her malaise: "The mental life! Suddenly she hated it with a rushing fury, the swindle!" (*LCL* 111). Self-awareness is unfreedom: the loss of natural spontaneity and the fall into the mechanical tic-like jerkings and twitchings that remind us of our "buried life" even as they parody spontaneity. The "true self," on the other hand, is "not aware that it is a self" (*Phoenix* 382). This self is "not by any means a Logos. It precedes any knowing. It is the fountainhead of everything: the quick of the self" (*Phoenix* 709). And we must seek it in the "mysterious labyrinth of the body" (*Phoenix II* 620–21).

Cure for the malaise is, then, by way of the denied body—not by way of what Clifford offers. For him the "real secret of marriage" is that "little by little, living together, two people fall into a sort of unison, they vibrate so intricately to one another. That's the real secret of marriage, not sex. . . . You and I are interwoven in a marriage" (*LCL* 82). This is the mental-reflective life raised to incandescence: pure denial of otherness. But neither is the cure by way of the flawed body of Michaelis, whose ejaculations represent the mental tainting of orgasm.

Return to the untainted body comes only with the recognition of otherness, but for someone like Connie, long committed to mental life, such recognition demands "vision": "Yet in some curious way it was a visionary experience: it had hit her in the middle of the body. She saw the clumsy breeches slipping down over the pure, delicate, white loins, the bones showing a little, and the sense of aloneness, of a creature purely alone, overwhelmed her" (*LCL* 107). When Connie finds Mellors washing himself, what she sees is, simply, "a body," and on the level of her impersonal consciousness she experiences the "shock of [this] vision in her womb." But, Lawrence adds, "with her mind," where she remains Constance Chatterley, she ridicules the sight.

If we wish to see where Lawrence's critique of this corrosive mental self and his insistence on a self that precedes reflection overlap with the concerns of existentialism, we should turn to the work of Sartre. In Sartre's critique of the ego and in his general novelistic response to what he calls "human reality" we are closer to the world of Lawrence the *novelist* than in the other canonical texts of existentialism. It is impossible to attempt here anything more than a sketch of Sartre's account of the self, but certain aspects of that account do bear on Lawrence's own work. These include the notion that consciousness is not first a means of reflection but a way of living in the world; the ego's status as an object *of* consciousness and a mask assumed by the latter to deny its inherent freedom; and the refusal to distinguish consciousness from the body.

While Sartre does not offer a critique of "mental life" or attempt (as Lawrence *sometimes* seems to do) to deny the value of reflection, his conception of man—of "Being For-itself"—grants no privilege to the ego. He argues that the self operates at two levels of consciousness: prereflective and reflective. But the "consciousness which says *I think*"—the reflective form—"is precisely not the consciousness which thinks."[11] In that primary, prereflective consciousness, the ego has no place; for this consciousness is "empty"; it is a "nothingness," a wind blowing against objects that brings us into living relationship with them: "When I run after a streetcar, when I look at the time, when I am absorbed in contemplating a portrait, there is no *I*. There is consciousness *of the streetcar-having-to-be-overtaken*, etc., and nonpositional consciousness of consciousness. In fact, I am then plunged into the world of objects; it is they which constitute the unity of my consciousness; it is they which present themselves with values, with attractive and repellant qualities—but *me,* I have disappeared; I have annihilated myself. There is no place for *me* on this level" (*TE* 48–49). For Lawrence it is on "this level" that *life* is to be found: impersonality, the "inhuman," and the "true, deeper spontaneous self." Like Sartre, he would agree that if we tried to live by the ego it would come between us and the world.

Sartre, however, does not deny reality to the ego. Rather, he refuses to build on it his conception of freedom. Freedom, he thinks, has nothing to do with freedom of the will, a phenomenon of reflective life and thereby in league with the ego.[12] The latter is simply the self as it is seen by reflective consciousness. We find the ego when we pause to read our life-histories. Thus Sartre would agree with Lawrence's remark in *Psychoanalysis and the Unconscious* that the ego "is merely the sum total of what we conceive ourselves to be."[13] It is what we take to be the meaning of the past of the self, of the style of its past activity and inactivity. But prereflective consciousness—what Sartre calls a "monstrous spontaneity"—is always in principle free to choose for itself another ego.

Like Lawrence, Sartre believed that we fear this monstrous spontaneity because it leaves us perpetually open to that "unknown" that lies before us, in the future. Thus the for-itself tries to act as though it were only what it *has been.* It tries, that is, to live under the patronage of the ego. In this "fear of itself" Sartre finds the source of "psychasthenic ailments" that bring malaise to the body (*TE* 102). However, the for-itself cannot be its past as my typing-paper is white. It is always *in question* for itself. What is not in question is "being-in-itself": the sidewalk, typing-paper, trees, the ego—all that is other than consciousness. We come to the "present" of our spontaneous life trailing behind us a certain form of the in-itself with which we share intimate relations: this ego we find whenever we pause to look over our shoulder. And because we fear our freedom we may seek to *coincide with* that ego and thereby become, in Lawrence's word, "predictable"—as Sartre notes apropos of the ego of Genet, in a remark that recalls Lawrence's etymological critique of personality: "It is his soul, the governing principle of his behavior, his entelechy. It is a *person* in the Latin sense of *persona*—I mean a mask and a role whose behavior and speeches are already set down."[14]

Later I will suggest that in the sexual episodes of *Lady Chatterley's Lover* Lawrence offers a kind of analogue to the for-itself's desire for coincidence with its ego. At issue is the desire of the for-itself to coincide with flesh insofar as, by a kind of erotic "white magic," the for-itself seeks to capture ("in the flesh") the freedom of its sexual partner. It is necessary first, however, to point to what it is in the existentialist conception of the self that not only parallels Lawrence's own but makes possible a critique of Lawrencean sexuality.

So profoundly does consciousness dream of freedom from freedom that, Sartre concludes, it desires to provide for itself a "foundation" that would guarantee it stability *without* extinguishing the unstable play of consciousness. Sartre calls this ideal the "in-itself-for-itself," the "*Ens causa sui* which religions call God" (*BN* 615). This human "passion" for freedom within unfreedom (e.g., to be a free consciousness that is "nothing more" than an ego) is, in Sartre's notorious term of dismissal, "useless."

Useless, but not baseless. That other point of resemblance between Sartre and Lawrence—their insistence that consciousness is embodied—permits us to understand how a spontaneous consciousness might be tempted to imagine itself a freedom-thing. Not only must Lawrence's Christ give up the illusion of his divinity but he must abandon the illusion of being a privileged spirit-self enclosed within the arbitrary limits of a body: "I wanted to be greater than the limits of my hands and feet."[15] Or, in Sartre's terms, the body "is what consciousness is; it is not even anything except body" (*BN* 329–30). Moreover, this embodied self is a self "in situation," engaged in modifying the world (which in turn is always modifying it) in the light of what Sartre calls its "project," and what, in *Fantasia,* Lawrence calls a "great predominant purpose" (*FU* 191).

But this embodied, situated self is also composed of the flesh and bone that can be "recalled" to the in-itself. While climbing a stairway, the for-itself may slip on a roller skate and be returned to the physicochemical world of gravity, friction, bruises, and so forth. Nor need its flesh and bone be merely a danger to it. Like the mental image of the ego, the flesh may offer a promise of stability, the vegeto-mineral stability of the "natural." No accident, then, that the flesh can be made to serve the for-itself's desire to find forms of completion and fulfillment: "Thus this perpetually absent being which haunts the for-itself is itself fixed in the in-itself. It is the impossible synthesis of the for-itself and the in-itself" (*BN* 90). This "impossible synthesis" would provide for the self the "translucency of consciousness" along with the coincidence with itself of being in-itself. On the plane of the ego, Sartre's "Saint Genet" tries to coincide with a regularity of criminal behavior that others have assured him is his. On the plane of the flesh, the attempt at self-completion may reveal itself in so trivial a form as chronic nail-biting (to be the thing chewed and the self that chews). Or, as I will indicate shortly, the attempt may be made sexually.

Thus this embodied self is poised in paradox: other than nature and yet composed of nature. A "decompression in being," other than the in-itself of ego and of flesh, always a thrust forward into the future—the for-itself "is not what it is and it is what it is not." In this matter of embodied consciousness or bodily self, what distinguishes Lawrence from Sartre is the relative emphasis each puts on the terms at issue. For Lawrence we seem first to be bodies that *find ourselves conscious*. For Sartre, it is as if, first, there is a consciousness that *finds itself embodied*. Lawrence seems to grant a privilege to the body and to a spontaneity that mimes the spontaneity of nature. For Sartre, however, we lose in authenticity whenever we seek to become what we cannot be: *natural*. As we would lose in authenticity if, by reference to an ego, we sought to be no more than that "introvert" or "extrovert" we have been.

Thus *existential* freedom lies on the far side of nature. Nature is what it is and not some other thing. It is not "in question" for itself. But neither Lawrence nor Sartre will grant to the personalized self of limitations and recurrences any priority in the self. Each challenges that self by positing an ur-self that precedes reflection. However, where Lawrence seeks to make us yearn for coincidence with nature— one that will come as naturally as the orgasms of Mellors and Connie come together—Sartre's for-itself can never slip outside of existence and into natural consciousness.

I am suggesting, then, that Mailer's honorific "existential" is most clearly relevant to Lawrence's critique of the mental-reflective life and the incorporeal ego to which it gives birth. But two dangers face such a critique. First, the return to the impersonal self may be seen as an advocacy of "primitivism" or "irrationalism." Second, the return to the body may entail a corporeal isolation every bit as "menacing" as the "individualism" (a "mental" phenomenon) to which Lawrence objects in his essay "A Propos of *Lady Chatterley's Lover*" (*Phoenix II* 513). The charge of irrationalism has also been made—with equal irrelevance—against existentialism. As has the more telling charge of individualist isolationism.

Tommy Dukes recognizes the first danger and warns his listeners, "I wasn't talking about knowledge. . . . I was talking about the mental life. . . . Real knowledge comes out of the whole corpus of the consciousness . . ." (*LCL* 74). For Lawrence the "resurrection of the body" and the "democracy of touch" have epistemological consequences, although not, perhaps, those we have come to admire since the seventeenth century.[16] Once we become impersonal we will see the world as in itself it really is, for we will no longer see it through a film of Spirit. It is with such a film that Clifford Chatterley coats the world: "[Connie] was angry with him, turning everything into words. Violets were Juno's eyelids, and windflowers were unravished brides. How she hated words, always coming between her and life: they did the ravishing, if anything did: ready-made words and phrases, sucking all the life-sap out of living things" (*LCL* 137). Remove that film and one can apprehend the life of the wood: "Constance sat down with her back to a young pine-tree, that swayed against her with curious life, elastic, and powerful, rising up. The erect, alive thing, with its top in the sun!" (*LCL* 129). After she and Mellors have made love, this sensitivity to the world rises to a pitch of acuteness. Then, as she "ran home in the twilight the world seemed a dream; the trees in the park seemed bulging and surging at anchor on a tide, and the heave of the slope to the house was alive" (*LCL* 234).

In such passages we hear the voice of the pantheistic—or, perhaps, the pagan—Lawrence of *Birds, Beasts and Flowers, Twilight in Italy, Mornings in Mexico,* and *Etruscan Places.* In those books it is the unmediated rapport between the narrator and the living world that we sense. And in such passages no existentialist philosopher is more likely to come to mind than the Heidegger who also *went back,* before Rome, before Plato, to a world that had not yet lost sight of Being. "It must have been a wonderful world," Lawrence writes, "that old world where everything appeared alive and shining in the dusk of contact with all things, not merely an isolated individual thing played upon by daylight."[17]

But the voice of the lyric poet and of the traveler across the out-of-the-way places of past and present is not the object of the novelist's gaze. That gaze must register the self in relationship with others and not merely a plurality of I's, each apprehending the world's body. In fact, one of the consolations of Clifford's spirit-world is that it is not lonely! Intimacy—the interweaving of spirit with spirit—is what his world offers, and Clifford knows that the barrier to such intimacy is the body. Thus he entertains theories of evolution that promise we will leave behind the corporeal shells that (for this man of spirit) we now inhabit.

Indeed, when Mellors first makes love to Connie she senses in this alien body the great problem of embodiment—the distance it imposes between selves: "The man lay in a mysterious stillness. What was he feeling? What was he thinking? She did not know. He was a strange man to her, she did not know him" (*LCL* 164). It goes without saying that Connie's response has nothing to do with her limited "personal" knowledge of Mellors. And to the extent to which this distance *is* a problem, Lawrence's way round it requires that we accept our embodi-ment. Nor does he believe such an "acceptance" to be inevitable: all of the ego stands as a tribute to our capacity to deny the body. But if we do accept embodiment, Lawrence assumes that what can hold between the self and nature—Connie's sense of the swaying life of a tree, or, in *Fantasia,* Lawrence's sense of the life of a forest—can also hold *between selves* authentically embodied. Return with the Other to the body and together you will take the straight line of existence and turn it round on itself into a circle.

Mailer finds the "existential" encounter with the "unknown" in

Lawrence's work in such normative moments as those of *Lady Chatterley's Lover* when Lawrence imagines this two-part solution to the isolation of embodiment (acceptance of the body and rapport with the Other). But from the perspective of Sartrean existentialism this is to bring in through the back door what has been thrown out the front door: stability, recurrence, and coherence—an existence that is providing itself with a foundation. At the same time, however, those scenes of sexual love in Lawrence's fiction must put us in mind of the most famous existentialist meditation on sex: Sartre's, in *Being and Nothingness*. If those Lawrencean scenes seem doubtfully existential and yet also call to mind an existentialist account of sexual life, this is owing, in each case, to the role of "nature." Recall Connie's disgust with "words" that form over living nature a spiritual coating. As she grows impersonal no word stands between her and a swaying pine-tree or a heaving slope of earth. Within her and without her is the same nature. All we need to do is undertake, as she does, the self-purification that will make us present to nature: "It is a question . . . of relationship. We *must* get back into relation, vivid and nourishing relation to the cosmos and the universe. The way is through daily ritual, and the re-awakening" ("A Propos of *Lady Chatterley's Lover*," *Phoenix II* 510). This is the dialectic of the infinite—in short, of romanticism's myth of the "circuitous return" of man to what he has lost. M. H. Abrams's account of Lawrence's *Apocalypse* makes clear what is at issue on this journey: "What Lawrence has done . . . is to revise the Scriptural account of the fall and apocalypse, as Blake had done before him, by accepting, as a literal truth of the imagination, the myth of the catastrophic division of the Primal Man who once did, and will again, incorporate heaven and earth and god and man."[18] And, we can add, "man and woman," as they journey together on the royal road of sex.

Now in Sartre's *Nausea* there is also a critique of words and of the reflective life that uses them to establish distance from nature. And, like Connie, Antoine Roquentin has *seen through* words and known vision: "And suddenly, suddenly, the veil is torn away, I have understood, I have *seen*." What he sees is that "words had vanished and with them the significance of things, their methods of use, and the feeble points of reference which men have traced on their surface."[19]

He realizes not the similarity of man to nature but the terrible difference between them. He understands that men, the measurers of all things, have used those measures for protection; but now the "veneer" of verbal measurement has "melted, leaving soft, monstrous masses, all in disorder—naked, in a frightful, obscene nakedness" (*N* 127). And Roquentin, too, comes to know the being of a tree. In his case, a chestnut tree. But once "chestnut" loses its "use," Roquentin sees that the "world of explanations and reasons is not the world of existence." Circles are not absurd, but then they don't exist: "This root, on the other hand, existed in such a way that I could not explain it. Knotty, inert, nameless, it fascinated me, filled my eyes, brought me back unceasingly to its own existence. In vain to repeat: 'This is a root'—it didn't work any more" (*N* 129). This is the dialectic of the finite that, in *The Devil and the Good Lord*, Sartre's Goetz adumbrates when he announces, "No more Heaven, no more Hell; nothing but earth." And earth is *de trop*. This is all it has in common with the for-itself. Nor will it do to say of Roquentin's response to the root that it represents a "neurotic" response to nature. This is a game that two can play, and the immediate riposte is to point to forms of "neurotic" closeness ("oral" in character) to nature in the romantic tradition.

As for Roquentin's ego, it is also out of commission: "Now when I say 'I,' it seems hollow to me. I can't manage to feel myself very well. . . . The only thing left in me is existence which feels it exists. I yawn, lengthily. No one. Antoine Roquentin exists for no one. That amuses me. And just what is Antoine Roquentin. An abstraction. A pale reflection of myself wavers in my consciousness. Antoine Roquentin . . . and suddenly the 'I' pales, pales and fades out" (*N* 170). What remains are "anonymous walls, anonymous consciousness. That is what there is: walls, and between the walls, a small transparency, alive and impersonal." Embodied, isolated, Roquentin concludes his diary by dreaming of circularity, of a work of art.

If we turn to those encounters with the "unknown" in Lawrence's work that Mailer calls existential, we must recognize that Lawrence intends them to be solutions to the dangers of isolation within anonymous walls: "She felt the glide of his cheek on her thighs and belly and buttocks, and the close brushing of his moustache and his soft thick hair, and her knees began to quiver. Far down in her she felt a new stirring, a new nakedness emerging. And she was half afraid. Half she wished he would not caress her so. He was encompassing her somehow" (*LCL* 174). She is "half afraid" of her body, her spontaneity's assertion of itself. Then comes her moment of bad faith, as she wills herself "into separateness," returns to her ego, and *reflects on* the "buttocks" ("supremely ridiculous") of the creature who is with her.[20]

When she does allow her will to lapse, it is only after a fight: "Her old instinct was to fight for her freedom. But something else in her was strange and inert and heavy. His body was urgent against her . . ." (*LCL* 182). The "something" "inert and heavy" is her authentic freedom (not the personal freedom of which she thinks), represented here as a troubling of the flesh brought about by Mellors's caresses. Later, when she sees his erect penis, Connie's "own mind melted out" in harmony with the "changed . . . direction" of Mellors's "stream of consciousness" (*LCL* 271). In such passages two things occur. There is, first, the drama of a double "resurrection of the body": the body de-situated, become curiously inert, and yet at a pitch of activity. And, second, the imagery is consistently as much of liquid (meltings, waves, surges, plasms) as it is of the flesh (belly, buttock, thigh). Those images of liquescence suggest that in the inertness of the heavy flesh there is the ecstasy of consciousness. Furthermore, all of this is suspended in the most urgent and insistent rhetoric. The lovers are, of course, silent. It is their reflective creator, the third party at the double resurrection, who is speaking. These paradoxes of liquefaction and bodily substantiality, of activity and passivity, are all in order, for Lawrence is being his "passionately religious" self. He is imagining a miracle.

Anyone who admires Lawrence's fiction soon comes up against the problem of those representations of sexual love. What do those passages *mean*? Is Lawrence not being too serious, too "puritanical" about sex? The voice of Hip Enlightenment. Are such passages not sentimental? The voice of Hard-Boiled Criticism (ca. 1956)—that always has a follow-up question: has Lawrence not failed to find an "objective correlative" for such scenes? All these questions hang suspended from the first, the question of meaning that may be rewritten as "What does sex mean?" Here, from *Saint Genet,* is what I think it means for the "priest of love": "Is not the religious moment par excellence that in which a subjectivity, ceasing to disperse itself indefinitely in everyday reality, regains its eternal being, becomes a calm totality in full possession of itself?" (SG 63).

In effect, then, I am arguing that the meaning of sex for Lawrence can be understood by reference to what Sartre calls the for-itself's quest to become *Ens causa sui* (what Abrams calls the reincorporation of "heaven and earth and god and man"). The for-itself would like to *be* the prefabricated self that is the ego and thereby never know anguish. But it would like to *know itself* prefabricated: always, out of the corner of a residually impersonal eye, to see itself become "purely" personal. In that surreptitious glance, of course, it deconstructs the character it builds for itself. On the sexual plane, however, things are more complicated. There the for-itself seeks to resolve the general problem of a life of otherness. Under the eyes of the Other it can become an object: ugly, shameful, inadequate, handsome, proud, adept. Become an object (in-itself), it can recover its freedom only by turning on the Other a counter-glance so rich with subjectivity that it can reduce the Other to thinghood. Or, with Saint Genet, it may seek to catch up with the objectivity conferred upon it by others. As in Ransom's poem on Paolo and Francesca, there is "no end to this."

Unless, perhaps, we can lay a trap for Being. And perform—in a bedroom, or a hut in a wood—a certain kind of ceremony that will allow us—I and the beloved—to be *both* subject (free and desiring) and object (flesh and desired): "Desire is an attitude aiming at enchantment. Since I can grasp the Other only in his objective facticity, the problem is to ensnare his freedom within this facticity. It is necessary that he be 'caught' in it as the cream is caught up by a person skimming milk. So the Other's For-itself must come to play on the surface of his body . . . ; and by touching this body I should finally touch the Other's free subjectivity" (*BN* 394). This is sex-as-reenchantment. The impossible ideal of desire is to overcome isolation by having consciousness touch consciousness at the very instant when each of the partners is reduced to flesh. The ceremony demands a certain act of "incarnation" (double, reciprocal) whereby I and the beloved step outside the situations of everyday living and bring ourselves into the presence of our living bodies by removing those bodies from the world of activity. It is *gesture*—action performed for its own sake—that we seek in sexual love. To borrow some terms from formalist criticism, we must "foreground" our bodies by "defamiliarizing" them, and to accomplish this we call on the master-gesture of desire, the caress: "It is my flesh alone which knows how to find the road to the Other's flesh, and I lay my flesh next to her flesh so as to awaken her to the meaning of flesh. In the caress when I slowly lay my inert hand against the Other's flank, I am making that flank feel my flesh, and this can be achieved only if it renders itself inert. The shiver of pleasure which it feels is . . . the awakening of its consciousness as flesh" (*BN* 396). It is as difficult to bring this off as it is to overcome that linguistic obstacle to the for-itself's effort to become God that Jacques Derrida calls "*différance.*"

Thus, for the existentialist, existence is enmeshed in the dialectic of finitude, and desire's goal is doomed to failure. Consciousness seeks to entrap itself in its flesh and, by means of a caressing hand, to entrap in her flesh the consciousness of the Other. It is a strategy that "while aiming at the body as a whole attains it especially through masses of flesh which are very little differentiated, grossly nerveless, hardly capable of spontaneous movement, through breasts, buttocks, thighs, stomach . . ." (*BN* 396). This strategy (to be body-as-subject-and-body-as-object) works against the threat to incarnation posed by the lived-body's need to act, to *initiate* the routines of sex that return the gesture to the world of action. And, worse, at the moment of orgasmic ecstasy, the lived-body returns to itself:

> But pleasure is the death and the failure of desire. It is the death of desire because it is not only its fulfillment but its limit and its end. This, moreover, is only an organic contingency: it *happens that* the incarnation is manifested by erection and that the erection ceases with ejaculation. But in addition pleasure closes the sluice to desire because it motivates the appearance of a reflective *consciousness of* pleasure, whose object becomes a reflective enjoyment; that is, it is *attention to the incarnation of the For-itself which is reflected-on* and by the same token it is forgetful of the Other's incarnation. [*BN* 397]

What Lawrence (in *Fantasia*) calls the "circuit of coition" is an effort by both partners to achieve spontaneity-without-a-subject, to become with each other *natural consciousness.* From Sartre's perspective, however, that circuit cannot be completed. This is not to say, of course, that sex is somehow unpleasant! Rather, Sartre's point is that it cannot achieve its ideal aim.

If Lawrence shows us nothing like the Sartrean drama, it is because he is *not concerned to show failure*. Note, however, both the importance of the caress and the liquefaction of the lovers that are meant to suggest perfect fusion between consciousness and body: "He took her in his arms again and drew her to him, and suddenly she became small in his arms, small and nestling. It was gone, the resistance was gone, and she began to melt in a marvellous peace. And as she melted small and wonderful in his arms, she became infinitely desirable to him, all his blood-vessels seemed to scald with intense yet tender desire, for her, for her softness, for the penetrating beauty of her in his arms, passing into his blood" (*LCL* 228). The lived-body is becoming the object-body, and it is doing so in harmony with—and through the aid of—the transfiguration of the Other's body. The heart has reasons that reason can never know. The secular response is to say reason knows them *all too well*. And to add that we are witnessing here the attempt of all lovers—including the Hip-Enlightened and the Hard-Boiled—to make of two separate bodies one circuit of Being. That failure to establish the circuit of Being may account for why we respond to Lawrence's accounts of sexual experience with nostalgic sympathy or embarrassed disdain.

Lawrence would scorn this interpretation, but I suspect he would not deny that the "facts" in question are the same for him as for Sartre. Here, for example, is that ritual agent of transfiguration, the caress, moving along the "grossly undifferentiated" parts of the body in order to reach the presence of incarnated consciousness: "And softly, with that marvellous swoon-like caress of his hand in pure soft desire, softly he stroked the silky slope of her loins, down, down between her soft warm buttocks, coming nearer and nearer to the very quick of her. And she felt him like a flame of desire . . . and she felt herself melting in the flame" (*LCL* 228–29). Connie and Mellors alone in the world of gesture. Lawrence, the third party, alone in the world of action, of *reflection on* the desire of the lovers, of writing.

In *S/Z* Roland Barthes argues that "in the most realistic novel, the referent has no 'reality': suffice it to imagine the disorder the most orderly narrative would create were its descriptions taken at face value, converted into operative programs and simply *executed.*"[21] "*The novelistic real is not operable,*" Barthes emphatically concludes, with that solemnity and failure of nerve typical of the linguistic fetishism of post-structuralism. Now Lawrence could be solemn, but his novelist's nerve never failed him. We see the solemnity and the boldness in his remark that "I think . . . I have inside me a sort of answer to the *want* of today" (*CL* 183). For the "third party" in the hut, the novelistic real *is* operable; and yet, in the light of the existentialist meditation on selfhood, Lawrence's "answer" puts us in the presence not of completed consciousness but of that incomplete consciousness—immanent in his text—that is Lawrence's. However, *pace* Barthes, Lawrence's textual "referent" does have a "reality"; and if this reality is "inoperable," it is owing to the impossibility of lived sexual experience to satisfy the desire for completion that it can *imagine* in the "signifiers" of a "realistic novel."

If Lawrence and Sartre might be said to share a sense of the self's desire for completion-in-sexuality, there is yet another matter on which they seem to agree. If I "de-situate" my body, deprive it of its instrumental relation to the world, and live it as flesh, then the world must also change; for, in Sartre's words, it is "as a reference to my flesh that I apprehend the objects in the world" (*BN* 392). The lawn on which you make love is not the lawn you mow. Here Sartre's account of sexual life suggests a kind of positive dimension of his thought at variance with the generally gloomy outlook he offers on man's erotic ideals. What the return to the flesh offers is something *perceptual,* as one of Sartre's commentators has noted: "Through the destructuring of the everyday environment, we come to grasp the textural harmony of world and incarnate consciousness. We apprehend that we are not only *in* the world but *of* the world."[22]

In Lawrence's work this changed relationship to the world is an explicit concern—as in those books I mentioned earlier by reference to Heidegger's quest for Being. But for Lawrence this quest for Being is a consequence of his extraordinary sensitivity to the existential de-situation of sex and to its implications for our apprehension of the texture of the world's body. I have mentioned Connie's alertness to the heaving and surging earth. At the moment of orgasm, appropriately, she feels as if she is "the sea, nothing but dark waves rising and heaving, heaving with a great swell." As the "slope of the hill" heaves—nature outside—so does nature within. At the moment of orgasm one becomes moralized seascape. Then, "in a soft, shuddering convulsion, the quick of all her plasm was touched, she knew herself touched, the consummation was upon her, and she was gone. She was gone, she was not, and she was born: a woman" (*LCL* 229). Death of the ego. Resurrection of the Body. Moment of Orgasm. "Behold the God!"

Is there an objective correlative for such scenes? Are they sufficiently "dramatized"? The drama is to be found not in the presence of a god but of a voice—of Lawrence's desire, rising above the lovers. It is the voice of reflection, attending to pleasure, and distancing us from the natural consciousness it wants us to touch. After all, it is not simply the touch of the lovers upon *each other* that Lawrence wants to present. He wants *us* to touch *them*. Recall Mailer's words: "I learned from Lawrence that the way to write about sex was not to strike poses, but be true to the logic of each moment. There's a subtle logic to love." Notice the segue from the "logic of love" (out there in the world) to a *writing about* love that, despite its textuality, is homologous with that logic. To write is to touch, for Mailer and Lawrence. Each wants to put us in the unmediated presence of the God. And if we recall the sexual rapport that Mailer's Stephen Rojack achieves with Cherry, in *An American Dream,* in that Lower East Side equivalent to Lawrence's hut in a wood, it becomes obvious why he responds as he does to Lawrence. But is it the "unknown" we encounter in *An American Dream* and *Lady Chatterley's Lover,* or is it another form of the unreachable fruit that haunted Tantalus?

If sex offered the possibility of an encounter with the unknown, Lawrence turned away from it. If he is correct to warn against the primacy of the ego and to remind us of the prereflective life of the body, and if he also senses the burden of otherness (it is also a grace) that the body imposes, then he seems to have failed to draw from the dialectic of embodiment a possible conclusion: that it entails not heterosexuality but bisexuality (I do not say homosexuality). Instead he chose a stern division of sexual labor we all know already. Doing with men. Being with women. One sex the for-itself. The other the in-itself. However, we need only recall the suppressed "Prologue" to

Women in Love and that novel's concern with blood brotherhood to recognize that psychological intrusions into "ontological fiction" may have turned Lawrence from—made it impossible for him to accept—a vision of bisexuality.

In this respect the Mailer of *Why Are We in Vietnam?* risked more, was more "existentially" willing to confront the unknown, when he suggested that Tex and D.J. might have overcome their masculine blood-lust had they given in to homosexual yearning for each other. The Alaska hunting-expedition that prepares them for the rice-paddies of the tropics must recall Sándor Ferenczi's astonishment at the extent to which "present-day men have lost the capacity for mutual affection and amiability. Instead there prevails among men decided asperity, resistance, and love of disputation"—qualities that Ferenczi regarded as "defence symptoms erected against affection for the same sex."[23] Elsewhere I have discussed these "psychological intrusions" that made it impossible for Lawrence to enact imaginatively the bisexual possibility to which they also made him alert—an alertness and an impossibility implicit in the "gladiatorial" embrace that is all the embrace Birkin and Gerald can know.[24]

If the possibility of bisexuality exists at all in *Lady Chatterley's Lover*, it is kept secret. I am thinking of the lovemaking between Mellors and Connie on the night before Connie leaves for Venice, when Mellors burns out "the deepest, oldest shames, in the most secret places" (*LCL* 312). "Shame" recalls the chapter-title of *The Rainbow*'s account of Ursula's homosexual affair, and it reminds us of all the other places where anal intercourse and intimations of homosexuality enter Lawrence's fiction. At this point in his career, after *Women in Love* and the fiasco of the leadership novels, if Lawrence had chosen not secrecy but transparency and had extended to *impersonal* beings of the same sex the privileges he reserves for those of different sexes, the often anxious masculinity of his work (apparent in *Aaron's Rod* and *Kangaroo*) might have been overcome in a spectacularly "existential" confrontation with the unknown. But to use his word, he "funked" a consequence of his own existential critique of the ego: that Self and Other might rise, in their anonymity, above gender, to pursue bisexually the will-o'-the-wisp of natural consciousness. Once more, now in a novel that celebrates its own candor, he retreated: into a hut, where, yet again, he wrote of unspeakable practices, unnatural acts. And on the door of the hut he hung, discreetly, a sign that read "Do Not Disturb."

NOTES

1. Norman Mailer, *Cannibals and Christians* (New York: Dial, 1966), pp. 197–98, where Mailer also says why he thinks *Lady Chatterley's Lover* "is not a very good book."

2. Norman Mailer, *The Prisoner of Sex* (Boston: Little, Brown, 1971), pp. 147–48; emphasis added.

3. Why must one return to "bodily life with another self?" Because, as Mailer argues, in an "existentialist" critique of masturbation, in the fantasy world of masturbation it is precisely *risk-taking* that one avoids. See Mailer's *The Presidential Papers* (New York: G. P. Putnam's Sons, 1962), pp. 139–42.

4. Norman Mailer, *Existential Errands* (Boston: Little, Brown, 1972), p. 104.

5. Jean Wahl, "Sur D. H. Lawrence," *La Nouvelle Revue Française* 42 (1934): 116–17. See also Eliseo Vivas, *D. H. Lawrence: The Failure and the Triumph of Art* (Bloomington: Indiana University Press, 1964), p. 109.

6. Gabriel Marcel, "In Memoriam D. H. Lawrence," *La Nouvelle Revue Française* 34 (1930): 571.

7. In view of the connection I will draw between Lawrence's critique of the ego and that of Sartre, it is worth noting that a major French philosophical work of the post-existentialist generation—but one marked by Sartre's influence—again sees fit to praise Lawrence for his awareness that men and women are not "clearly defined personalities, but rather vibrations, flows." Gilles Deleuze and Félix Guattari, *Anti-Oedipus: Capitalism and Schizophrenia*, trans. Robert Hurley, Mark Seem, and Helen R. Lane (New York: Viking, 1977), p. 362.

8. It is pointless to try to make precise distinctions among these terms. Lawrence does not make them, and those occasionally employed by Sartre are too finely tuned for my purpose.

9. See Sartre's discussion of "respectability" (*la distinction*) in his *Critique of Dialectical Reason*, trans. Alan Sheridan-Smith (London: New Left Books, 1976), pp. 770–81.

10. I have discussed these tensions of otherness in "*The Rainbow* and 'Otherness,' " *D. H. Lawrence Review* 7, no. 1 (Spring 1974): 58–77; for a discussion of the ego's life of "surplus-anxiety," see my "Invention or Discovery? The Surplus-Anxiety of Good Taste," *Dalhousie Review* 59 (1979): 475–86.

11. Jean-Paul Sartre, *The Transcendence of the Ego: An Existentialist Theory of Consciousness*, trans. Forrest Williams and Robert Kirkpatrick (New York: Noonday,

1957), p. 45; hereafter cited in the text as *TE*. In *TE* Sartre's terms are "unreflected" and "reflected" consciousness; however, I am using the later distinction ("prereflective," "reflective") of *Being and Nothingness*.

12. See Jean-Paul Sartre, *Being and Nothingness: An Essay on Phenomenological Ontology*, trans. Hazel E. Barnes (London: Methuen, 1957), pp. 443 ff.; hereafter cited in the text as *BN*.

13. D. H. Lawrence, *"Fantasia of the Unconscious" and "Psychoanalysis and the Unconscious"* (London: Heinemann, 1961), p. 225; hereafter cited in the text as *FU*.

14. Jean-Paul Sartre, *Saint Genet: Actor and Martyr*, trans. Bernard Frechtman (New York: George Braziller, 1963), p. 60; hereafter cited in the text as *SG*.

15. D. H. Lawrence, *The Escaped Cock*, ed. Gerald M. Lacy (Santa Barbara, Calif.: Black Sparrow Press, 1978), p. 24.

16. "But the two ways of knowing, for man, are knowing in terms of apartness, which is mental, rational, scientific, and knowing in terms of togetherness, which is religious and poetic. The Christian religion lost, in Protestantism finally, the togetherness with the universe, the togetherness of the body, the sex, the emotions, the passions, with the earth and sun and stars" ("A Propos of *Lady Chatterley's Lover*," *Phoenix II* 512).

17. D. H. Lawrence, *Etruscan Places* (London: Martin Secker, 1932), p. 120.

18. M. H. Abrams, *Natural Supernaturalism: Tradition and Revolution in Romantic Literature* (New York: Norton, 1971), p. 324.

19. Jean-Paul Sartre, *Nausea*, trans. Lloyd Alexander (New York: New Directions, 1964), pp. 126–27; hereafter cited in the text as *N*.

20. Connie's response to her "emerging nakedness" represents her lingering commitment to what has been described as an Augustinian view of bodily spontaneity: "[St. Augustine] sees the sexual act as a kind of spasm. All the body . . . is shaken by terrible jerks. One entirely loses control of oneself." Michel Foucault, "Sexuality and Solitude," *London Review of Books* 3 (21 May to 3 June 1981), 5. For Lawrence such "spasms" and "jerks" are only that parodic form of spontaneity Connie experiences while she endures the "mental life."

21. Roland Barthes, *S/Z*, trans. Richard Miller (New York: Hill and Wang, 1974), p. 80.

22. Monika Langer, "Sartre and Merleau-Ponty: A Reappraisal," in *The Philosophy of Jean-Paul Sartre*, ed. Paul Arthur Schilpp (LaSalle, Ill.: Open Court, 1981), p. 316.

23. Sándor Ferenczi, "The Nosology of Male Homosexuality," *First Contributions to Psycho-Analysis*, trans. Ernest Jones (London: Hogarth, 1952), p. 315. On the general issue of bisexuality, see Gad Horowitz, *Repression: Basic and Surplus Repression in Psychoanalytic Theory* (Toronto: University of Toronto Press, 1977).

24. See the following articles: "Intimacy at a Distance: Sexuality and Orality in *Sons and Lovers*," *Mosaic* 13 (1980): 71–89; "The Father of All Things: The Oral and the Oedipal in *Sons and Lovers*," *Mosaic* 14 (1981): 69–88.

FREDERICK P. W. MCDOWELL

"Moments of Emergence and of a New Splendour": D. H. Lawrence and E. M. Forster in Their Fiction

Of all his major contemporaries, E. M. Forster appealed most to D. H. Lawrence. Lawrence recognized his affinity with Forster toward the end of his own career by maintaining in 1924 that "he is about the best of my contemporaries in England" (*CL* 800) and to Forster himself that "there's not a soul in England says a word to me—save your whisper through the willow boughs."[1] Forster in his turn maintained, in an obituary, that Lawrence "was the greatest imaginative novelist of our generation," and engaged in a spirited controversy with T. S. Eliot to uphold that judgment.[2] These words of mutual admiration were the sequel to a closer but brief and unsatisfying relationship between the two writers during Lawrence's period at Greatham in 1915, after they had met in January at Garsington, Lady Ottoline Morrell's mecca for the intellectuals of the age. Lawrence was becoming a major figure: *The White Peacock* (1911), *Sons and Lovers* (1913), and *The Prussian Officer and Other Stories* (1914) were already behind him, and he was readying *The Rainbow* for its ill-starred publication later that year. A link at that time between Forster and Lawrence was the relaxed sexuality propounded by the homoerotic intellectual Edward Carpenter, whom Forster knew well and whose influence upon Lawrence Emile Delavenay has convincingly established, despite Lawrence's failure ever to mention him.[3] Temperamental differences meant that a close friendship between Forster and Lawrence could not last: Lawrence's shrillness and distrust of Forster's unassertiveness and intellectuality and

Forster's diffidence and aversion to Lawrence's violence of manner and his heterosexual proselytizing obscured, for the moment, their fundamental similarities. As Paul Delany notes, Forster ought to have persisted more than he did in a friendship with a man of Lawrence's integrity;[4] yet the two men continued to exchange books and to maintain a distant cordiality, though they seem never again to have met. The affinities that led to the 1915 meetings were never obliterated in either man's consciousness, affinities that come out in their work.

Despite the fact that Forster was to outlive Lawrence by forty years, his work as a writer of fiction was mostly over by the time the two met in 1915. Forster still was to revise at least twice his unpublished homosexual novel, *Maurice*, finished in its first form in 1914, and these revisions reveal Lawrencean influence. His greatest novel, *A Passage to India* (1924), has many parallels in its situations, characters, and ideas to those found in Lawrence's fiction; and the posthumously published short stories that date after 1920 in *The Life to Come and Other Stories* (1972) owe something to Lawrence's example. Lawrence had read *Howards End* by 1911; the Lawrences added *Where Angels Fear to Tread*, *The Longest Journey*, and *The Celestial Omnibus and Other Stories* (notably "The Celestial Omnibus" and "The Story of a Panic") in the Greatham period of 1915, and Frieda Lawrence apparently read *Howards End* then for the first time.[5] Forster sent Lawrence *Alexandria: A History and a Guide* (1922), *Pharos and Pharillon* (1923), and *A Passage to India* (1924), books that Lawrence seems to have read; and Lawrence in turn sent Forster copies of his books through *St. Mawr* (1925).[6] Each writer had reservations about the other: Forster felt that Lawrence was extreme and idiosyncratic in his views and actions, and Lawrence disliked the Bloomsbury aspect of Forster—the intellectual, detached, and ironic sensibility that so often informed his work and his personality.

The similarities in outlook and values are interesting to consider even if direct influence cannot always be proved. In any case, the facts as I have presented them argue that most of the resemblances in the work of the two writers emerged after 1915, though *Howards End* could have exerted an earlier influence on Lawrence, and *The White Peacock* (1911) probably contributed to the initial conception of Alec Scudder, the gamekeeper in *Maurice*. Julian Moynahan has stressed the essential truth about the relationship when he says, "So often Forster can be seen as a precursor—sometimes a faint-hearted one—of Lawrentian insights and emphases."[7] This is the point of view from which I will consider the two writers, and I shall deal more specifically with their works than have previous writers on the subject. I will use *Lady Chatterley's Lover,* especially the second version, *John Thomas and Lady Jane,* as the work that illustrates Lawrence's essential values, though some scholars might regard *Women in Love* as the more central work.

Since Lawrence knew *Howards End* by 1911 and since it summarizes Forster's prewar outlook and values, one can begin by ascertaining the relations between this novel and Lawrence's work. Though in *The Rainbow* Lawrence draws mostly on Louie Burrows and Frieda for his Ursula Brangwen, she is related as a young woman, in her constant testing of experience and her search for truth, to the conscientious Margaret Schlegel. Margaret is more genteel and enjoys the wealth that capitalist culture has provided for her; but she constantly criticizes the values of the materialistic Wilcoxes, even if with some facets of her mind she appreciates them. She tries to establish the connections between her disparate experiences as does Ursula in the last section of *The Rainbow.* Ursula is the sensitive and persistent female truth-seeker in Lawrence's work, who appears also as Louisa Durant in "Daughters of the Vicar," as Lou Witt in *St. Mawr,* as Kate Leslie in *The Plumed Serpent,* and as Yvette Saywell in *The Virgin and the Gipsy.*

Anton Skrebensky, Ursula's deficient lover in *The Rainbow,* suffers from a failure in sensibility and imagination similar to Henry Wilcox's. These two men organize their lives on the externals that shape them: the army or the life of business. In both cases they prefer to serve the empire rather than to deepen the knowledge of the self. Anton is unable to take Ursula into the unknown, and Henry is insensitive to the influence of the "unseen," an influence that continually informs Margaret's sensibility. The image of the rainbow acts as a symbol of spiritual harmony in the two works, though a common origin in the Bible or in Wagner is likely.

Howards End also prefigures *Women in Love,* with contrasting sisters sharing the writer's focus in each book. Margaret and Ursula are the questing intellectuals, alive to the significance of forces that transcend the intellectual and that are of potentially greater value. Helen Schlegel and Gudrun Brangwen are also comparable in being more instinctual and passionate than their sisters, yet they are sometimes given to a spiritual rigidity or to an overintellectualizing of their instincts; their energies have destructive ramifications despite their intelligence and their capacity to feel. In the personal realm the strength of these women has fateful results: the unmanning of Leonard Bast in *Howards End* and the death of Gerald Crich in *Women in Love*. The intensity of both women, however, gives them a complexity and a distinction often lacking in the destructive women in Lawrence's later work, or for that matter in Hermione Roddice of *Women in Love*.

Though Lawrence in a well-known letter reproved Forster "for glorifying those *business* people in *Howards End*" (CL 716) Forster is ambiguous toward them in his novel. He acknowledges their role in making England powerful and in providing the wealth that allows culture to flourish, but he is even more aware of their spoliation of England and of their insensitivity, of their being responsible for the "inner darkness in high places that comes with a commercial age."[8] The red rust of London that threatens the rural fastness of Howards End house is allied to the blight that is overtaking the midlands as a result of the coal-mine operations in *Women in Love* and *Lady Chatterley's Lover*. Henry Wilcox is a fully envisioned man of business, antedating the complex figures of Gerald Crich and Sir Clifford Chatterley. Another figure of like complexity in the Lawrence canon is Godfrey Marshall in "England, My England." He is an entrepreneur who has some degree of vision and a vigor, which are lacking in his sensitive but ineffectual son-in-law, Egbert. At the end of the tale Egbert has become a deracinated man from the countryside (recalling Leonard Bast of Forster's novel), though earlier he had enjoyed an idyllic relationship with his wife Winifred, before the injury to their daughter. Ruth Wilcox in *Howards End,* as a person who is great by virtue of what she is and whose power and authority transcend death, resembles many of the instinctively confident figures of Lawrence, some of whom also remain powerful after their disappearance or their physical death: Count Dionys in *The Ladybird,* the gipsy in *The Virgin and the Gipsy,* and Alan Anstruther in "The Border Line" (though he has died, his spirit frees Katherine

Farquhar from her present effete husband, Philip, by causing his death). As in the rest of my discussion, I am being suggestive rather than exhaustive, but the parallels between *Howards End* and the works of Lawrence that I have cited establish a consistency of vision in the two writers.

Philosophically, Forster in *Howards End* adumbrates Lawrence's preoccupation, after the writing of *Sons and Lovers*, with the interplay, the conjoining, and the final transcending of opposites. In Forster's fiction before *Howards End*, the ability or the inability of the characters to make "connections" of the sort described or dramatized in *Howards End* had led respectively to their success or failure in life; and the same is true of the figures in *Howards End*. Margaret Schlegel is able not only to relate to the materialism of the Wilcoxes, the intense idealism of Helen Schlegel, and the mysticism and nature worship of Ruth Wilcox, but she also espouses a philosophy of achieving proportion by the forging of such connections. She emphasizes that proportion is an ongoing process; it is to be used as a last resource, but it is often a crucial one: only "prigs" would act from a scheme of proportion worked out in advance, Margaret asserts. In an existence characterized by difficulty and by the unexpected, she would urge "the building of the rainbow bridge that should connect the prose in us with the passion."9

Forster's emphasis on the need to achieve by positive effort a creative synthesis of opposing entities is allied with the philosophy elucidated by Lawrence between 1913 and 1915 in his nonfiction (and in *The Rainbow* and, later, in *Women in Love*). In his posthumously published "Study of Thomas Hardy" (written in 1914) Lawrence saw the need to reconcile the "polarities" of the male principle (of Love, of God the Son) with the female principle (of Law, of God the Father) in the Holy Spirit, the Comforter who transcends while He includes the two principles. In "The Crown" (1915) the juxtaposition lies between the Lion and the Unicorn, and the fight between them "under the Crown." The truth lies less in the fusion of Lion and Unicorn than in the struggle between them, which is to be forever maintained, as the only dynamically creative state: "There are the two eternities fighting the fight of Creation, the light projecting itself into the darkness, the darkness enveloping herself within the embrace of light. And then there is the consummation of each in the other, the consummation of light in darkness and darkness in light, which is absolute. . . . The lion and the unicorn are not fighting for the Crown. They are fighting beneath it. And the Crown is upon their fight" (*Phoenix II* 371). This provocative essay, which underlies the separateness-in-unity doctrine enunciated by Birkin in *Women in Love,* was published in 1915 when Forster and Lawrence had become friends. Evidently Forster found that Lawrence had expressed something in which he could also centrally believe, for Lawrence some years later said that "E. M. Forster said he liked them. [*The Crown* essays] best of all my small things."[10]

Early in 1913 Lawrence began a novel of contrasting personal, social, and national types, *The Insurrection of Alvina Houghton,* which he laid aside in March (after writing two hundred pages, which have not survived) in order to complete *The Rainbow* and *Women in Love.* He returned to the work in 1920, using it as the basis for *The Lost Girl.*[11] Since Frieda by 1915 had read *Where Angels Fear to Tread,* one can hazard some minimal influence of that novel upon *The Lost Girl.* In any case, the two works are strikingly congruent in general conception and in some of the characters.[12] Ciccio, the primitive Italian in a traveling circus, challenges the conventionality of the provincial Alvina, who decides that only with her "demon" lover can she find the motivation to reject British convention and lead a fuller life. Ciccio is unrefined and has a streak of brutality in him, as does Gino Carella in Forster's novel, especially toward his ill-fated wife, Lilia Herriton. Italy changes Alvina as it does Forster's Caroline Abbott. Caroline falls in love carnally with Gino, but unlike Alvina she is unable to break from her past and to express her sensual self. Yet she is forever changed as a result of exposure to Gino's vitality. In her difficult life in Italy Alvina finds a challenge rather than entire fulfillment, but her nature would not have allowed her to remain "respectable" in Woodhouse in England. Caroline returns to the respectable Sawston that she had wished to renounce, but is a different person, as is Philip Herriton. While she admits the necessity for the sensual, she cannot achieve the power to communicate her reoriented vision to Gino, the man whom she loves and who might have been capable of loving her—and requiting her passion—if he could have divined her feelings.

In 1915 Forster gave Lawrence *The Celestial Omnibus and Other Stories,* and to "The Story of a Panic," at least, Lawrence reacted in detail. In the Forster tale a group of British tourists recoils in fright from a gust of wind which betokens Pan's presence. Only the boy Eustace lingers to receive the full blessing of Pan, but he is later confined to a hotel room. Breaking loose, he disappears forever into a nearby wood to take up his life as a disciple of Pan—or perhaps as the god himself. Lawrence asserted that Forster had kept the tale too near the "undifferentiated root and stem drawing out of unfathomable darkness" and that, at the moment, he was more interested himself in "the flower into which we strive to burst."[13] But a few years later Lawrence was to become preoccupied with Pan in just the way he had criticized Forster for being. Actually, in Annable, the gamekeeper of *The White Peacock* (1911), Lawrence had already conceived a Pan figure who represented "a stooping back to the well-head." Annable is "a malicious Pan," a demonic force who balances the other somewhat anemic characters, and he stands apart from the action of the tale, a figure unintegrated with the whole. Lawrence has to kill him off, but he represents the independent natural force that George Saxton ought to have become. Saxton is a man of the soil who lacks the moral strength which a close rapport with nature ought to have given him and which Annable personifies. Arthur Pilbeam, the gamekeeper in "The Shades of Spring" (1913), is another vital personification of nature and by implication a Pan figure as well as an early and tentative version of the gamekeeper figure in Lawrence.

It is not until the American period in Lawrence's career that Pan gains supremacy in his imagination, especially in the writings between 1924 and 1926.[14] By that time Lawrence would probably have known *The Longest Journey* as a result of Frieda's having read it in 1915. In that novel Stephen Wonham is an authentic scion of nature and exerts a purifying, iconoclastic influence upon the Failings, the Pembrokes, and his half-brother Rickie, all in some degree individuals belonging to the party of convention. Stephen, with whom Forster associates the Virgilian phrase "Pan, the keeper of sheep," represents the primeval vitality that Lawrence finds in the god Pan. Both the god and his disciple Stephen illustrate the primary quality that Lawrence associates with the god in his essay "Pan in America," a "vivid relatedness between the man and the living universe that surrounds him" (*Phoenix* 27).

In the 1924–1926 works Pan is a central presence, a vital—in some degree even obsessive—presence, as in *The Plumed Serpent*. In *St. Mawr*, for example, St. Mawr himself, the regal and violent stallion, suggests a descent from some primitive time, and he has for Lou Witt all the force and vitality of "unfallen Pan." Both Lou and her mother are searching for such a presence in a man; they do not find it in any of the men of their acquaintance, except in the groom Lewis. Lewis's unspoiled sensibility has allowed him to catch oblique glimpses at night of the Pan-God, who is the core of life in all living things. Stephen Wonham in *The Longest Journey* is an analogous figure and shares with Lewis an expertise in the managing of horses and an identification with all the forms of wild life. Lewis's sense of self-integrity is strong, with the result that he cannot listen to Mrs. Witt's proposal of marriage; he feels that she would try to unman him, as she had attempted to do, Delilah fashion, when she insisted on cutting his hair. A like kind of self-worth animates Stephen, who refuses, for example, to remain merely a symbol to Rickie, a surrogate for Rickie of their dead mother. As for Lou Witt, when she comes to America she finds the spirit of Pan in the wild New Mexico landscape, which predates "the God of Love," nature becoming at once a source of vitality and renewal and a cruel and destructive force. Cipriano in *The Plumed Serpent* is also a Pan figure, emanating the vitality of the cosmic energies, with something of the fateful and the demonic about him. "A face like Cipriano's is the face at once of a god and a devil, the undying Pan face"; and his whole figure suggests to Kate Leslie "the bygone mystery of the twilit, primitive world," as well as "ancient phallic mystery."[15]

In a short story from the period, "The Last Laugh," Lawrence may have appropriated Forster's technique in indicating the presence of Pan. In "The Story of a Panic" Pan reveals his presence through a sinister catspaw of wind and then through some large hoofprints, being otherwise invisible. Similarly, Pan obtrudes only obliquely in

"The Last Laugh," through his incessant laughter, through his giving off an intriguing almond scent, through wind and storm, and through the gratuitous malice of his acts (causing a policeman to acquire a goat's foot, and Marchbanks, the man who first heard his laughter, to be killed). If Lawrence found hints for his own dramatizings of Pan in the fiction of Forster, he developed his god with greater force and poetic intensity.

By 1960 Forster had read *Lady Chatterley's Lover*, since he defended it in the well-known "trial" of that book. In the proceedings he not only asserted that the book "had very high literary merit," but he expressed once again his 1930 judgment that Lawrence was "the greatest imaginative novelist of our generation."[16] Lawrence in 1928 had mentioned Forster as a possible subscriber to the privately printed Florence edition of the work (*CL* 1058), and Forster probably read it sometime in the 1930s. The original version most likely circulated in the bohemian group of J. R. Ackerley and others with whom Forster associated at that time in London. In any case, he must have read one of the numerous expurgated editions published in England in 1932 and after, as authorized by Frieda Lawrence; he might even have read *The First Lady Chatterley*, published in London in 1944. In pointing out some of the similarities in Lawrence's and Forster's world view, I shall use *Lady Chatterley's Lover* as my basis in Lawrence, since it is a representative work. In my discussion I shall refer often to Forster's *Maurice*, which seems to owe something to Lawrence's novel and to some of Lawrence's other works.

Of the three versions of *Lady Chatterley*, I shall consider mostly the second, *John Thomas and Lady Jane*, although it is the one that Forster could not have known unless he had read it in the 1954 Italian version (it was first published in English in 1972). *John Thomas and Lady Jane* is close enough in content to the third version, known as *Lady Chatterley's Lover*, to make this approach justifiable; and it presents in clearer form the overriding obstacle of class in the formation of enduring sexual relationships, which was Forster's obsessive concern in *Maurice*. This concern with class is even more nagging in *The First Lady Chatterley* (the version that Frieda preferred); in *John Thomas and Lady Jane* it is also central, but the character of Constance is more developed so that the work presents the Lawrencean ethos and mythos (with Constance as spokesman) more truly than the first version. It is a more representative text for Lawrence than *The First Lady Chatterley* (of which it is an elaboration), but it does not mute the issue of class barriers to free sexual expression, which the portrayal of Mellors in *Lady Chatterley's Lover* does. The subject of social class as it relates to sex is, moreover, of insistent concern to Forster in *Maurice,* and draws the book closer to *John Thomas and Lady Jane* than to the standard *Lady Chatterley.* The paradox obtrudes: the version of *Lady Chatterley's Lover* that Forster most likely did not know is the closest in situation, character, conception, and tone to *Maurice.* While I shall refer most often to *John Thomas and Lady Jane* in discussing Lawrence and Forster, I shall also refer to *Lady Chatterley's Lover* when that version of the novel has special relevance to Forster and his work.[17]

Forster in a 1930 talk on Lawrence asserted that Lawrence both wrote from his instincts and preached instinct.[18] The various versions of *Lady Chatterley's Lover* support Forster's assertion. As do most of his other books, this late novel illustrates Lawrence's famous assertion of 1913: "My great religion is a belief in the blood, the flesh, as being wiser than the intellect" (CL 180). Lady Chatterley achieves renewal when she heeds the desires of the flesh and rejects the debilitating forces that surround her as a social being. Twenty-five years after this 1913 statement, Lawrence would express himself similarly in *John Thomas and Lady Jane:* "Man is a creature, like all other creatures. And all creatures alike are born of complex and intricate passion, which will for ever be antecedent to reason" (JTLJ 130). Passion, or what he calls in his discussions relating to *Lady Chatterley's Lover* "the phallic consciousness,"[19] makes Lady Chatterley come alive.

Though Forster is less strident, less assertive, and more intellectual than Lawrence, he believed, as Lawrence did, that the rational must yield to the irrational, the intuitions, the unconscious, if men are to achieve a valid standard for the meaningful conduct of their lives. Thus, Rickie Elliot must acknowledge the elemental in his half-brother Stephen Wonham in *The Longest Journey,* if he is to break out of his inner torpor; thus, Margaret Schlegel, in contrast to the Wilcoxes, can see life whole as well as seeing it steadily, supplementing her knowledge gained from the social realm with intimations from the "unseen"; thus the Bloomsbury-oriented intellectuals Fielding and Adela Quested, of A *Passage to India,* are inadequate to the mystery and the challenge of India because that challenge is in large part transcendental and outside their past experiences. In like manner, the sentimental Christianity of Mrs. Moore must yield to the sinister echo that she encounters in the primordial Marabar Caves. Because she is sensitive, however, to the mysteries in life that are not to be apprehended by the intelligence alone, she is able to exert an irrational influence after death, when as a spiritual presence she causes Adela Quested to retract her charges of rape against Aziz and when, eventually, she becomes one of a multitude of Hindu goddesses.

"Blood consciousness" can reach back into the primitive, which for Lawrence exists as a source of renewal but not precisely as a model to be followed. So in *John Thomas and Lady Jane,* Parkin seems to Connie in the act of sex to be "far back almost as the snake itself" and his voice is like "something pre-human" (*JTLJ* 169). For the student of Forster such phrases bring to mind Stephen Wonham of *The Longest Journey,* the man of nature who is also in part a primitive and so reaches back into the mythic racial past: he "had been back somewhere—back to some table of the gods, spread in a field where there is no noise, and . . . he belonged for ever to the guests with whom he had eaten."[20]

Opposed to "blood consciousness" is "mental consciousness," which, if it dominates unduly, becomes the primary enemy of the individual who aims to be in a positive relationship with the life-energies. The inflexible operations of the mind, in Lawrence's view, can stifle the intimations of the blood. The individual who idealizes or mentalizes his experience and so excludes from his purview the element of spontaneity does so at his peril. According to Lawrence, the role of "the idealist philosophies and religions" (*Phoenix II* 512) has been disastrous for the modern individual, who has been deprived thereby of reacting firsthand to the multifarious phenomena associated with life at its most full. Lady Chatterley herself had been at first a self-conscious intellectual, preferring art, for example, to sex. Clifford, partly in compensation for his bodily injuries, has become interested only in the life of the "spirit"—its resurrection and its immortality. To Constance his very mysticism is mentalized and egoistic: "This

Mystic One was like a great pompom on the top of his cap, to show his personal superiority and importance" (*JTLJ* 80).

In Forster's work it is people like the Pembrokes (*The Longest Journey*), the Wilcoxes (*Howards End*), Cecil Vyse (*A Room with a View*), and Adela Quested (*A Passage to India*) who, as exponents of "mental consciousness," reduce and thereby falsify the complexities and the abundances of life. Of these figures Cecil Vyse most completely corresponds to Sir Clifford: Cecil so intellectualizes his love for Lucy Honeychurch that as a woman she ceases to exist for him.[21] At the same time, Cecil lacks the capacity to become a power in the great world in which Clifford makes his mark. Although Rickie Elliot is a more complex and admirable character than Clifford, Rickie like Clifford falls in love "through the imagination" rather than "through the desires."[22] And admirable as she is in her honesty and integrity, Adela Quested is as limited by her rational powers as Clifford; she cannot apprehend, let alone comprehend, the ineffable and the visionary, except possibly at the time of the trial of Aziz when the spirit of Mrs. Moore causes her to retract her accusation against him.

Although Lawrence and Forster regarded intuition as antecedent to rationality and of greater value as a source of truth and renewal, they were concerned essentially with harmonizing the human powers—mind and body, reason and instinct—into a meaningful synthesis. But both writers felt that instinct, intuition, and the unconscious comprise the aspect of our life that is the most easily disregarded in the modern age, and the one most in need of "rescue" and emphasis. Modern fragmentation has resulted from an elevation of the mental, the rational, the rigidly ideal, the conscious: "there is no balance and no harmony now" (*Phoenix II* 492). In an effort to establish once more the provenance of instinct and intuition and to reconcile these powers with the mental and the rational, Lawrence wrote *Lady Chatterley's Lover:* "As I say, it's a novel of the phallic Consciousness: or the phallic Consciousness versus the mental-spiritual Consciousness: and of course you know which side I take. The *versus* is not my fault: there should be no *versus*. The two things must be reconciled in us. But now they're daggers drawn."[23] Like Lawrence, Forster would also connect "the prose . . . with the passion," "the beast and the monk,"[24] but would emphasize most the role of the instincts in a culture that tended to turn from them in fear and aversion.

One form that mental consciousness can take in modern man is a glorification of the Will at the expense of the other elements in the psyche. Even in the leadership novels of the early 1920s wherein Lawrence advocated the positive aspects of power—and the Will upon which such power must be based—he recognized the necessity for the fullness of the psyche rather than its reduction. In the modern age the Will, as it operates in an individual whose horizons are limited, often finds expression and satisfaction, according to Lawrence, in industrial enterprise. Sir Clifford Chatterley (in the third version of the novel) begins as a writer whose modish and conventional narratives gain him critical acclaim; these stories are deficient in passion and are products of a rational mind rather than a ranging imagination. The stories recall those early pallid efforts of Rickie Elliot in *The Longest Journey*, which were also the results primarily of mental consciousness and which, consequently, his half-brother Stephen ridiculed.

In *John Thomas and Lady Jane* (and in *Lady Chatterley's Lover*) Clifford, at the suggestion of Mrs. Bolton, transfers his energies from his intellectual pursuits to managing his coal mines efficiently. His will is no longer merely a will-to-live: it is an impersonal and inhuman force that needs to fasten on something external by which it can sustain itself. Thus the egoistic entrepreneur gains his greatest satisfaction in exerting power over his subordinates. Whereas Gerald Crich had other facets to his nature—especially his obsessive sexual drive—and was a more complicated person, Sir Clifford Chatterley becomes almost a caricature in the singleness of his energies and interests. He is motivated, moreover, by a hatred of the lower classes, incited by Mrs. Bolton's stories of the antagonism that the miners feel toward him; and he lacks the sense of benevolent despotism that had characterized his father's attitude toward his workers. Henry Wilcox in *Howards End* reveals a similar distrust of the working classes; he has Clifford's narrowness and some of his emotional hypocrisy about sex, but Henry's instincts are healthier than Clifford's. Henry is able to appreciate, if he cannot fully understand, those whose values are different from his own—Ruth Wilcox and Margaret Schlegel, who are his successive wives. It is, rather, his sons Charles and Paul who reveal most blatantly the constricted outlook of power-hungry practical men such as Clifford Chatterley. Bast and Parkin are the victims of Henry Wilcox and Clifford Chatterley respectively, in the sense that each man loses economic security as a result of the actions of his social superior. Yet in both novels the oppressed man has his victory, since the future of England lies with the child he has sired.

In *John Thomas and Lady Jane* Constance expresses her dissatisfaction with the destruction of rural England and an apprehensiveness as to what England is becoming, a preoccupation shared by Mellors of *Lady Chatterley's Lover* but not by Parkin. In *John Thomas and Lady Jane*, Constance is appalled at the ugliness that is settling over England in towns like Tevershall, at the deterioration of the countryside, and at the disappearance of the forests and the stately homes, monuments of an older England. She feels that dignity, beauty, and decency are becoming irrelevant to the miners who lead such hard lives; but she concedes that if a "more awful" world is coming, it may be one with more life. The miners have at least their "elementality," which Parkin shares though he is not one of them, but that trait is also in danger of being extinguished.

These regrets at the passing of a pastoral England, Forster also expressed in his work. The downs to which Stephen Wonham could retreat and lead his life as elemental man failed to survive the Great War in their pristine state, as Forster asserted in his introduction to the 1960 edition of *The Longest Journey:* "For the England that Stephen thought so good and seemed destined to inherit is done for."[25] And even in *Howards End* (1910) Forster had sensed this wasting of rural England with the uprooting of Leonard Bast from the soil, with Howards End in danger of being sold by the Wilcoxes, and with the Hertfordshire fields being increasingly exposed to the sprawling metropolis. Maurice's dream of retreat to the greenwood with his lover was becoming an anachronism even at the time Forster wrote *Maurice*, with the result that he dropped the epilogue describing their idyllic life together. Maurice and Alec are fated to become outcasts, but they will have to secure their anonymity elsewhere than in the English woodlands, perhaps in the jungle of the large city.

Though the wood at Wragby estate is threatened, it yet serves as a source of the life-energies and provides the scene for Lady Chatterley's regeneration. In the wood there survives still "some of the old inviolate mystery of Britain, even Druid Britain" (*JTLJ* 20). The gamekeeper, Parkin, is the overseer, or rather the priest, of the woodland; his ministrations restore Connie to life and bring about her "resurrection of the body" (*JTLJ* 63). Through his talismanic touch, which, as with his breeding of the pheasants, brings forth new life, Connie undergoes her metamorphosis from a deadened to an incandescent self, becoming at one with the energies of the cosmos as the woodland embodies them. Nature represents in the nonhuman world the steadying force that enlightened marriage represents in the human: "Mankind has got to get back to the rhythm of the cosmos, and the permanence of marriage" (*Phoenix II* 509). The rhythms of nature and the rituals of marriage have a parallel significance and consecrating power. The wood, though its continued existence is precarious, acts as a transforming influence: under its spell Parkin achieves a new freedom, "a new space in life . . . this was one of his moments of emergence and of a new splendour," and Connie attains a new strength of insight: "the man had caused her soul to turn, to become aware in a different way" (*JTLJ* 171). Though the wood is in danger of being destroyed, the powers that it contains provide the only hope for the renewal of human beings in an ailing society.

John Thomas and Lady Jane reveals a provocative relation to Forster's *Maurice*, for similarities to and differences from that work. Most obviously, *Maurice* is a novel about homosexual love, and *John Thomas* is a novel celebrating the renovative power of heterosexual passion. Yet the books are allied by their central situation in which a lower-class man, a gamekeeper who is identified with nature, acts as a regenerative agent for an individual who needs to be awakened from emotional lethargy. In his elemental purity of feeling, Parkin has ties with the other gamekeepers in Lawrence's fiction, with some of Lawrence's other "instinctual" characters, with Alec Scudder in *Maurice*, and with Stephen Wonham of *The Longest Journey*. First, we can consider the sources for Parkin in Lawrence's work. Annable in *The White Peacock*, the Pan-like and self-sufficient man of the forest, is akin to Parkin; in his former connection with an upper-class wife, he is closer even to Mellors, whose social connections are higher than Parkin's. As the epitome of primitive vitality, the game-keeper Arthur Pilbeam in a 1911 story, "The Shades of Spring," is another precursor of Parkin. The heroine of this tale rejects an intellectual in whom she is genuinely interested, in favor of the physical satisfaction she finds with the keeper, much as Lady Chatterley turns from Clifford to Parkin. Parkin, whose origins go far back into the history of the race, resembles the archetypal demonic men in Lawrence's previous fiction: Count Dionys in *The Ladybird* and General Cipriano in *The Plumed Serpent*, for example. Parkin also shares with Stephen Wonham of *The Longest Journey* a spirited self-sufficiency, an easy accord with nature, and a sense of fulfillment in being close to it. These qualities are even more intensely the possession of Stephen's father, the farmer Robert.

Although Forster in the "Terminal Note" to *Maurice* claims that Alec Scudder owes nothing to the "prickly" gamekeepers of Lawrence, we need to qualify that observation.[26] Forster, for one thing, appreciated quite early *The White Peacock*. In addition to the Stephen Wonham analogue in the gamekeeper Annable, there is also in this novel the deflected son of nature, George Saxton, whose ruin recalls that of Leonard Bast in *Howards End*, and there is the intimate relationship between Cyril Beardsall (the first-person narrator) and George when the men dry each other and embrace after swimming. Forster evidently found the homoerotic overtones in this situation genuine enough, though he recognized in a letter to E. J. Dent that Lawrence seemed to be unconscious of them, not having "a glimmering from first to last of what he's up to."[27] The relationship of George and Cyril may have been the prototype for that of Maurice and Alec Scudder in *Maurice*, which Forster had finished in its first form by the time that he wrote this letter and knew Lawrence personally.

Lawrence seems not to have divined Forster's homosexuality at this point, although Forster undoubtedly was aware of that element in Lawrence's psyche, whatever may have been Lawrence's own attitudes toward it.[28] Lawrence condemned homosexuality outright as mistakenly oriented emotion, though he celebrated with fervor the love of comrades in the first version of "Whitman" in his *Studies in Classic American Literature* and Birkin's erotic fervor for men in the suppressed "Prologue" to *Women in Love*.[29] In his revisions to *Maurice* in 1932 and then again in 1959, Forster may have intensified the Maurice-Scudder relationship by remembering the other well-known homo-erotic scenes in Lawrence's fiction: the wrestling scene in *Women in Love* between Rupert Birkin and Gerald Crich, the massage sequence in *Aaron's Rod* when Lilly ministers to the ill Aaron Sisson, and the scene in *The Plumed Serpent* when Cipriano and Don Ramón merge mystically with the cosmos while in physical contact with each other. Since Forster's revisions of *Maurice* in 1932 were concerned largely with making the physical relationship between Maurice Hall and Alec Scudder more realistic,[30] he may have written more frankly by the example of Lawrence's candor concerning physical love in *Lady Chatterley's Lover*. Philip Gardner in his study of *Maurice* informs us that Forster wrote in 1959 the last two pages of chapter 45 (after Maurice leaves Mr. Borenius at the boat pier on learning that Alec has decided not to emigrate).[31] In these pages an authentic poetry, a heightened eroticism, and a tenderness toward the loved one reveal a Lawrencean sensibility; in effect, the spirit of *Lady Chatterley's Lover* suffuses these additions to the novel.

Parkin and Alec have in common the vitality of the unsophisticated man close to nature; and each one acts as the intrusive stranger who upsets the normal existence of a person whom he comes to know intimately. Alec enjoys his career as gamekeeper and loves the woodland, but he has been infected more than Parkin by the desire to advance in "the great world": "it was only by accident that he had appeared as an untamed son of the woods. Indeed, he liked the woods and the fresh air and water, he liked them better than anything and he liked to protect or destroy life, but woods contain no 'openings,' and young men who want to get on must leave them."[32] Yet Alec seems at home in the outdoors and brings with him an intensity of animal life that Maurice has never known before. There are some other likenesses between Parkin and Alec. Both are resentful of the classes above them; both hesitate to involve themselves personally with individuals from a higher stratum; and both with some reluctance assume the role of outcast in order to be with the person whom they love physically. Maurice foresees that he and Alec will be outcasts, whereas it is Parkin who suggests to Connie that if other people knew the nature of their intimacy, they would be outlawed. If Parkin is hesitant about beginning a life with Connie, it is Connie who is even more hesitant. In *Lady Chatterley's Lover*, however, these reservations almost cease to exist, since Mellors impresses Connie favorably from the beginning: "He might almost be a gentleman" (*LCL* 85). In contrast, in *John Thomas and Lady Jane*, Connie wishes for a long time "the selfish pleasure of the contact, but not the submission to the subtle interweaving of her life with his, in creative fate" (*JTLJ* 295). Like Maurice, she fights against the passion that inevitably subdues her.

Maurice Hall also feels many reservations about his lover. Even before he meets Alec, he had once thought: "The feeling that can impel a gentleman towards a person of lower class stands self-condemned."[33] The day after his first contact with Alec, Maurice still dislikes playing cricket with his social inferiors, and he resents the fact that Alec is the son of a butcher. Then when he receives the notes from Alec with their threats of blackmail, he thinks that he may be undergoing the retribution that results when a man goes outside his class to establish an intimacy. Maurice also realizes that the transports of physical love are so extreme that they can beget fear and cruelty, as they seem to have done, temporarily, with Alec; physical love, Maurice thinks, is "panic in essence."[34]

Both Alec and Connie realize that social class is irrelevant in the face of genuine emotion. As a result of her talks with Archie Blood in France, Connie loses her mistrust of the lower class. She sees that social differences mean little in comparison with genuine distinction. With the upheaval caused by the Great War, she realizes that there are now no more classes, and that mankind in the lump now forms "one vast proletariat." Most people, no matter what their social origins, belong to this proletariat of the "cold-blooded" and the "cold-willed," in opposition to "the warm-blooded . . . sons and daughters of god," with whom she and Parkin, she feels, are to be aligned (*JTLJ* 288–89). Parkin is, in short, a natural aristocrat, despite the fact that his father was a collier. Like Connie, Maurice sees that his own upper middle class is vitiated by moral convention, repression of emotion, and unreasonable desire for security. The only recourse for the individual who desires to preserve his spiritual identity, Maurice finds, is to live outside society, without relatives or money—to become, in short, one of the natural aristocracy of whom Forster speaks in "What

I Believe": "an aristocracy of the sensitive, the considerate and the plucky."[35]

Through the successive drafts of *Lady Chatterley's Lover* Lawrence virtually erased the element of class, and Mellors (though not Parkin) is as articulate as any other Lawrencean hero. Despite his intellectual championing of a natural aristocracy, Forster regrets in *Maurice* that considerations of class form an obstacle to free sexual expression. But he acknowledges also that Maurice could have responded only to a man from Alec's class. Forster himself gravitated toward men of the lower class and asserted in a rather poignant statement of 1935: "I want to love a strong young man of the lower classes and be loved by him and even hurt by him. That is my ticket."[36] It would have been possible for the Lady Chatterley of *John Thomas* to make this statement, but it would have been an irrelevance for the Lady Chatterley in the final version of the novel. Forster virtually declared that homosexual love can be meaningful only when class taboos as well as sexual taboos are consciously flouted. Forster, in fact, causes us to wonder whether homosexual passion could even exist in a classless society.

The Lady Chatterley of *John Thomas and Lady Jane* is closer to Ursula Brangwen than to any of Lawrence's other characters. She lacks, moreover, some of the initial strident sophistication of the Lady Chatterley of the final version. She has intelligence and culture, sensitivity and a quickened sensibility; she is constantly alive to impressions from without, and she attains an increased awareness and comprehension in the course of the novel. In her search for truth, she has affinities with Paul Morel, Kate Leslie, and Richard Somers among other Lawrence characters, and she reveals some of the qualities possessed by the early, uncorrupted Rickie Elliot of *The Longest Journey* and by Margaret Schlegel of *Howards End.* Constance's seriousness and candor ally her to Adela Quested of *A Passage to India,* though her emotional range is broader; Constance has also the penetrating social sympathies of Fielding in *Passage* and his openness of temper, but she is more available to the implications of the transcendental than he is. In her emotional moments she has some of the force of Helen Schlegel; in her moments of doubt and confusion, she undergoes some of the painful soul-searching of Forster's Maurice Hall—though they both decide, ultimately, that the world is well lost for love.

Sir Clifford Chatterley is, in essence, one of the bourgeois-minded English of whom Forster wrote cryptically in his "Notes on the English Character." When these men leave the public school and the university, they go forth, Forster maintained, "into a world of whose richness and subtlety they have no conception. They go forth into it with well-developed bodies, fairly developed minds, and undeveloped hearts. . . . An undeveloped heart—not a cold one."[37] Except for his being maimed in body, the description fits Clifford in the early pages, before he muffles his emotions and imagination. Clifford becomes in the course of the novel an individual whose singleness of purpose and numbness of sensibility align him with Herbert Pembroke of *The Longest Journey,* the Wilcoxian entrepreneurs of *Howards End,* and the convention-bound Anglo-Indians of *A Passage to India.* He differs from these Forsterian types, in that he retrogresses into their frame of mind from having been initially a more sympathetic presence. He also reveals some of the characteristics of Clive Durham, Maurice's first and Platonic lover, who is overly concerned, as is Clifford, with the perquisites of the aristocracy and who reveals an inflexible intellectualism like Clifford's. In both men the mind or the will interferes with their being able to achieve valid perceptions of reality. Perhaps Sir Clifford reveals, too, some of the acquisitiveness and possessiveness of Harcourt Worters in Forster's story "Other Kingdom." These qualities prove so intolerable to Worters's wife Daphne that she runs off from her husband to become a dryad in the wood that he had bought for her but had, against her wishes, fenced in. The character of Tommy Dukes in *John Thomas,* more fully and appealingly developed than in the third version of the book, may owe something to Fielding in *A Passage to India:* a conscientious intellectual, Dukes perceives many truths about modern man—the need to live by touch, for example— but he is unable himself to live by the light of these truths. Like Fielding, he is a man of good will who is less effective than he ought to have been—though, of course, Dukes has been more greatly disabled spiritually by the Great War than Fielding has.

In two major works that appeared in the middle twenties, *A Passage to India* (1924) and *The Plumed Serpent* (1926), Forster and Lawrence juxtaposed a fragmented European culture with one that reached back through the centuries and had, by implication, a sturdiness and strength absent from the modern. Lawrence was impressed with Forster's novel when he read it in 1924, although he thought that Forster did not understand Hinduism (CL 811); and Forster in his 1930 obituary regarded *The Plumed Serpent* as Lawrence's greatest work. Lawrence also referred scornfully to the Caves sequence with its disorienting echo, and he criticized Forster for not being primarily concerned with the "religious relationship" or "the X" in our existence.[38] But Forster's radical disillusion projected in Mrs. Moore's horror at the Marabar Caves and his presentation of the Shri Krishna rituals in "Temple," for all of Lawrence's criticism, undoubtedly did influence him. Like Forster, Lawrence tried in *The Plumed Serpent* to use the rituals of an ancient culture to find some source of renewal. The sequences in the novel which feature the chanted hymns and the patterned dances of Quetzalcoatl-worship ("The Plaza," "Lords of the Day and Night," "Auto da Fé," and "The Opening of the Church") parallel the formalized dramatization of the birth of Shri Krishna in the "Temple" sequence in *Passage*.

In both books there is a reaching down and through the present-day civilizations of India and Mexico to something that is central and permanent in their traditions. In the two novels the expression of these rites and of this racial heritage is both ordered and chaotic. Too much order would extinguish the vitality in the traditions, and too much confusion would entail a failure to communicate their essence. Judith Wilt suggests with insight that the whole of *The Plumed Serpent* may be Lawrence's answer to what follows the retreat to the desert undertaken by Lou Witt in *St. Mawr* (1925), in her protest against the triviality of modern life.[39] Like Ursula Brangwen at the end of *The Rainbow*, Lou Witt at the end of *St. Mawr* is in a state of expectancy and awaits the coming of the fully vital man who will offer her the chance of renewal. Cipriano, as the god-demon Pan, comes to Kate Leslie (in Wilt's view a surrogate in *The Plumed Serpent* for the Lou Witt of *St. Mawr*) and offers her a deliverance, by exposing her to the stark force yet to be found in the living religion of Quetzalcoatl. Kate's reactions toward Cipriano's double-edged gift—the religion assimilates violence and cruelty as well as vitality—are ambiguous, but at the end she commits herself to a mode of life that sometimes repels her judgment. In Forster's novel the rich life-giving confusion of the Hindu ceremonies offsets the paralyzing ramifications of the echo in the Marabar Caves which reduces all aspiration to nullity. The living religions of Quetzalcoatl and Hinduism offset in Lawrence's novel and Forster's the spiritual barrenness inherent in a torpid and fragmented modern culture.

Lawrence's radical cynicism concerning European culture in *St. Mawr* and *Lady Chatterley's Lover* probably owes something to Mrs. Moore's disillusionment in the Marabar Caves, despite his professed lack of interest in "Bou-oum" or "all the universe."[40] Mrs. Moore's trauma has become a central metaphor for the modern sensibility, so arresting is this scene in its dramatization of the total paralysis likely to overtake a person unprepared for the stark realities of the cosmos at its most uncompromising: "the echo began in some undescribable way to undermine her hold on life. Coming at a moment when she chanced to be fatigued, it had managed to murmur, 'Pathos, piety, courage—they exist, but are identical, and so is filth. Everything exists, nothing has value.' If one had spoken vileness in that place, or quoted lofty poetry, the comment would have been the same—'ou-boum.' "[41] Some parallels to Mrs. Moore's vision occur when Lou Witt in *St. Mawr* rides with her superficial friends to the Devil's Chair in Shropshire overlooking Wales, "one of those places where the spirit of aboriginal England still lingers."[42] (Her appreciation of the Welsh spirit may also owe something to Margaret Schlegel's fascination with the Celtic sensibility when she visits Oniton Grange in Shropshire in *Howards End*.) At the Devil's Chair, Lou succumbs to some overpowering realizations, rivaling in intensity those of Mrs. Moore in the Marabar Caves: "And she had a vision, a vision of evil. Or not strictly a vision. She became aware of evil, evil, evil, rolling in great waves over the earth. Always she had thought there was no such thing—only a mere negation of good. Now, like an ocean to whose surface she had risen, she saw the dark-grey waves of evil rearing in a great tide."[43] A like stultifying vision descends on Mrs. Witt, Lou's mother, a vision which, like that of Mrs. Moore, renders her incapable of action. On the ride with Lewis, the groom, she muses that "nothing in all my life has ever truly affected me," and the narrator summarizes her radical pessimism: "In such a world there was nothing even to conquer. It gave everything and gave nothing to everybody and anybody all the time. . . . A great complicated tangle of nonentities ravelled in nothingness. So it seemed to her."[44] In New Mexico, she becomes totally indifferent and wishes never to make another decision—neither to die nor not to die. Mrs. Witt never transcends the pessimism that engulfs her, however, as Mrs. Moore was about to do when she was leaving India. Mrs. Witt will die apparently unreconciled either to life or to death.

Some of the starkness of *A Passage to India* also helps establish the tone of *John Thomas and Lady Jane* and *Lady Chatterley's Lover*. In *John Thomas* Connie sees that the men who have participated in the war have lost the will, or even the capacity, to live. Tommy Dukes, the best of them in her circle, is not a possible lover for her, despite his integrity, because "the weight of disillusion" hangs too heavy on him: "But the old thing, the dead civilisation, was clamped down on him too hard. . . . She could have loved Tommy Dukes, but for the dark, cold death that was still at the centre of his heart" (*JTLJ* 58, 62). In *Lady Chatterley's Lover* Connie discovers that the fine-sounding words that used to inspire mankind no longer mean anything to her, in a passage that seemingly combines the disillusionment of Mrs. Moore in the Marabar Caves and the cynicism of Frederic Henry in *A Farewell to Arms:* "All the great words, it seemed to Connie, were cancelled for her generation: love, joy, happiness, home, mother, father, husband, all these great, dynamic words were half dead now, and dying from day to day" (*LCL* 102). She experiences, before her resurrection in the wood, a total desiccation, comparable to that undergone by Mrs. Moore: "Poor Connie! As the years drew on it was the fear of nothingness in her life that affected her. Clifford's mental life and hers gradually began to feel like nothingness. Their marriage, their integrated life based on a habit of intimacy, that he talked about: there were days when it all became utterly blank and nothing. It was words, just so many words. The only reality was nothingness, and over it a hypocrisy of words" (*LCL* 89).

Yet with neither writer does the pessimism remain unmitigated. For Parkin and for Constance there has occurred the great resurrection of the body under the healing aegis of nature and the animistic benefi- cence of the forest. The cosmic powers exert their healing influence, as the battered lovers plan their life together. If Byron's line, "There's not a joy the world can give like that it takes away!" (*JTLJ* 367), suggests in the closing sequences the tragic, the very existence of joy and love implies the possibility of transfiguration. In *Lady Chatterley's Lover* the aspect of tenderness in love is a positive value and more completely stressed than in *John Thomas*. For the alienated characters in *A Passage to India*, a meaningful connection and understanding takes place, again under the aegis of nature and the healing rains of the monsoon. Symbolically, the characters are reborn when they are thrown into the Mau tank, and the absent characters, such as Adela Quested and Mrs. Moore, are present by proxy. The Mau festivities have, in essence, wiped out the Marabar and its undermining reverberations upon the spirit, just as the forest in *John Thomas* negates the trivialities of Clifford and of the visitors to Wragby Hall.

What Forsterian similarities can we discern in some of Lawrence's other fiction, written during the war and after, and what Lawrencean influences can we discover in Forster's posthumously published stories (in *The Life to Come and Other Stories*, 1972), written in the 1920s and after? There are many analogous characters and situations that betoken a similar sense of human destiny and similar values, and some direct influence too of one writer upon the other. The world views, sensibilities, and ideas of the two writers are at times uncannily alike. To adopt a Lawrencean metaphor used in *John Thomas* to describe the ideal marriage, the two writers are like ships that steer parallel courses, only occasionally touching one another. But sometimes they draw together unmistakably.

In *Aaron's Rod* (1922), the most interesting pages are those that describe Italy and Aaron Sisson's experiences there. The re-creations of Florence have a vitality and an immediacy that recall the early Italian novels of Forster and a sense of place that Lawrence had already revealed in *Twilight in Italy* (1916) and elsewhere. The "spirit of place," as it is revealed in a foreign culture, animates the works of Lawrence at the time: Australia in *Kangaroo* (1922), New Mexico in *St. Mawr* (1925), and Mexico in *The Plumed Serpent* (1926). Forster in his Italian novels is an engaging satirist and an accomplished novelist of manners, and, as such, he became one antecedent for Lawrence, the commentator upon social life, often in a foreign setting, and its satirist. The people whom Aaron meets in Italy, Lawrence etches in with the finesse of a writer who has some flair for the comic—a sense for the incongruous and the exaggerated aspects of an individual's personality or behavior. Among the satirically envisioned characters in *Aaron's Rod* are the vulgar financier Sir William Franks and his aggressive wife; the effete expatriates Francis Dekker and Angus Guest; the contentious Argyle; and the sensuous but sterile Marchese del Torre (the American expatriate with whom Aaron has a somewhat unenthusiastic affair in Florence). This satiric exposé of modern types who are deficient in some respect forms part of *John Thomas and Lady Jane* when Lawrence writes of the Christmas guests at Wragby; it is even more evident in *Lady Chatterley's Lover* in the presentation of the shallow and self-important Michaelis with whom Connie has a frustrating affair and in Clifford's circle of shallow intellectual friends. Lawrence emerges in *Aaron's Rod,* in novellas such as *St. Mawr* and *The Captain's Doll,* and in some of the shorter works written after the war, as a competent though hardly great practitioner of the comedy of manners. If he were more accomplished as a writer in this genre, he would have been guilty of an excessive degree of intellectuality in his writing, of the "mental consciousness" against which he was always to inveigh.

Like Forster, Lawrence is expert at painting social surfaces as well as exploring psychic depths. This satiric approach informs many of the short fictions that Lawrence wrote toward the end of his career. In works like "The Rocking Horse Winner" (1926), "The Lovely Lady" (1927), and "Mother and Daughter" (1929), Lawrence exposed, with satiric emphasis, the dominating mother figure, the destructive matriarch. These women have some of the insensitivity, the possessiveness, and the latent cruelty characteristic of Forster's most formidable women: Mrs. Herriton in *Where Angels Fear to Tread,* Mrs. Failing and Agnes Pembroke in *The Longest Journey,* and the memsahibs of *A Passage to India.* In one of Lawrence's most arresting fables from his late career, "The Man Who Loved Islands" (1927), it is difficult to separate the elements of satire and tragedy. Cathcart, the protagonist, is deficient in imagination and awareness so that potentially positive values end by being dehumanizing. "Blood consciousness" in him congeals by slow degrees into "mental consciousness," without his quite realizing what has happened. So in *The Longest Journey* Rickie

Elliot's supple imagination in the wrong environment hardens into uncritically assimilated abstractions.

Some of Lawrence's other excellent short fictions reveal notable likenesses to the situations and characters found in Forster's narratives: "The Blind Man" (1918) is such a work. In this tale Lawrence matches an elemental protagonist, Maurice Pervin, the blind man who is reminiscent of Stephen Wonham, with Bertie, an effete intellectual who cowers away from physical contact with Pervin. Bertie is a less substantial Rickie Elliot figure for whom touching the vital blind man is psychologically shattering. His recoil from the physical surely symbolizes his fear of "blood consciousness." In compensation, he is led to an excessive intellectualizing of his consciousness; he is therefore in part a harbinger of Clifford Chatterley in *John Thomas and Lady Jane*. Bertie has elements in him also of Clive Durham in *Maurice*; Bertie turns with aversion from the blind man just as Clive reacts with stridency to the idea of Maurice's allying himself with a gamekeeper. The woman in the triangular relationship of "The Blind Man," Isabel Pervin, is the perceptive individual of goodwill who has the capacity to develop, in the manner of Ursula Brangwen and Margaret Schlegel, though she lacks their large dimensions.

In his late, homosexually oriented stories Forster retreated from the irony that had encompassed his vision through *A Passage to India* and revealed in them a more direct participation in, and celebration of, desire.[45] So the spontaneous and the instinctive are of greater importance in this fiction than they had been even in Forster's early Italian novels; in this respect, Forster became more Lawrencean with the years. *Maurice*, perhaps to its detriment as a work of art, also partakes of this openness and directness of manner. The unashamed expression of emotion, advocated as a program for living in "What Does It Matter? A Morality," results sometimes in a reduction of the complexity of these stories, although a few of them gain thereby added force. I will discuss only "Dr. Woolacott" and "The Other Boat" as representatives of this late fiction, though Lawrencean analogues and parallels are present in all these stories.

"Dr. Woolacott" (1927) is allied imaginatively and conceptually with *Lady Chatterley's Lover*, though it was written slightly before. It is also reminiscent of Forster's own early story "The Road from Colonus."

In that work Mr. Lucas is unable to stay in the vicinity of the votive tree in Greece which had given him a sense of intense life when he entered its hollow trunk and found a pure stream inside. Rather, his assertive, mentally conscious daughter hustles him away and back to his meaningless existence in London. It would have been preferable for him to have remained in Greece, despite the fact that the tree where Mr. Lucas's soul awakened had fallen the night the visitors left and destroyed the inn in which they would have had to stay. They would have been killed; but psychic death is far more to be deplored than mere physical death; and this is the lesson that Clesant also learns in "Dr. Woolacott." A youth from nowhere—an agricultural worker, formerly a student—visits Clesant and instills in him a feeling of abundance until Clesant's mention of the deadly and conventional Dr. Woolacott dispels their rapport with one another. On the return of the boy, Clesant chooses him as opposed to the regimen of Dr. Woolacott which might have preserved him as a physical entity for many years. As he embraces the youth, the excitement kills him, but an apotheosis in physical death is more meaningful than the torpor of a vegetative existence. The intruder from outside who brings regeneration to another who needs him—such is the youth's role in "Dr. Woolacott," such is Henry Grenfel's role in Lawrence's "The Fox," and such is Parkin's role in *John Thomas and Lady Jane*. And Woolacott is a sinister analogue to the soul-destroying Sir Clifford Chatterley.

The best of these stories, "The Other Boat" (1957–58), exploits some of the same themes, but with a difference. The conflicts in the story are sinister and incapable of resolution except in death, a death that is associated, moreover, with fulfilled passion itself. It is as if Forster were dramatizing in a short narrative the full implications of the extreme position that Whitman—in Lawrence's view—had found himself in, as a result of his compulsion to merge his identity with that of another: the most extreme sort of fusion is not with another individual, says Lawrence, but with death:

> Merging! And Death! Which is the final merge.
> The great merge into the womb. Woman.
> And after that, the merge of comrades: man-for-man love.
> And almost immediately with this, death, the final merge of death.[46]

In this discussion of Whitman, Lawrence is almost certainly describing his own predisposition and—by inference—Forster's, at least in "The Other Boat."

In "The Other Boat" the great enemy to the spontaneous expression of the self is society; such, of course, is one basic premise in most of Forster's and Lawrence's fiction. In the story the conventions of early twentieth-century society impede an affair of the heart, on an outward-bound boat to India, between Captain Lionel March and a middle-class youth from India, Cocoa. The complicating factor of race acts additionally as a barrier to the free expression of desire. March is divided in his allegiance to a lover from another class and race and to the society which has produced him and which is powerfully entrenched in the figure of his mother. The conflict is the same as in "The Life to Come," but it is more focused: denial of sex results in psychic desiccation, whereas indulgence in sex, counter to the dictates of convention, is likely to result in physical death. Infuriated at Cocoa's attempts to blackmail him into becoming his permanent lover, March strangles him, only to jump overboard when he realizes the ramifications of the crime that his manipulative lover had caused him to commit.

"Dr. Woolacott" and "The Other Boat" are among Forster's best works; the completion of them owes much to Lawrence, though Lawrence might have been uncomfortable with them. In these stories Forster asserts that the denial of desire is more disastrous for the individual than its satisfaction. Lawrence, too, in his late works such as *Lady Chatterley's Lover* and *The Escaped Cock*, urged a more direct, less mediated, expression of the passions than he had advocated in the works of his prime. Aesthetically, the absence of struggle in his characters as they make their adjustments to love simplifies these late works to a degree, and this criticism is even more valid for the late stories of Forster. Forster and Lawrence began writing with similar ideas concerning the repressiveness of English middle-class society, and in one way or another, they advocated throughout their careers the need for the unimpeded, though responsible, expression of the emotions and the instincts. The watershed between the two writers is in the matter of sexual preference. That aside, they worked from the same large blueprint.

Despite their moments of disillusionment, Forster and Lawrence did much to preserve all that is most vital in the romantic tradition. Above all else, they asserted the sanctity of the individual and his need to assume a life of spiritual responsibility. According to them, he must become freely responsive to experience and attempt to attain an increased awareness, he must be open to influences from within the self and from outside the self (especially to those of nature, art, religion, myth, and human relationships), he must be sensitive to visionary impulses, and he must learn to savor—and to act in accordance with—the infinite possibilities that the subjective life offers to those who are willing to follow it with imagination and with dedication. From such an enlarged perspective of human potentialities, both men wrote their fiction, creating "moments of emergence and of a new splendour" for which we are immensely in their debt.

NOTES

1. P. N. Furbank, *E. M. Forster: A Life*, vol. 2, *Polycrates' Ring (1914–1970)* (London: Secker and Warburg, 1978), p. 163. A fuller documentation of the points of contact between the two men than I can give here will be found in John Beer, " 'The Last Englishman': Lawrence's Appreciation of Forster," in *E. M. Forster: A Human Exploration*, ed. G. K. Das and John Beer (New York: New York University Press, 1979), p. 245–68, and in Paul Delany, *D. H. Lawrence's Nightmare* (New York: Basic Books, 1978), pp. 48–57 (for the Greatham period especially). Also helpful is C. E. Baron, "Forster on Lawrence," in Das and Beer, pp. 186–95. I shall mention a few excellent studies which compare individual works of the two writers at appropriate places in my text and notes. The most informed short discussions of the two writers are Martin Price, "E. M. F. and D. H. L.," *Yale Review* n.s. 55 (Summer 1966): 597–601, and Wilfred Stone, *The Cave and the Mountain: A Study of E. M. Forster* (Stanford: Stanford University Press, 1966), pp. 378–87.

2. E. M. Forster, "D. H. Lawrence," *Nation and Athenaeum* 46 (29 March 1930): 888. For T. S. Eliot's remarks see "D. H. Lawrence," *Nation and Athenaeum* 47 (5 April 1930): 11; for Forster's rejoinder, see "D. H. Lawrence," *Nation and Athenaeum* 47 (12 April 1930): 45. See also Forster's tribute in "D. H. Lawrence," *Listener* 3 (30 April 1930): 753–54, and his praise of Lawrence in 1927 in *Aspects of the Novel* (New York: Harcourt, Brace and World, 1956), pp. 143–44.

3. See "Terminal Note" to Forster's *Maurice* (New York: Norton, 1971), pp. 247–55; Emile Delavenay, *D. H. Lawrence and Edward Carpenter: A Study in Edwardian Transition* (New York: Taplinger, 1971); and Margaret Bolsterli, "Studies in Context: The Homosexual Ambience of Twentieth Century Literary Culture," *D. H. Lawrence Review* 6, no. 1 (Spring 1973): 71–85.

4. Delany, *D. H. Lawrence's Nightmare*, p. 56.

5. See letter to Louie Burrows, 23 June 1911, *Lawrence in Love*, ed. James T. Boulton (Nottingham: University of Nottingham, 1968), pp. 113–14; postscript by Frieda Lawrence to Lawrence's letter to Forster, 28 January 1915, in Furbank, *Forster: A Life*, vol. 2, p. 7 (*Angels*); letter, 3 February 1915, in Furbank, *Forster: A Life*, vol. 2, p. 8 ("The Story of a Panic"); letter, Frieda Lawrence to Forster, 1915, in *E. M. Forster: The Critical Heritage*, ed. Philip Gardner (London and Boston: Routledge and Kegan Paul, 1973), p. 97 (*Journey*); letter, Frieda Lawrence to Forster, 5 February 1915, in Furbank, *Forster: A Life*, vol. 2, p. 8 (*Howards End*). One can assume, I think, that if Frieda had read a book, Lawrence would have read it himself or else would have known about it from her, since Frieda was always voluble.

6. Rose Marie Burwell, "A Catalogue of D. H. Lawrence's Reading from Early Childhood: Addenda," *D. H. Lawrence Review* 6, no. 1 (Spring 1973): 92; letter to Martin Secker, 23 July 1924 (*CL* 799); letter to Secker, 13 August 1925, quoted in Beer, " 'The Last Englishman,' " *E. M. Forster: A Human Exploration*, p. 245.

7. Julian Moynahan, "Lawrence, Woman, and the Celtic Fringe," *Lawrence and Women*, ed. Anne Smith (London: Vision Press, 1978), p. 128.

8. E. M. Forster, *Howards End* (New York: Vintage Books, 1934), p. 331.

9. Ibid., p. 186.

10. Letter, "Mr Jester," 23 May 1925, *The Centaur Letters by D. H. Lawrence*, introduction by Edward D. McDonald (Austin: Humanities Research Center, University of Texas, 1970), p. 19.

11. For the facts about the composition of *The Lost Girl*, see Keith Sagar, *D. H. Lawrence: A Calendar of His Works* (Austin: University of Texas Press, 1979), pp. 33–38, 98–101, and *The Lost Girl*, ed. John Worthen (Cambridge: Cambridge University Press, 1981), pp. xix–xxxi.

12. For a complete discussion of this subject see Jeanne Delbaere-Garant, "The Call of the South: *Where Angels Fear to Tread* and *The Lost Girl*," *Revue des Langues Vivantes* 29 (1963): 336–57, and Calvin Bedient, "Lawrence and Forster in Italy," in his *Architects of the Self: George Eliot, D. H. Lawrence, and E. M. Forster* (Berkeley and Los Angeles: University of California Press, 1972), pp. 183–95.

13. Furbank, *Forster: A Life*, vol. 2, p. 8.

14. A full discussion of E. M. Forster and D. H. Lawrence as writers preoccupied with the Pan legend will be found in Patricia Merivale's standard *Pan the Goat-God: His Myth in Modern Times* (Cambridge: Harvard University Press, 1969), pp. 180–91 for Forster and pp. 194–219 for Lawrence. I am much indebted to this study.

15. D. H. Lawrence, *The Plumed Serpent* (New York: Vintage Books, 1959), p. 341.

16. *The Trial of Lady Chatterley: Regina v. Penguin Books Limited*, ed. C. H. Rolph (Baltimore: Penguin, 1961), pp. 112–13.

17. *John Thomas and Lady Jane* rates highly with some critics. Harry T. Moore maintained that in it Lawrence presented his story more intensely and that the characters are more believable and vital than in *Lady Chatterley's Lover*. L. E. Sissman

feels that *John Thomas and Lady Jane* is the better novel because it is less didactic and allegoric than *Lady Chatterley's Lover*. See Harry T. Moore, "John Thomas and Lady Jane," *New York Times Book Review*, 27 August 1972, p. 7; and L. E. Sissman, "The Second Lady Chatterley," *New Yorker* 48 (6 January 1973): 73–75. I feel that the books are closely related but different novels, and I find virtues in each, though I have come to favor *John Thomas* because for me Lawrence is more resolute in it in his analysis of his characters under conditions of great, and sometimes intolerable, stress.

18. E. M. Forster, "D. H. Lawrence," *Listener* 3 (30 April 1930): 753–54, reprinted in *D. H. Lawrence: The Critical Heritage*, ed. R. P. Draper (New York: Barnes and Noble, 1970), pp. 343–47. Reference is on p. 345.

19. As in his letters about the novel and in "A Propos of *Lady Chatterley's Lover*" (*Phoenix II* 487–515).

20. E. M. Forster, *The Longest Journey* (New York: Vintage Books, n.d.), p. 231.

21. See especially chapter 9, "Lucy as a Work of Art," in E. M. Forster, *A Room with a View* (New York: Vintage Books, n.d.), pp. 110–25.

22. Forster, *The Longest Journey*, p. 66.

23. Letter to Earl and Achsah Brewster, 1928, in Earl and Achsah Brewster, *D. H. Lawrence: Reminiscences and Correspondence* (London: Secker, 1934), p. 166.

24. Forster, *Howards End*, pp. 186, 187.

25. E. M. Forster, *The Longest Journey* (Oxford: Oxford University Press, World's Classics, 1960), p. xiii.

26. E. M. Forster, *Maurice* (New York: Norton, 1971), p. 252.

27. 6 March 1915, Furbank, *Forster: A Life*, vol. 2, p. 12.

28. An article that I have encountered since writing my study, Dixie King's "The Influence of Forster's *Maurice* on *Lady Chatterley's Lover*," *Contemporary Literature* 23, no. 1 (Winter 1982): 65–82, covers some of the ground that I do. King's article is valuable for indicating the parallels between *A Room with a View* and *The White Peacock*, though there is no explicit reference to *Room* available to me either in Lawrence's or Frieda Lawrence's work (or in Furbank's life of Forster). The chances are good, however, that Lawrence knew *Room*. King also points out some parallels between *Maurice* and *Lady Chatterley* that I do not mention, a number of them suggestive. I cannot accept, however, her principal arguments that Lawrence was one of the close friends to whom Forster showed his manuscript of *Maurice* and that, as a result, *Maurice* is to be regarded as a chief source of Lawrence's novel. There exists no documentation or other convincing evidence to lend credence to her arguments. The uneasy relationship between the two writers, which tended to become abusive on Lawrence's side, suggests that the reticent Forster would have been reluctant to offer Lawrence the opportunity of reading a manuscript to which he would have been sure to react with abrasiveness and satire rather than with sympathy. I agree with one of our best Lawrence scholars, Keith Sagar, when he says, "Forster cannot have told Lawrence [in 1915] of his recently completed, unpublishable, homosexual novel *Maurice*," in *The Life of D. H. Lawrence* (New York: Pantheon Books, 1980), p. 83.

29. See Lawrence's remarks on sodomy in the letter to Bertrand Russell, 12 February 1915 (*CL* 319). For "Whitman," see D. H. Lawrence, *The Symbolic Meaning: The Uncollected Versions of "Studies in Classic American Literature,"* ed. Armin Arnold (London: Centaur Press, 1962), pp. 253–64 (in the 1923 version Lawrence scorns the love of comrades). For the "Prologue" to *Women in Love,* see *Phoenix II,* 92–118. That the intimate and homoerotic relationship between Rupert Birkin and Gerald Crich may have been partly formative upon Forster in dramatizing the relationship in *A Passage to India* between Aziz and Fielding with its erotic overtones is suggested by Forster's having transcribed into the manuscript of *Passage* the concluding paragraphs of *Women in Love,* in which Birkin still asserts that he wishes for as fulfilling a relationship with a man as with a woman. See *The Manuscripts of "A Passage to India,"* ed. Oliver Stallybrass (New York: Holmes and Meier, 1978), p. 580.

30. According to Evelyne Hanquart in "Maurice et E. M. Forster," *Études Anglaises* 28, no. 3 (July–September 1975): 281–99, most of the substantive changes occurred in the 1932 version. Forster, following the advice of Lytton Strachey and others, added the chapter describing Maurice's and Alec's night together at the London hotel and thereby made the love affair more physical in character.

31. Philip Gardner, "The Evolution of Forster's *Maurice,*" in *E. M. Forster: Centenary Revaluations,* ed. Judith Scherer Herz and Robert K. Martin (Toronto: University of Toronto Press, 1982), pp. 204–23 (see especially p. 221).

32. Forster, *Maurice,* p. 219. Christopher Orr notes that George Saxton and Alec Scudder are similar in their spontaneity and instinctive behavior and in their discontent with life in rural England. See "D. H. Lawrence and E. M. Forster: From *The White Peacock* to *Maurice,*" *West Virginia Association of College English Teachers Bulletin* 2, no. 2 (1975): 22–28.

33. Forster, *Maurice,* p. 151.

34. Ibid., p. 226.

35. E. M. Forster, "What I Believe," in his *Two Cheers for Democracy* (New York: Harcourt, Brace, 1951), p. 73.

36. Quoted in Oliver Stallybrass's "Introduction" to Forster's *The Life to Come and Other Stories* (London: Edward Arnold, 1972), p. xiv.

37. E. M. Forster, *Abinger Harvest* (New York: Harcourt, Brace, 1936), p. 5.

38. Letter to Forster, 23 July 1924, in Das and Beer, *E. M. Forster: A Human Exploration,* p. 256.

39. Judith Wilt, *Ghosts of the Gothic: Austen, Eliot, and Lawrence* (Princeton: Princeton University Press, 1980), pp. 289–91.

40. Letter to Furbank, 23 July 1924, quoted in Furbank, *E. M. Forster: A Life,* vol. 2, p. 124.

41. E. M. Forster, *A Passage to India* (New York: Harcourt, Brace, 1924), p. 149.

42. D. H. Lawrence, *"St. Mawr" and "The Man Who Died"* (New York: Vintage Books, 1959), p. 63.

43. Ibid., pp. 68–69. This episode is also discussed by M. L. Raina in "A Forster

Parallel in Lawrence's *St. Mawr*," *Notes and Queries* (London) n.s. 13, no. 3 (March 1966): 96–97.

44. Lawrence, *St. Mawr*, in "*St. Mawr*" and "*The Man Who Died*," pp. 97, 96.

45. I am indebted for this insight to Alan Wilde. See his "Depths and Surfaces: Dimensions of Forsterian Irony," *English Literature in Transition* 16 (1973): 257–74.

46. D. H. Lawrence, "Whitman," in *Studies in Classic American Literature* (New York: Viking, 1971), p. 169.

JAMES C. COWAN

Lawrence, Joyce, and the Epiphanies of *Lady Chatterley's Lover*

D. H. Lawrence and James Joyce never met, but they read and despised each other's work. Their mutual dislike sprang in part from their commitment to contrasting theories of literary art. They represent opposing tendencies in modernism that are clearly visible in their differing treatments of the epiphany.

For a writer who had experienced so many censorship problems himself, Lawrence was surprisingly uncritical in echoing the popular charge of obscenity against Joyce's *Ulysses.* Dorothy Brett reports a conversation in Taos in 1924 in which Frieda's calculated statement that *Ulysses* "is a wonderful book" provoked the predictable, vehement response from Lawrence: "The last part of it is the dirtiest, most indecent, obscene thing ever written. Yes it is, Frieda. . . . It is filthy."[1]

After Lawrence read a section of Joyce's *Work in Progress,* he declared, "My God, what a clumsy *olla putrida* James Joyce is! Nothing but old fags and cabbage-stumps of quotations from the Bible and the rest, stewed in the juice of deliberate, journalistic dirty-mindedness— what old and hard-worked staleness, masquerading as the all-new!" (*CL* 1075).[2] And he told Harry Crosby, whose Black Sun Press published both Lawrence's *Sun* (unexpurgated ed., 1926) and Joyce's *Tales Told of Shem and Shaun* (1928), "James Joyce bores me stiff—too terribly would-be and done-on-purpose, utterly without spontaneity or real life" (*CL* 1087). Lawrence thought Giovanni Verga a better writer. Although Verga's style "gives at first the sense of jumble and incoherence" in an effort to convey the "muddled" thought processes of the peasant mind, Lawrence says, "he is doing, as a great artist, what men like James Joyce do only out of contrariness and desire for a sensation" (*Phoenix* 250).

The clue to Lawrence's dislike for Joyce is his repeated use of words like "would-be" and "sensation," terms which in Lawrence's criticism usually mean overconscious and deliberate, mechanical and inorganic. That is why he categorizes Joyce among the modern novelists whose "dominant note is the repulsiveness, intimate physical repulsiveness of human flesh" (*Phoenix* 270). It is also why he ridiculed the stream-of-consciousness novelists for "the death-rattle in their throats," for "dying in a very long-drawn-out fourteen-volume death-agony, and absorbedly, childishly interested in the phenomenon. 'Did I feel a twinge in my little toe, or didn't I?' asks every character of Mr. Joyce or of Miss Richardson or M. Proust" (*Phoenix* 517).

For his part, Joyce returned the ill opinion in repeated condescension toward Lawrence's work. In one letter he mockingly calls Lawrence's book "*Lady Chatterbox's Lover*," and in a later letter, Joyce says of "*Lady Chatterli's* [sic] *Lover*": "I read the first 2 pages of the usual sloppy English which is a piece of propaganda in favour of something which, outside of D.H.L.'s country at any rate, makes all the propaganda for itself."[3] Joyce's derisive parodies of Lawrence's title convey the same sort of judgment (or misjudgment) as Lawrence's derisive parody of the stream-of-consciousness character's obsession with his own sensations. But the real clue to Joyce's judgment of Lawrence is his charge against *Lady Chatterley's Lover* of "propaganda," a charge related to Stephen Dedalus's declaration, in chapter 5 of *A Portrait of the Artist as a Young Man*, that "pornographical or didactic" arts, which excite "kinetic" feelings of "desire or loathing," are "improper arts."[4] As Richard Ellmann comments, Joyce "was anxious that his books should not commit propaganda, even against institutions of which he disapproved."[5]

Yet both Joyce and Lawrence employed scenes of the type that Joyce called "epiphany" and Lawrence called "visionary experience," although they arrived at these scenes by different routes and from opposing theoretical positions. The theory set forth in *A Portrait of the Artist as a Young Man* is a classical, mimetic theory in which "the esthetic emotion" "arrests the mind" because "the tragic emotion is static. . . . The mind is arrested and raised above desire and loathing." "Beauty expressed by the artist," Stephen declares, "cannot awaken in us an emotion which is kinetic or a sensation which is purely physical." Rather, it should awaken or induce "an esthetic stasis, an ideal pity or an ideal terror, a stasis called forth, prolonged and at last dissolved by what I call the rhythm of beauty" (*Portrait* 204–6).

Lawrence recognized the validity of classical theory for certain types of literature. His statement in "Poetry of the Present" that the "poetry of the beginning and the poetry of the end" have a "finality" and "perfection" "conveyed in exquisite form" fits Joyce's aesthetic theory and practice. "But," Lawrence suggests, "there is another kind of poetry: the poetry of that which is at hand: the immediate present. In the immediate present there is no perfection, no consummation, nothing finished. The strands are all flying, quivering, intermingling into the web, the waters are shaking the moon. . . . If we try to fix the living tissue, as the biologists fix it with formalin, we have only a hardened bit of the past, the bygone life under our observation."[6]

Joyce in *A Portrait of the Artist* and Lawrence in "Art and the Individual" set forth the theories in which their views of the epiphany and of art are rooted, although both go beyond these theories in their artistic practice. Stephen Dedalus's celebrated aesthetic theory in the fifth chapter of *A Portrait of the Artist* is drawn, of course, from the teachings of Saint Thomas Aquinas on the three principles required for beauty, "*integritas, consonantia, claritas,*" which Stephen translates as "*wholeness, harmony and radiance,*" qualities which, he believes, "correspond to the phases of apprehension." The "synthesis of immediate perception," as the object is first seen as a unified image, "self-bounded and selfcontained" against the background of all that is not it (*integritas*), is followed by the "analysis of apprehension" as the image is seen to be "complex, multiple, divisible, separable, made up of its parts, the result of its parts and their sum" (*consonantia*). Finally, having rejected as "literary talk" the idea that radiance is "the artistic discovery and representation of the divine purpose" or universality of the object, Stephen concludes that having perceived the object's wholeness and having analyzed its form, "you make the only synthesis which is logically and esthetically permissible. You see that it is that thing which it is and no other thing" (*claritas*), which Stephen takes to be identical with "the scholastic *quidditas*, the *whatness* of a thing" (*Portrait* 212–13).

In "Art and the Individual," a youthful essay of the Croydon period, Lawrence's concept of "two schools of Aesthetic thought," the mystical and the sensual, prefigures his later theory of the two kinds of poetry, that of the beginning and the end and that of "the immediate present." In the first, "Art. Beauty is the expression of the perfect and divine Idea." In the second, "Art is an activity arising . . . from sexual desire and propensity to play" or from some other pleasurable emotion. In the interpretation that Lawrence accepts, "these two, the mystical and the sensual ideas of Art are blended. Approval of Harmony—that is sensual—approval of Adaptation—that is mystic—. . ." (*Phoenix II* 223). Despite his differences from Joyce, Lawrence's definition of *harmony*, using the example of a swan, as approval of "the silken whiteness, the satisfying curve of line and mass," is compatible with Stephen Dedalus's definition of *consonantia* as the "analysis" that follows *integritas* as "you pass from point to point, led by [the object's] . . . formal lines; you apprehend it as balanced part against part within its limits; you feel the rhythm of its structure" (*Portrait* 212). But whereas Joyce relies on Aristotle and Aquinas, Lawrence's idea of art depends on Herbart's "classification of interests," from which Lawrence arrives at categories according to the source of the interest and arranges these in an aesthetic progression from the concrete to the universal (empirical, speculative, aesthetic, sympathetic, social, religious). "Since Aestheticism embraces all art," the aesthetic image in Lawrence's work may be seen as incorporating all six planes on ascending levels of experience (*Phoenix II* 221–23).

Turning to the question of epiphany in the context of Joyce's and Lawrence's theories of art, I want to consider first the nature of the experience to which the term refers, then some distinguishable types of literary epiphany. Joyce originally used the term to refer to the genre of some seventy short prose pieces he wrote between 1900 and 1904, recording actual experiences and moods; forty extant examples of these epiphanies are published in *The Workshop of Daedalus*, edited by Robert Scholes and Richard M. Kain.[7] As Joyce explains Stephen Dedalus's use of the term in *Stephen Hero*, "By an epiphany he meant a sudden spiritual manifestation, whether in the vulgarity of speech or of gesture

94

or in a memorable phase of the mind itself. He believed that it was for the man of letters to record these epiphanies with extreme care, seeing that they themselves are the most delicate and evanescent of moments."[8] This statement is clearly the source of Morris Beja's definition of *epiphany,* in *Epiphany in the Modern Novel,* as a "sudden spiritual manifestation, whether from some object, scene, event, or memorable phase of the mind—the manifestation being out of proportion to the significance or strictly logical relevance of whatever produces it."[9] In a critical exchange with Scholes, Florence Walzl comments that "the term *epiphany* has several meanings in current Joyce criticism. It may refer to an early prose type, to a spiritual and intellectual illumination of the nature of a thing, and also, by extension, to the artistic insights and means by which such a revelation is achieved."[10] Whereas Beja barely mentions Lawrence, Ann Shealy, in "The Epiphany Theme in Modern Fiction: E. M. Forster's *Howards End* and D. H. Lawrence's *Sons and Lovers,*" treats Lawrence's epiphanies in light of the second and third meanings of the term as given by Walzl.[11]

Irene Hendry Chayes, in her seminal essay "Joyce's Epiphanies," correctly observes that "the epiphany is not peculiar to Joyce alone":

> Virtually every writer experiences a sense of revelation when he beholds a fragment of his ordinary world across . . . 'psychic distance'—dissociated from his subjective and practical concerns, fraught with meaning beyond itself, with every detail of its physical appearance relevant. It is a revelation quite as valid as the religious; in fact, from our present secular viewpoint, it perhaps would be more accurate to say that the revelation of the religious mystic is actually an esthetic revelation into which the mystic projects himself—as a participant, not merely as an observer and recorder—and to which he assigns a source, an agent and an end, called God. What Joyce did was give systematic formulation to a common esthetic experience, so common that few others—writers, if not estheticians— have thought it worth considering for its own sake.[12]

Where Lawrence is concerned, the question is not the presence in his work of revelatory experience of this kind but the breadth of the "psychic distance" across which such fragments of ordinary experience are seen in the transforming light.

There is no need to rehearse Chayes's whole discussion of Joyce's work. Indeed, two of her four types of epiphany are largely irrelevant to Lawrence's work: the first, achievement of *claritas* "through an apparently trivial incident, action, or single detail which differs from the others . . . only in that it illuminates them, integrates them, and gives them meaning"; and the third, the emergence of *claritas* from *quidditas* as "character is sacrificed to the *integritas* of the esthetic image" which resynthesizes the generalities of the individual. The other two types of epiphany, however, are in accord with Lawrence's practice.

In the second type, "although *claritas* is ultimately generated by *quidditas*, we are first aware of an effect on the beholder—Stephen, or ourselves through Stephen—not of an objectively apprehensible quality in the thing revealed." For Joyce this method may have been regressive in terms of his aesthetic goal of refining the artist's personality out of existence, but it had the advantage, Chayes says, "of realizing the three principles, *integritas*, *consonantia*, and *claritas*, in a single image" (209). For Lawrence, whose third-person narratives often center in the consciousness of a focal character, this method is predominant, especially in scenes that emphasize the importance of a visionary experience in the education into instinctual or sensual being of the focal character. Examples of this type of epiphany include Ursula Brangwen's encounter with the horses near the end of *The Rainbow*, her recognition of the meaning of Gerald Crich's brutal subjugation of the Arab mare and of Rupert Birkin's stoning of the moon's reflection in *Women in Love*, and Lou Witt's vision of the "mysterious fire" of St. Mawr's body in *St. Mawr*.

In the fourth type, *quidditas* has the function "to identify rather than to abstract." The character, "broken down into its separate parts," is then reduced to an image associated with him. "Only one or two of the detached 'parts'—'the vulgarity of speech or of gesture,' . . . a detail of figure or expression, an item of clothing"—are recombined to create the individual *quidditas*, a technique that "represents the ultimate in 'objective' characterization, 'revealing' an individual essence by means of a detail or an object to which it has a fortuitous relation"; for example, Father Dolan's pandybat or Mr. Casey's "three cramped fingers." "Through Joyce's fourth epiphany technique (in which *claritas* is a tiny, perfunctory flash, all but absorbed by *quidditas*) we can trace out a virtual iconography of the characters, like the systematic recurrence of emblems and attitudes among the figures in sacred art" (Chayes 216–18).

There are emblems aplenty in Lawrence—Will Brangwen's phoenix butter-mold, Count Dionys's ladybird, Ramón Carrasco's "eye of Quetzalcoatl," or even Anna Brangwen's gargoyle faces, Ursula's rainbow, and Aaron Sisson's flute. But these deliberate emblems, except perhaps for the last one, are not the same as the metonymic images with which Joyce's characters have a "fortuitous relation." A nearer example in Lawrence can be found in the clothes imagery by which characters throughout his work are defined—William Morel's collar, Gudrun Brangwen's stockings, Gerald Crich's elegant robe, Hermione Roddice's feathered hat.[13] But this epiphany technique is perhaps most evident in the close association Lawrence evokes between a character and an image that clearly objectifies his essential quality as a human being—Henry Grenfel and the fox, Jill Banford and the dead tree, or Sir Clifford Chatterley and the motorized wheelchair. Lawrence's identification of character with iconographic image, however, cannot often be called the "ultimate" in objectivity. It must be said also that his insight is never a "perfunctory flash" of meaning absorbed in the "whatness" of the object, but a clear metaphorical statement in which the image, rather than merely "standing for" the character, is so interpenetrated with his essential quality that it effectively becomes him: Sir Clifford's motorized chair *is* his very being.

Both Joyce and Lawrence employed epiphanic scenes to present ideas by means of revelation rather than by thematic statement. But because Lawrence's narrative technique involved more discursive statements about the characters and less aesthetic or psychic distance from them than is typical of Joyce, Lawrence has not often been described as an epiphanic writer. The first three chapters of *Lady Chatterley's Lover*, written from the point of view of an assumed narrator relating a general history, lack the artistic objectivity necessary to the Joycean epiphanic style. Rather, the technique corresponds to Stephen Dedalus's definition of the "epical form" (*Portrait* 214), mediating between artist and reader through the narrative point of view. But the scenes present what usually happens in the ongoing relationship, and the potential for epiphanic distillation inherent in the dramatic situation and a few concrete details is undercut by Lawrence's inveterate explanations. In contrast, the opening chapter of *A Portrait of the Artist,* although it also has an expository function, is fully visualized, concrete, specific, and not interpreted by a narrator.

In chapter 4 of *Lady Chatterley* the discussion of the "mental lifers" who visit Wragby parallels in several ways that of the Christmas dinner scene in chapter 1 of *A Portrait of the Artist.* Both involve a dramatic situation in which a group of people, family and visitors, engage in a lively discussion which is registered on the perceiving consciousness of one member of the family (Stephen and Connie) who takes little part in the discussion but whose perceptions of the discussants and the issues involved motivate a change in the observer. Whereas Joyce used Mr. Casey's "three cramped fingers" as an epiphanic identification of his character, Lawrence, in his brief character sketch of the Wragby visitors, associates the first two with institutional abstractions—Tommy Dukes with the army, Charles May with the science of the stars, only in the case of Arnold B. Hammond identifying and distilling the character by means of an epiphanic image: "a tall thin fellow with a wife and two children, but much more closely connected with a typewriter" (*LCL* 68). Joyce's judgment of Dante Riordan for the narrowness of her religious politics in supporting the Irish clergy even in their treatment of Parnell is clear if unstated. Similarly, when Tommy Dukes compares the sexual and property instincts in terms of the "craving for self-assertion and success," when Charles May speaks of sex as "just an interchange of sensations instead of ideas," or when Arnold Hammond, in Graham Holderness's phrase, "equates sexual emotions with excretory functions,"[14] Lawrence's judgment of them is clear.

The violent rhetoric of the Christmas dinner scene in *A Portrait of the Artist* brings to vivid life the "nets" of family, church, and nation that the soul of the youthful artist will later determine to "fly by." The ostensibly intellectual conversation of the "mental lifers" in *Lady Chatterley* embodies, in its emotional vacuity and its desperate wit, the triviality and deadness which the instinctual self, in order to live at all, will have to escape. Joyce maintains Stephen's point of view throughout; the epiphanic experience is registered on his consciousness from the beginning to the end of the scene when "Stephen, raising his terrorstricken face, saw that his father's eyes were full of tears" (*Portrait* 39). Lawrence begins in a general, historical perspective, moves to a concrete dramatization, and brings the potential for epiphany to the surface by returning increasingly to Connie's point of view. As in the second type of epiphany defined by Chayes, the reader of both scenes is conscious not so much of "meaning" as of an "effect" registered on an observer. Connie says nothing at first but "put another stitch in her sewing" (*LCL* 72), an ironic link with the faithful Penelope, since Connie's thoughts reveal her real attitude of contempt for both the "suitors" and the returned soldier husband. The men discuss Plato and Socrates, Bolshevism and Capitalism, and the meaninglessness of sex. They ignore Connie's presence, but Lawrence does not let the reader forget that the scene is being played out on her consciousness. When Dukes speaks of Renoir's saying that "he painted his pictures with his penis" and confesses, "I wish I did something with mine. God! when one can only talk," Connie responds to his despair: "There are nice women in the world," thus revealing how closely she has been attending the conversation (*LCL* 77). The potential for epiphany is not realized in the kind of objective revelation that Connie will experience later but is inherent in the dawning realization of sterility and death that precede rebirth and growth. Connie's disillusionment with this kind of mental life is comparable to the disillusionment with Irish patriotism motivated by Stephen Dedalus's experience of the Christmas dinner scene.

Chapter 5 of *Lady Chatterley* begins, appropriately, with an objective statement: "On a frosty morning with a little February sun, Clifford and Connie went for a walk across the park to the wood. That is, Clifford chuffed in his motor-chair, and Connie walked beside him" (*LCL* 78). The shift from the generalized historical perspective of the first three chapters to the dramatic scene of the fourth chapter and thence to the concrete narrative mode of the fifth establishes the necessary context not only for the contrast between Clifford and Mellors introduced in this chapter but also for several important epiphanic images.

One of these may be called the denuded knoll epiphany: "The chair chuffed slowly up the incline, rocking and jolting on the frozen clods. And suddenly, on the left, came a clearing where there was nothing but a ravel of dead bracken, a thin and spindly sapling leaning here and there, big sawn stumps, showing their tops and their grasping roots, lifeless. And patches of blackness where the woodmen had burned the brushwood and rubbish" (*LCL* 79). The narrative explanation as Connie surveys the wasteland scene directs without stating the interpretation: "This was one of the places that Sir Geoffrey had cut during the war for trench timber. The whole knoll, which rose softly on the right of the riding, was denuded and strangely forlorn. On the crown of the knoll where the oaks had stood, now was bareness; and from there you could look out over the trees to the colliery railway, and the new works at Stacks Gate. Connie had stood and looked, it was a breach in the pure seclusion of the wood. It let in the world. But she didn't tell Clifford" (*LCL* 80). Considered in the light of the Fisher King motif in the novel, the war has caused both the sexual maiming of Clifford (the Fisher King) and the destruction of the phallic trees of Wragby (his kingdom): both have been reduced to lifeless stumps. There is even an echo of T. S. Eliot's imagery: as in *The Waste Land,* where the question "What are the roots that clutch?" (line 19) is ultimately answered in "And other withered stumps of time" (line 104),[15] so in this passage from *Lady Chatterley's Lover,* the implied question of what caused the destruction of "big sawn stumps, showing their tops and their grasping roots, lifeless" is answered in the explanation: Sir Geoffrey had cut the trees "during the war for trench timber." The progression of imagery leads as inevitably as the colliery train to "the new works at Stacks Gate."

The denuded knoll is not only a symbolic image but an epiphanic one as well, a self-contained microcosm of the wasteland over which Sir Clifford Chatterley presides, though its meaning is revealed at different levels to the two observers. To Clifford, in anger, it conveys the destruction by the war of a legacy of the heart of "the old England," which had been entrusted to the stewardship of his generation to keep inviolate. To Connie, in pathos, it is "a breach in the pure seclusion of the wood," an assault on the private self and on organic nature. The fact that for both it is also linked with the destruction of Clifford's potency is signaled by their conversation, in this context, on Clifford's inability to sire a son and his suggestion that Connie might have a child by another man. But the mechanistic quality of Clifford's love of tradition and his wish for paternity is exposed by the difference between his attitude and Connie's toward the prospect. "I don't believe very intensely in fatherhood," he says in a Lawrencean blasphemy,[16] and refers to the hypothetical heir as an "it," not as a person. He does not think it matters much who the father is. Connie, already an organicist, wonders "how could she know what she would feel next year," and says that while she agrees with Clifford theoretically, "life may turn quite a new face on it all." It is at this point, as if in response to Connie's prophetic statement, that Oliver Mellors, the gamekeeper, emerges with his symbolic red mustache, dark green velveteens, and phallic gun (*LCL* 81–84).

Another major epiphanic image introduced in this chapter is Clifford's motorized wheelchair. Clifford, who has chuffed into the wood in the chair, calls to Mellors to "turn the chair round and get it started." Mellors, "curiously full of vitality, but a little frail and quenched," pushes "the chair up the steepish rise of the knoll in the park." Set in opposition to the wood, the chair symbolically embodies all of the forces that account for the denuding of the knoll (*LCL* 84–86).

The chair is the focal image in a recurrent pattern of imagery culminating in the long scene in chapter 13 in which the motor stalls and Mellors is again called to help. The mindless war of machine against nature is set forth in admirable, uninterpreted specificity as the chair puffs slowly on: "Connie, walking behind, had watched the wheels jolt over the wood-ruff and the bugle, and squash the little yellow cups of the creeping-jenny. Now they made a wake through the forget-me-nots." An epic simile presents the chair, "washed over with blue encroaching hyacinths," as the ship of Western civilization, and Clifford, with an ironic allusion to Whitman's Lincoln, as its mock-heroic captain: "Oh last of all ships, through the hyacinthian shallows! Oh pinnace on the last wild waters, sailing in the last voyage of our civilisation! Whither, Oh weird wheeled ship, your slow course steering! Quiet and complacent, Clifford sat at the wheel of adventure: in his old black hat and tweed jacket, motionless and cautious. Oh captain, my Captain, our splendid trip is done!" (*LCL* 240–41). The simile of the ship identifies the chair with Clifford's mines, for Mrs. Bolton has told him: "Oh, there's been some money made in Tevershall. And now the men say it's a sinking ship, and it's time they all got out. . . . It seems soon there'll be no use for men on the face of the earth, it'll be all machines" (*LCL* 151).

Throughout the novel, the chair is compared, sometimes directly, sometimes subtly, to Clifford's sexual being, which is held in contrast to that of the organicist Mellors, who confesses his incompetence "about these mechanical things." In chapter 13 (*LCL* 244–48), Lawrence employs a number of sexual double entendres. Clifford's attempts to force the wheelchair to go are compared to masturbation. Connie warns him, "You'll only break the thing down altogether, Clifford, . . . besides *wasting your nervous energy.*" Calling for Mellors to examine the motor, Clifford asks pointedly, "Have you looked at *the rods underneath?*" Grimly determined, "[Clifford] began *doing things* with his engine, running her fast and slow as if to get some sort of tune out of her. . . . Then he put her in gear with a jerk, having *jerked off* his brake." Finally, he turns to the gamekeeper: " 'Do you mind *pushing her home,* Mellors!' he said in a cool, superior tone." The irony of the question escapes Clifford, but Lawrence does not allow it to escape the reader.[17] As Mellors pushes the wheelchair home, he takes Connie's wrist in a caress behind Clifford's back, and she bends to kiss Mellors's hand (*LCL* 249). Clifford is identified and defined throughout the novel by the metonymic image of the wheelchair, which is as much a part of Clifford as Mellors's penis is of Mellors. Considered in terms of the fourth epiphanic method discussed by Chayes, this motorized chair is his whole mechanistic being, a mechanical contrivance that he possesses instead of a self.

In chapter 6, Connie, walking in the old wood, from which comes "an ancient melancholy, somehow soothing to her" (*LCL* 106), comes upon the gamekeeper's cottage. Because the scene presents the major epiphany of the novel, I should like to quote it in full and to examine its development in Lawrence's conception:

> She turned the corner of the house and stopped. In the little yard two paces beyond her, the man was washing himself, utterly unaware. He was naked to the hips, his velveteen breeches slipping down over his slender loins. And his white slim back was curved over a big bowl of soapy water, in which he ducked his head, shaking his head with a queer, quick little motion, lifting his slender white arms, and pressing the soapy water from his ears, quick, subtle as a

weasel playing with water, and utterly alone. Connie backed away round the corner of the house, and hurried away to the wood. In spite of herself, she had had a shock. After all, merely a man washing himself; commonplace enough, Heaven knows!

Yet in some curious way it was a visionary experience: it had hit her in the middle of the body. She saw the clumsy breeches slipping down over the pure, delicate, white loins, the bones showing a little, and the sense of aloneness, of a creature purely alone, overwhelmed her. Perfect, white, solitary nudity of a creature that lives alone, and inwardly alone. And beyond that, a certain beauty of a pure creature. Not the stuff of beauty, not even the body of beauty, but a lambency, the warm, white flame of a single life, revealing itself in contours that one might touch: a body! [*LCL* 106–7]

Lawrence's revisions of the scene in the three versions of the novel show clearly the evolution of his thinking. In *The First Lady Chatterley*, the epiphanic vision, although not so well-structured aesthetically, is interpreted directly as a showing forth of the god, a revelation of the "divine body." Having discovered Parkin with his shirt off washing himself, ducking his head in the water like an animal, Connie retires to the wood: "But in the dripping gloom of the forest, suddenly she started to tremble uncontrollably. The white torso of the man had seemed so beautiful to her, splitting the gloom. The white, firm, divine body with that silky firm skin! Never mind the man's face, with the fierce moustache and the resentful hard eyes! Never mind his stupid personality! His body in itself was divine, cleaving through the gloom like a revelation" (*FLC* 11).

In *John Thomas and Lady Jane*, the increased emphasis on beauty moves the second version of the scene closer to the Joycean conception of such an epiphany, but the intensification of emphasis on the divinity of the body shows that Lawrence's conception remains thoroughly religious rather than secular or aesthetic:

The white torso of the man had seemed so beautiful to her, opening on the gloom. The white, firm, divine body, with its silky ripple, the white arch of life, as it bent forward over the water, seemed, she could not help it, of the world of the gods. There still was a world that gleamed pure and with power, where the silky firm skin of the man's body glistened broad upon the dull afternoon. Never mind who he was! never mind what he was! She had seen

> beauty, and beauty alive. That body was of the world of the gods, cleaving through the gloom like a revelation. And she felt again there was God on earth; or gods. [*JTLJ* 43–44]

The emphasis on power, divinity, and, in particular, the "gleaming whiteness" of the body suggests a biblical source that is appropriate to Lawrence's purpose. In the liturgical calendar, in addition to the feast of the Epiphany, which commemorates the visitation of the three wise men to the Christ child, there is another epiphanic feast day, the Transfiguration, which commemorates the event and the vision which took place when Jesus took the disciples Peter, James, and John up to a high mountain and was there, with Elijah and Moses, "transfigured before them": "And his raiment became shining, exceeding white as snow; so as no fuller on earth can white them" (Mark 9:3). Because "the broad, gleaming whiteness" of the man's body "had touched her soul," Connie cherishes the vision not merely as an aesthetic but as a transfigurative experience: "A great soothing came over her heart, along with the feeling of worship. The sudden sense of pure beauty, beauty that was active and alive, had put worship in her heart again. Not that she worshipped the man, nor his body. But worship had come into her, because she had seen a pure loveliness, that was alive, and that had touched the quick in her. It was as if she had touched God, and been restored to life. The broad, gleaming whiteness! It was the vision she cherished, because it had touched her soul" (*JTLJ* 44). The effect of the experience on Connie is profound: "When she was home again, she seemed haunted by another self inside herself. It was a self which had seen powerful beauty, seen it alive, and in motion, seen it as the greatest vision of her life" (*JTLJ* 46). The language, "herself" and "another self," recalls that of Lawrence's letter to Edward Garnett about *The Rainbow:* "You mustn't look in my novel for the old stable *ego*—of the character. There is another *ego*, according to whose action the individual is unrecognisable, and passes through, as it were, allotropic states . . ." (*CL* 282). The first self sees only the man's face and the external trappings of his working-class position. It is "another self," the "soul" touched by the epiphanic image, which responds to the divinity in the man's body, not to worship the body, Lawrence makes clear, but to worship the divinity that shines through this matter as a revelation.

In the third version of the novel, *Lady Chatterley's Lover*, Lawrence omits the direct references to God, the world of the gods, and revelation of the divine and concentrates instead on the human quality of Connie's visionary experience. The contrast between "herself" and "another self" is made more concrete in the distinction between mind and womb: "Connie had received the shock of vision in her womb, and she knew it. . . . But with her mind she was inclined to ridicule" (*LCL* 107). The shift from "the vision . . . had touched her soul" (*JTLJ* 44) to "the shock of vision in her womb" (*LCL* 107) is a greater change than it may at first appear. In the former, the visionary experience is still spiritual, opening to Connie "the world of the gods," putting "worship in her heart again" (*JTLJ* 44). In the latter, the experience is fully human without being "social." It is concerned not with "personality" but with "the warm, white flame of a single life, revealing itself in contours that one might touch: a body!" (*LCL* 107). Lawrence was possibly already considering the idea of a risen man, a Christ figure returning to the fulfillment of instinctual being through sexuality instead of to fulfillment of spiritual mission through sacrifice. Thus, in the second version, the effect of Connie's vision of Parkin's body is "as if she had touched God, and been restored to life" (*JTLJ* 44), an allusion to the healing by faith of the woman with the "issue of blood" who had touched Christ's garment (Mark 5:25–34). But perhaps concerned that readers might be misled by such comparisons to Christian divinity, Lawrence discarded most of these allusions in the third version and reserved the fuller treatment of the risen man theme for *The Escaped Cock.*[18] The significant biblical allusions that remain in *Lady Chatterley's Lover* use biblical language, often in parody, to present the theme of rebirth through phallic experience: "Go ye into the streets and byways of Jerusalem, and see if ye can find *a man*" (*LCL* 105); "Ye must be born again! I believe in the resurrection of the body! Except a grain of wheat fall into the earth and die, it shall by no means bring forth" (*LCL* 128); "Lift up your heads o' ye gates, that the king of glory may come in" (*LCL* 270).[19] These allusions support a consistent movement in the third version from the divine to the human, from the spiritual to the carnal.

In the third version, the bathing scene, an example of the second type of epiphany discussed by Chayes, combines aesthetic and religious visions. It may be instructive to compare it to a scene in Joyce's *A Portrait of the Artist* which parallels it in both subject matter and structure—the "bathing girl" epiphany at the end of chapter 4, which I shall also quote in full:

> A girl stood before him in midstream, alone and still, gazing out to sea. She seemed like one whom magic had changed into the likeness of a strange and beautiful seabird. Her long slender bare legs were delicate as a crane's and pure save where an emerald trail of seaweed had fashioned itself as a sign upon the flesh. Her thighs, fuller and softhued as ivory, were bared almost to the hips where the white fringes of her drawers were like featherings of soft white down. Her slateblue skirts were kilted boldly about her waist and dovetailed behind her. Her bosom was as a bird's soft and slight, slight and soft as the breast of some darkplumaged dove. But her long fair hair was girlish: and girlish, and touched with the wonder of mortal beauty, her face.
>
> She was alone and still, gazing out to sea; and when she felt his presence and the worship of his eyes her eyes turned to him in quiet sufferance of his gaze, without shame or wantonness. Long, long she suffered his gaze and then quietly withdrew her eyes from him and bent them towards the stream, gently stirring the water with her foot hither and thither. The first faint noise of gently moving water broke the silence, low and faint and whispering, faint as the bells of sleep; hither and thither, hither and thither: a faint flame trembled on her cheek.
>
> —Heavenly God! cried Stephen's soul, in an outburst of profane joy. [*Portrait* 171]

If Vivian de Sola Pinto and F. Warren Roberts are correct in their suggestion that Joyce's "bathing girl" epiphany was a source for Lawrence's poem "The Man of Tyre,"[20] then possibly the same scene also influenced Connie's "visionary experience" of Mellors bathing. Although I have found no evidence that Lawrence had read *A Portrait of the Artist as a Young Man*, there are significant parallels between the two scenes. In both Joyce and Lawrence, the point-of-view character, beset with personal difficulties (Stephen confronting a choice of vocation, Connie experiencing spiritual and physical atrophy) and walking outdoors in a state of mind that represents a crisis of conscience and personal psychology, comes upon a person of the opposite sex who is alone and self-absorbed in a ritual of bathing and whose image passes into the consciousness of the observer in a revelatory experience. In both scenes, the figure is isolated in a setting that symbolically parallels the character's sense of nullity and desolation, Stephen amid "a waste of . . . brackish waters and . . . veiled sunlight" (*Portrait* 171), Connie in a "dying," "grey," "inert," "hopeless" world, itself in need of renewal. Both figures are compared to animals in grace, the bathing girl to a dove, Mellors to a weasel, and their motion in the water is emphasized. The girl's thighs are "bared almost to the hips," where her skirts are kilted about her drawers and "dovetailed" behind her. Mellors is "naked to the hips," where his breeches have slipped down "over the pure, delicate, white loins, the bones showing a little." In both scenes, the sexual content of the figure's half-nudity is sublimated into quasi-religious epiphany, with the observer's attitude of worship a common element of the scenes in both *A Portrait of the Artist* and *John Thomas and Lady Jane.* In both images, the color white is prominent, although in Joyce's it is not predominant. In both scenes, the observer sees the figure of the bather as a "flame"-body: Stephen observes that "a faint flame trembled on her cheek," and Connie discovers "the warm white flame of a single life" in the "contours" of the man's body. There is, however, one apparent difference between the two scenes: in Joyce's epiphany, "her image had passed into his soul," whereas in Lawrence's final conception of the scene, Mellors's image "had hit her in the middle of the body"—"Connie had received the shock of vision in her womb, and she knew it . . ." (*LCL* 107). As a result of their experiences, both Stephen and Connie take a new direction, toward life, and the difference between "soul" and "womb" as the organ of reception for the epiphany may be attributable to the distinction in aim between Stephen's move toward his true vocation as an artist and Connie's move toward liberation of her instinctual and psychological being. As Richard Ellmann points out, however, Stephen "receives a *call*, hears 'a voice from beyond the world,' but what it summons him to is not the priesthood but life, including sexual love, and an art that would content body and soul alike."[21] Connie is also summoned toward an awakening, in the sexual relationship with Mellors, of a new life of body and soul together.

The difference in means by which the image impresses itself upon the consciousness of the observer is an aesthetic difference that has its source in the opposing aesthetic theories from which the two scenes emerge. Aesthetically, Joyce's epiphany follows the pattern of Stephen Dedalus's artistic theory drawn from Saint Thomas Aquinas. It moves from the *integritas* of the isolated figure of the girl standing before Stephen in midstream, through the *consonantia,* the analysis of the rhythm and harmony of the component parts of the figure (legs, thighs, drawers, skirt, bosom, hair, face), and thence, in the reintegration of the image, to the *quidditas* or "whatness" of the unique object, from which the *claritas* of vision is registered on the observer's consciousness in the perception of the radiance of the bather's image. Lawrence's epiphany, on the other hand, follows aesthetically from his conception, as stated in "Art and the Individual," of the blending of "the mystical and the sensual ideas of Art." Sensually, the "approval of Harmony" is presented in the observation of Mellors's figure, which, no less than the observation of the bathing girl's figure, moves from the integrity of the image in aloneness as Mellors washes himself "unaware," through analysis of the "harmony" of the parts that make up the image (loins, breeches, back, head, arms), and finally to the reintegration of the image in the "solitary nudity," from which the "visionary experience" is registered on the observer's consciousness. The culmination of the epiphanic experience in Lawrence is not, as in Stephen Dedalus's theory, an ideal stasis, although Stephen's ecstatic cry and his movement "On and on and on and on!" suggest that the immediate effect of his epiphany, in practice, is not entirely static either. Whereas Stephen rejects the "literary" idea of radiance as the artistic representation of "divine purpose" (*Portrait* 213), Lawrence accepts a blending of the "mystical" conception of beauty, "the shining of the idea through matter," and the "sensual" conception of beauty, the expression of "pleasurable emotion." In his later poetic theory, these ideas emerge in the distinction between the poetry of the beginning and the end and that of "the immediate present," a poetic distillation of experience characterized by vital energy and relationship rather than by "perfection" or "consummation," as equal components of art. The order which Lawrence's images express is not the finality of stasis but the vitality of equilibrium, and the "morality" which they embody is "that delicate, for ever trembling and changing *balance* between me and my circumambient universe, which precedes and accompanies a true relatedness" (*Phoenix* 528).

The epiphanic vision of Mellors bathing propels Connie back to Wragby, where, at the beginning of chapter 7, she goes up to her bedroom for a critical examination of her own body, "naked in the huge mirror": "what a frail, easily hurt, rather pathetic thing a human body is, naked; somehow a little unfinished, incomplete!" What the lamp illuminates is a formerly "good figure," now "out of fashion," deprived of sun and warmth and "disappointed of its real womanhood." "Instead of ripening its firm, down-running curves, her body was flattening and going a little harsh." Connie takes note of her rather small, unripe breasts; her slack, thin belly; her "flat, slack, meaningless" thighs: "She was old, old at twenty-seven, with no gleam and sparkle in the flesh" (*LCL* 110–11). A consequence of what the mirror reflects in her deliberate examination of her own body, Connie's dawning "sense of injustice, of being defrauded," is motivated by the epiphany of Mellors bathing, and it leads, in turn, to her continuing visits to the wood. These visits increase her organicism, her identification of herself with nature, and establish the condition for the development of her psychological and sexual potential in the relationship with Mellors.

Nature imagery in chapter 8 reveals the change that is taking place in Connie, the newly awakened vision that frees her to see for the first time the manifestation in nature of the principles of sexuality, fecundity, and life. The following passage, presented from Connie's point of view, provides an example of how this epiphanic vision transforms her way of seeing:

> Constance sat down with her back to a young pine-tree, that swayed against her with curious life, elastic and powerful, rising up. The erect, alive thing, with its top in the sun! And she watched the daffodils turn golden, in a burst of sun that was warm on her hands and lap. Even she caught the faint, tarry scent of the flowers. And then, being so still and alone, she seemed to get into the current of her own proper destiny. She had been fastened by a rope, and jagging and snarring like a boat at its moorings; now she was loose and a-drift. [*LCL* 129]

No great powers of perception are required to recognize the phallic symbolism which associates the pine tree as fully with Mellors as with Connie, for as Lawrence emphasizes, the tree is "rising up" in elasticity and power, "erect" and "alive." More important is what the phallic symbolism itself signifies. Placed in the context of other nature symbolism (the sun, the daffodils), the pine tree becomes emblematic of far more than Mellors's sexual potency; it suggests the mythic powers that Lawrence evokes in "Pan in America" in the figure of the pine tree at Kiowa Ranch,[22] gathering up "earth-power from the dark bowels of the earth, and a roaming sky-glitter from above. And all unto itself, which is a tree, woody, enormous, slow but unyielding with life, bristling with acquisitive energy, obscurely radiating some of its great strength." "It vibrates its presence into my soul, and I am with Pan" (*Phoenix* 25). While this kind of symbolism is far from Joyce's carefully ordered and objectified concrete imagery, the organicism of the new life of the body to which Connie is just awakening comes to her, as Stephen Dedalus's earliest education in poetic imagery does, through the immediacy of sensory experience. Since Connie assumes Lawrence's own characteristic posture in writing the manuscript "at the Villa Mirenda, . . . sitting on the grass under a tree,"[23] the image conveys something of both the origin and the organicist philosophy of the novel. Connie could say, with Lawrence, "I have become conscious of the tree, and of its interpenetration into my life" (*Phoenix* 25).

The change in Connie is also signaled by her conversation with Clifford on her return home:

> ". . . Look, aren't the little daffodils adorable? To think they should come out of the earth!"
>
> "Just as much out of the air and sunshine," he said.
>
> "But modelled in the earth," she retorted, with a prompt contradiction, that surprised her a little. [*LCL* 129]

Whereas Clifford's emphasis on air and sunshine suggests the transcendent male forces of spirit and intellect, Connie's emphasis on the earth affirms the female generative function of incarnation. In contradicting Clifford, Connie is not only elevating her own femaleness and herself as a person but also signaling that she has come into relationship with transpersonal forces that allow her to affirm incarnation and mutability captured in the life cycle as equipotential to transcendental forces outside time and change. Her development to this point has prepared her for the recognition that to live in time as an individual woman with someone else who lives in time as an individual man is the ontological affirmation of being in the world. This change in Connie's character prepares for the epiphany of the chick and its consequences.

In chapter 10, a justly admired scene takes place at the chicken coop, where Mellors draws a peeping chick from under the mother hen and places it in Connie's hand:

> "There!" he said, holding out his hand to her. She took the little drab thing between her hands, and there it stood, on its impossible little stalks of legs, its atom of balancing life trembling through its almost weightless feet into Connie's hands. But it lifted its handsome, clean-shaped little head boldly, and looked sharply round, and gave a little "peep." "So adorable! So cheeky!" she said softly.
>
> The keeper, squatting beside her, was also watching with an amused face the bold little bird in her hands. Suddenly he saw a tear fall on to her wrist. [*LCL* 162]

Mellors, "suddenly . . . aware of the old flame shooting and leaping up in his loins, that he had hoped was quiescent for ever," stands away, but "there was something so mute and forlorn in her, compassion flamed in his bowels for her": "At the back of his loins the fire suddenly darted stronger. . . . Her face was averted, and she was crying blindly, in all the anguish of her generation's forlornness." Crouching beside her, Mellors returns the chick to the hen. "He laid his hand on her shoulder, and softly, gently, it began to travel down the curve of her back, blindly, with a blind stroking motion, to the curve of her crouching loins." The first of their sexual encounters begins with his quiet suggestion: "Shall you come to the hut?" (*LCL* 162–63).

Joyce's presentation of Thomas Aquinas's theory of beauty in the fifth chapter of *A Portrait of the Artist*, although not the basis for Lawrence's epiphanies, is a statement of principles so universal that the theory is applicable not only to certain Joycean epiphanies, such as the "bathing girl" scene, but also, with allowances for stylistic and thematic differences, to many scenes by other writers presenting the recognition of what in the largest sense must be called beauty. So it is that the epiphany of the chick, like the epiphany of Mellors bathing, corresponds structurally to the Thomist theory elaborated by Stephen Dedalus, moving from the initial *integritas* of the image (the chick in Mellors's hand), to the *consonantia* of the parts of the image ("its impossible little stalks of legs," "its almost weightless feet," "its handsome, clean-shaped little head"), to the *quidditas* of its unique individuality (its "peep" of "cheeky" defiance). It is from this reintegrated image that *claritas* emerges.

Connie's tears and Mellors's flame reveal that the experience has been epiphanic for both of them. The images at once recall the beginning and foreshadow the end of the novel. Connie's tears, in part for her own barren condition, both as a potential mother and as a potential creative human being, and in part for the vision of impossible vulnerability and indomitable bravery which the chick shows forth, are a catharsis that few experience in this forlorn generation of which the narrator says in the opening sentence of the novel: "Ours is essentially a tragic age, so we refuse to take it tragically" (*LCL* 37). Mellors's flame, which leaps in his body as his heart melts "like a drop of fire," will become "the forked flame" between him and Connie that constitutes the Pentecostal creed of his belief (*LCL* 373). Because of his reverence for life, even this tiny life, and his compassion for her, Connie recognizes Mellors as the man with whom mutual affirmation of earthly being is possible. Because her reaction reveals an equal reverence for life in a sense of tragedy that includes a recognition of the necessity of a fall into time and incarnation, Mellors recognizes Connie as the woman, unlike Bertha Coutts, with whom this mutual affirmation of earthly being is possible. For both, the epiphany is a vision of life, vulnerable and without defenses, except for its defiant selfhood.

As the scene continues in the hut, immediately after the epiphany of the chick, the medium through which Connie's growth in sensual consciousness is realized changes from sudden visionary experience to touch and direct sexual experience. After chapter 12, especially, the focus of the story shifts from Lady Chatterley to her lover and the working out of the realistic and symbolic details of their life together. There are still occasional changes through visual perception—Connie's sight of Mellors's "erect phallos rising darkish and hot-looking from the little cloud of vivid gold-red hair" (*LCL* 270); Connie's journey with her sister Hilda to Venice as a tour in hell (chapter 17)—but little that could be called epiphanic. A scene such as the one in chapter 15 in which Connie and Mellors dance naked in the rain, then decorate their pubic hair with forget-me-nots, Mellors's penis with creeping jenny, and their bodies with campion and bluebells, although certainly conducive to growth, involves acting out rather than sudden epiphany. In the first half of the novel, however, epiphany or visionary experience is the principal way through which Connie's development in consciousness is achieved.

NOTES

1. Dorothy Brett, *Lawrence and Brett: A Friendship* (Philadelphia: J. B. Lippincott, 1933), p. 81.

2. Lawrence read the section of Joyce's *Work in Progress* that became, with revisions, *Finnegans Wake*, III, ii, in *transition*, no. 13 (Summer 1928): 5–32. Lawrence's comment on Joyce was made in a 15 August 1928 letter to Aldous and Maria Huxley. He repeated the judgment in a letter to Earl Brewster on the same date (*CL* 1076).

3. The two letters, both to Harriet Shaw Weaver, dated respectively 27 September 1930 and 17 December 1931, are in *Letters of James Joyce*, vol. 1, ed. Stuart Gilbert (New York: Viking, 1957; rev. 1966), pp. 294 and 309. For a defense of the first two pages of *Lady Chatterley's Lover*, see the unsigned review "A Man in His Senses," *Times Literary Supplement* (London), 4 November 1960, p. 708. The author calls these pages "exemplary" and the novel "an extremely deliberated work."

4. James Joyce, *A Portrait of the Artist as a Young Man* (New York: Penguin, 1982), p. 205; hereafter cited in the text as *Portrait*.

5. Richard Ellmann, "On Joyce's Centennial," *New Republic* 186 (17 February 1982): 29.

6. D. H. Lawrence, "Poetry of the Present," in *The Complete Poems of D. H. Lawrence*, ed. Vivian de Sola Pinto and F. Warren Roberts (New York: Viking, 1971), pp. 181–83.

7. Robert Scholes and Richard M. Kain, *The Workshop of Daedalus: James Joyce and the Raw Material for "A Portrait of the Artist as a Young Man"* (Evanston, Ill.: Northwestern University Press, 1965). James Joyce, *Epiphanies*, with introduction and notes by O. A. Silverman (Buffalo, N.Y.: University of Buffalo, Lockwood Memorial Library, 1956) earlier published twenty-two epiphanies from the manuscripts in the

Lockwood Memorial Library. Scholes and Kain reprint these and add eighteen others from the Mennen Collection at Cornell University.

8. James Joyce, *Stephen Hero* (London and New York: Jonathan Cape and New Directions, 1944), p. 188.

9. Morris Beja, *Epiphany in the Modern Novel* (Seattle: University of Washington Press, 1971), p. 18.

10. Florence L. Walzl, in Robert Scholes and Florence L. Walzl, "The Epiphanies of Joyce," *PMLA* 82 (March 1967): 153.

11. Ann Shealy, "The Epiphany Theme in Modern Fiction: E. M. Forster's *Howards End* and D. H. Lawrence's *Sons and Lovers*," *The Passionate Mind: Four Studies Including "Julia Peterkin: A Souvenir"* (Philadelphia: Dorrance, 1976), pp. 3–27.

12. Irene Hendry Chayes, "Joyce's Epiphanies," in *Joyce's "Portrait": Criticisms and Critiques*, ed. Thomas E. Connolly (New York: Appleton-Century-Crofts, 1962), p. 206; hereafter cited in the text as "Chayes."

13. See Evelyn J. Hinz, "D. H. Lawrence's Clothes Metaphor," *D. H. Lawrence Review* 1, no. 2 (Summer 1968): 87–113.

14. Graham Holderness, *Who's Who in D. H. Lawrence* (New York: Taplinger, 1976), p. 49.

15. T. S. Eliot, *The Complete Poems and Plays* (New York: Harcourt, Brace, 1952), pp. 38, 40.

16. This statement may be compared with one reported by Jessie Chambers: " 'Fatherhood's a myth,' Lawrence declared. 'There's nothing in it. . . . There's no such thing as fatherhood.' " (E.T. [pseud. of Jessie Chambers], *D. H. Lawrence: A Personal Record* [New York: Knight Publications, 1936], p. 208.) In context, Lawrence, in a rather cynical mood after his breakup with Jessie, is commenting sardonically on a friend's attitude toward his new baby. In the background, too, is Lawrence's attitude toward his own father: "He hates his father," his mother told Jessie (p. 138). The fact that he places this sentiment in the mouth of Clifford Chatterley instead of Mellors, who embodies many of the positive qualities that Lawrence later found in his rejected father, is in keeping with the change in attitude. Through Clifford, Lawrence is also rejecting a side of himself that he finds shallow. As Frieda Lawrence commented in 1955, "The terrible thing about Lady C. is that L. identified himself with both Clifford and Mellors; that took courage, that made me shiver, when I read it as he wrote it." (*Frieda Lawrence: The Memoirs and Correspondence*, ed. E. W. Tedlock, Jr. [New York: Alfred A. Knopf, 1964], p. 389.)

17. The emphasis throughout this paragraph has been added to call attention to the thematic use of sexual puns employing slang usage current in Lawrence's day. See, for example, the definition "*To jerk one's juice or jelly (also to jerk off)* = to masturbate," in John S. Farmer and W. E. Henley, *Slang and Its Analogues: Past and Present*, vol. 4 ([London]: Printed for Subscribers Only, 1896), p. 47; reprinted in abridged form as *A Dictionary of Slang and Colloquial English* (London: George Routledge and Sons; New York: E. P. Dutton, 1912), p. 243. See also Taylor Stoehr, " 'Mentalized Sex' in D. H. Lawrence," *Novel* 8, no. 2 (Winter 1975): 101–22, which discusses

Lawrence's attitude toward masturbation in the context of the sexual mores and literature of his time.

18. This interpretation was suggested to me by Dennis Jackson. See also his "The Progression Toward Myth and Ritual in the Three Versions of D. H. Lawrence's *Lady Chatterley's Lover*" (Ph.D. diss., University of Arkansas, 1978), pp. 10–13, 153–54.

19. See C. J. Terry, "Aspects of D. H. Lawrence's Struggle with Christianity," *Dalhousie Review* 54, no. 1 (Spring 1974): 112–29; and Daniel J. Sheerin, "John Thomas and the King of Glory: Two Analogues to D. H. Lawrence's Use of Psalm 24:7 in Chapter XIV of *Lady Chatterley's Lover*," *D. H. Lawrence Review* 11, no. 3 (Fall 1978): 297–300.

20. In the notes to *The Complete Poems of D. H. Lawrence*, p. 1018, editors Vivian de Sola Pinto and F. Warren Roberts suggest that the middle stanza of "Man of Tyre" bears some striking resemblances to Joyce's "bathing girl" epiphany. T. A. Smailes, "Lawrence's Verse: More Editorial Lapses," *Notes and Queries*, n.s. 17 (December 1970): 465–66, refutes this idea and contends that Lawrence based the third stanza of the poem on his own experience rather than the scene in Joyce's novel.

21. Ellmann, "On Joyce's Centennial," p. 29.

22. For a photograph of this tree, see the *D. H. Lawrence Review* 5, no. 3 (Fall 1972): 133. The same tree became the subject of Georgia O'Keeffe's painting *The Lawrence Tree*, which is reproduced in *Georgia O'Keeffe* (New York: Viking Press, 1976), plate 57.

23. Giuseppe Orioli, *Adventures of a Bookseller* (New York: McBride, 1938), p. 233. The Villa Mirenda tree was an olive tree. For a photograph of Lawrence sitting under it with his back against the trunk, see Harry T. Moore and Warren Roberts, *D. H. Lawrence and His World* (New York: Viking Press, 1966), p. 105.

Lady Chatterley's Lover and Ulysses

D. H. Lawrence and James Joyce, the two giants of modern British fiction, did not, as has been often cited, think much of each other's writing. Lawrence, referring to Joyce's work, wrote to Aldous Huxley, "My God, what a clumsy *olla putrida* James Joyce is! Nothing but old fags and cabbage-stumps of quotations from the Bible and the rest, stewed in the juice of deliberate, journalistic dirty-mindedness . . . " (*CL* 1075). Of *Ulysses* Lawrence said, "The last part of it is the dirtiest, most indecent, obscene thing ever written. Yes it is, Frieda. . . . It is filthy."[1] While Joyce's plethora of detail annoyed Lawrence, Lawrence's language and didacticism annoyed Joyce. Referring to *Lady Chatterley,* Joyce wrote to Harriet Shaw Weaver, "I read the first 2 pages of the usual sloppy English which is a piece of propaganda in favour of something which, outside of D.H.L.'s country at any rate, makes all the propaganda for itself."[2] The two writers' styles were polemically opposed, their ideologies dissimilar, and so each refused to recognize the genius of the other, partly because of their divergent backgrounds and their rationalizations for their perceived shortcomings, and partly because of the nature of their aesthetic. But Joyce did buy *The Rainbow,* when he had little money, and Lawrence did admit to reading bits of *Ulysses.*

On the surface their work seems as divergent as any could be by two novelists who were such close contemporaries. Yet, in many ways *Ulysses* and *Lady Chatterley's Lover* are not so different. Each represents the mature work of its author and culminates his career. Joyce's great novel was to be followed by his magnificent experiment, *Finnegans Wake.* But *Ulysses* is a statement of middle age, and experimental as it is, it was his last work still recognizable as a novel. It is often said by Lawrence's critics that his last novel is a summation of themes developed through his entire canon. Both of the books had long and difficult trials in the courts and elsewhere before their publication, and both became the centerpiece for momentous legal decisions. Indeed the 1933 decision on *Ulysses* figures prominently as a precedent in the 1959 *Lady Chatterley* case. Both books were accused of being pornographic; both were widely popular before publication in England or the United States; and both were published in pirated editions. Lawrence's sympathy with Joyce, expressed by his joining other writers in signing a petition against Samuel Roth's unauthorized publication of *Ulysses*, was prophetic, because Roth was later to pirate *Lady Chatterley's Lover* in America.

Moreover, Lawrence and Joyce were each exiles from countries with which they had love-hate relations. Both felt themselves outsiders, yet curiously they were spokesmen for their heritage. Lawrence, born to a lower social class than Joyce, saw life in part as a contrast between the beauties of nature and the horrors of mechanization and the coal pits. Emancipated from a life of economic determinism, he married a woman of higher social standing. Joyce, of a moderately well-off middle-class parentage, saw his family's fortunes reduced to poverty. In Joyce's curiously egalitarian Irish-Catholic society, where everyone was poor, class distinctions did not loom as large as they did in England, divided by both aristocratic lineage and money into a more rigid structure. Joyce, if anything, married beneath his class, a B.A. taking up with a barmaid. Marriage evidently meant more to Lawrence than it did to Joyce, who refused—even after two children had resulted from his relationship with Nora—to succumb to the formal marital state until, worried that after his death inheritance rights might be denied his family, he officially married at age forty-nine. While Lawrence dwelt outside England and in later works portrayed foreign scenes and countries, Joyce, for all his exile, never left Ireland and more specifically Dublin in his fiction. Pastoral or rural scenes appear only in Joyce's poetry, whereas Lawrence often set his fictional scenes in nature, scarred by man and machine.

Yet both men did live in the same age and it would stand to reason that, for all their differences, some areas of commonality can be addressed. Certainly the alienation theme is a basis for the action both of *Lady Chatterley* and *Ulysses*, as I suppose it is for every twentieth-century work from *The Wizard of Oz* to *The Texas Chain-saw Massacre*. But in a number of ways the two novels in question bear a much closer resemblance than might be suspected on first reading, and some insights into each novel may be gained by comparing their treatment of sex, language, geography, social structure, characterization, and art.

The most apparent similarity and obviously the most prominent historically is their candid treatment of sex, which permeates all the areas to be considered in this paper. It is the topic invariably discussed by critics comparing Joyce and Lawrence and certainly a major preoccupation of Lawrence. I had not thought the same was true of Joyce until I began thinking about this essay. Molly Bloom's language and her general preoccupation with matters sexual, coupled with Bloom's memory of their lovemaking on Howth and his masturbation on Sandymount Strand seem to have caught the imaginations of the censors and prurient readers of *Ulysses* to the exclusion of almost everything else, but the preoccupation throughout Bloomsday with matters at least partially sexual had not seemed so far removed to me from everyday behavior that it called attention to itself. However, Strother Purdy sees *Ulysses* as a sexual epic, its heroism portrayed entirely in sexual terms of infidelities, comic masturbation, a heroine in bed throughout, a masochistic orgy in which the hero changes sex, etcetera. Its message, Purdy asserts, is "How inescapably sexual is life!"[3] Of course Bella Cohen's brothel and Molly Bloom's bed are by no means the entire essence of *Ulysses*. There are thoughts, conversations, and themes that deviate from the purely sexual. But fewer than I had thought: Stephen's day begins with Mulligan's blasphemous ribaldry; with Stephen's oedipal preoccupations, linked to Hamlet's own; with the rivalry for the favor of the old milkwoman, and by extension, Ireland; with Deasy's cattle and their fertility symbolism. Bloom's day begins with the sensuous Calypso, Molly, and his trip to the pork butcher's to walk home behind the moving hams of a female shopper. His odyssey includes trips to the cemetery, where he conjures up visions of the caretaker copulating; to All Hallows, where he hopes to stand "next to some girl" and leaves worrying about his trousers being unbuttoned; to the library, where Anne Hathaway seduces Shakespeare in a Dedalus analogue; to the Ormond bar, where siren songs are sung while the phallic white baton beer-pull is being fondled; to a maternity hospital, where all aspects of procreation are examined; to a brothel; and finally to Ithaca, where the quoits of the bedstead, which have occupied Bloom's thoughts during the day, jingle. Only, it seems, in Barney Kiernan's, with the citizen and assorted asexual barflies, is sex to be escaped, though not entirely even in this male bastion. Bloom, for all his Christian charity, is never far from awareness of his adulterous wife and the assignation about which his mind revolves during the entire day. Molly is at the center of his universe, a Gea-Tellus figure, the personification of the sexual experience. What makes *Ulysses* seem so normal is that it accurately depicts everyday life, which in itself is inextricably bound to sex.

G. Wilson Knight sees both Joyce and Lawrence as rump-oriented. For them the ultimate answers lie in the posterior. The affirmation of Knight's thesis is Bloom's kissing Molly's behind before he goes to sleep and the preoccupation of Mellors with the beauty of Connie's "arse." Both Joyce and Lawrence, Knight claims, "labour to interpret and redeem man in natural and human terms." But, "Lawrence tries hard to keep his mysticism close-locked to physical creation."[4] Therein lies one of the profound differences between the two. For Joyce, sex is an integrated part of life, which his characters accept as part of their beings, below as well as above the conscious level. Lawrence's characters constantly raise sex to the conscious level through rational discussion or the experience of spiritual sexual ecstasy. During the scene with the girl on the beach, at the end of chapter 4 of *A Portrait of the Artist as a Young Man*, Joyce attempts a Lawrencean combination of spiritual ecstasy and the eroticism of orgasm, but the conjunction is in Stephen's mind. The scene is parodied in "Nausicaa" by the all-too-fallible Gerty MacDowell and the literal-minded, masturbating Bloom. No topic is so sacred as to escape parody in Joyce's comic vision, in which importance and solemnity have nothing in common. This view is fundamentally different from the exultations of Lawrence's didacticism. Lawrence could describe the sublimity of the sex act without self-consciousness, through direct description, poetic language, and exalted emotion. Joyce, steeped in literary tradition, and a parodist by temperament, could never unblushingly relate a coital experience, even when its source is the mind of Stephen Dedalus. For Joyce, it was naive to deal didactically with subjects for which there were no ultimate truths and about which everything had been said centuries before. But for Lawrence, sex achieves an elegant mysticism, the fullest appreciation of it linked with a transcendental participation in the core of being. It is not like Joyce's view of everyday life as casually permeated by sex; it becomes rather the source of divine understanding in Lawrence's work, particularly *Lady Chatterley*.

The individual love scenes between Connie and Mellors mark new levels of increased spiritual awareness by Connie and dictate the pattern of her subsequent behavior. As such they are each important structural elements in the novel, as nature and a full life in communication with that nature are linked increasingly with the love scenes. The plot progression of *Lady Chatterley* is largely a history of Connie's developing sensibility. The sense of continuity in the book in large measure derives from explicit sexual conduct, resulting in Connie's progress toward a oneness with nature. The language of these scenes is elevated and lyrical, and the experience of sex, the orgasm in particular, is the pathway to life in harmony with transcendental being. The gamekeeper, after his and Connie's first sexual encounter, declares:

> "Now I've begun again."
> "Begun what?"
> "Life."
> "Life!" She re-echoed, with a queer thrill.
> "It's life," he said. "There's no keeping clear. And if you do keep clear you might as well die." [*LCL* 165]

It was not in Joyce, however, to deal so straightforwardly and explicitly with sex as the entry to God and the essence of being. It is there in *Ulysses*, but in Joyce's usual comic parody. If Bloom emerges triumphant over the suitors at the end of his Odyssean day, it is because he accepts with equanimity the outrages perpetrated upon him. In this he is not unlike Clifford, when he assumes initially that he will triumph over the men who merely plant seeds in Connie's womb and that the mental bond of friendship will overpower the passional bond of sex. Clifford is wrong; sex wins. But the case of Bloom is more ambiguous. His home is threatened, his peace of mind jarred, his existence impaired by the adultery of his wife and her sexual passion. His reflection on this subject is outlined in "Ithaca."

> Why more abnegation than jealousy, less envy than equanimity?
>
> From outrage (matrimony) to outrage (adultery) there arose nought but outrage (copulation) yet the matrimonial violator of the matrimonially violated had not been outraged by the adulterous violator of the adulterously violated.[5]

Like Mellors and Connie, Bloom finds equanimity in his recognition that sex is a manifestation of the natural order of things.

> Equanimity?
>
> As natural as any and every natural act of a nature expressed or understood executed in natured nature by natural creatures in accordance with his, her and their natured natures, of dissimilar similarity. As not as calamitous as a cataclysmic annihilation of the planet in consequence of collision with a dark sun. As less reprehensible than theft, highway robbery, cruelty to children and animals, obtaining money under false pretences, forgery, embezzlement, misappropriation of public money, betrayal of public trust, malingering, mayhem, corruption of minors, criminal libel, blackmail, contempt of court, arson, treason, felony, mutiny on the high seas, trespass, burglary, jailbreaking, practice of unnatural vice, desertion from armed forces in the field, perjury, poaching, usury, intelligence with the king's enemies, impersonation, criminal assault, manslaughter, wilful and premeditated murder. As not more abnormal than all other altered processes of adaptation to altered conditions of existence, resulting in a reciprocal equilibrium between the body organism and its attendant circumstances, foods, beverages, acquired habits, indulged inclinations, significant disease. As more than inevitable, irreparable. [*U* 733]

The question arises from these two parodies of catechism or scientific observation, whether this is a true picture of Bloom's views and identification with nature, or, like some other distorted views in "Ithaca," a false representation. Whatever falseness there is in "Ithaca" stems from the misimpressions of Bloom and not from their fidelity to his conscious or subconscious mind. The question of whether Joyce could handle the topic seriously, as Lawrence did, or whether he had to deal with it on the sophomoric level of a dirty joke is not the issue here. What is, is that in a curiously comic way the universe as Joyce depicted it is similar to Lawrence's universe. Their methods were entirely different, their self-consciousness of presentation and roots in the past widely divergent, but their views of the natural order coincide.

Lawrence's repeated explicit descriptions of foreplay, coition, and post-orgasmic satisfaction are erotic in their realism and essential to the author's intent. We participate with the characters in the immediacy of the action. Joyce, on the other hand, filters the actual sexual experience through the minds of his characters. The five sex scenes in *Ulysses* include both Bloom's and Molly's versions of the episode on Howth, Bloom's subconscious projection of Molly's copulation in the afternoon, Bloom's vicarious sex act with Gerty MacDowell and concomitant masturbation, and Molly's recapitulation of her afternoon with Boylan. While all of these are explicit and realistic in their narration, in none of them except the masturbation (vicarious in itself) does the act occur as an actual event in the book. Rather they occur in the minds of the characters either as speculation or retrospection. The secondhand quality of the sex in *Ulysses*, particularly in Molly's soliloquy, has prompted some harsh criticism of Joyce from critics such as Strother Purdy, who claims that Jung was mistaken in praising Joyce's knowledge of women's minds because Molly's is really only a compendium of male jokes and popular erotic literature.[6] Lawrence's realism, on the other hand, has just as often been seen as either courageous, honest art or adolescent indulgence.

Stemming from the sexual metaphor is the basic linguistic similarity between Joyce and Lawrence, the use of four-letter vernacular words by the two most basic characters, Molly Bloom and Oliver Mellors. When four-letter words occur elsewhere in *Ulysses*, as in the dialogue of Private Carr, they are such a natural part of the linguistic landscape that they go nearly unnoticed. Only Molly commands our special attention in her use of four-letter words in "Penelope" to describe the vitality of her feelings. This is not unlike Mellors's employment of "obscene" words to give an exalted quality to the paradox of the sublime arising from the ostensibly filthy. F. R. Leavis and the many others who find Lawrence's four-letter words objectionable criticize them as being out of place and hence an artistic flaw.[7] Even

W. W. Robson, who sees Lawrence's language as deliberate, is un-willing to excuse him for it:

> What the orthodox stigmatize as lust, as shamelessness, as unnatural sexual practices, become cardinal virtues. Essential to this undertaking is the notorious use of the four-letter words. The shocking effect is deliberate. This deliberateness is unattractive: and it suggests a certain falsity. *The class in which Lawrence was brought up was unprudish but decent* [italics mine]. Lawrence seems to have forgotten that when he drew Mellors. His motives were in part noble. He hoped to cleanse the sexual relationship of guilt and fear. But we suspect other motives. *Lady Chatterley's Lover* is one of those books . . . which seem to be written out of resentment. They are powerful, but the atmosphere is constricting. The reader feels he is being got at.[8]

Yet the use of such language by Mellors, who modulates his accent to project himself as either a gentleman or a peasant, seems perfectly natural as one of his affectations. Here the linguistic similarity between the two authors generally ends. Lawrence's use of dialect as a device by some of his male characters reflects his pre-occupation with class distinction. Joyce uses dialect for different purposes. In *Ulysses* a low Dublin accent is occasionally afforded characters for comic effect, as in the extensive use of dialect in "Cyclops," where the barfly-narrator has a comic patter all his own, and in "Eumaeus," where W. B. Murphy affects a low Dublin accent sprinkled with salty nautical metaphors. For Lawrence, the extensive use of linguistic variation and experimentation is neither an artistic nor a thematic concern. However, for Joyce, who attempted a microcosm of Western man in his universal novel, the experimentation in language is all-pervasive, from the history of rhetorical styles in "Oxen in the Sun" to the range of narrative devices in the last twelve chapters of *Ulysses*. It would be surprising if four-letter words did not appear somewhere in *Ulysses,* so closely linked is linguistic and rhetorical variety with the variety of human experience depicted in the microcosmic action of the book.

Growing out of the sexual metaphor and its relation to nature are the geography of the two novels and its relation to meaning. In Lawrence place is associated with fixed ideas, fixed classes, fixed metaphors, but with Joyce geography represents flux and the basis of ambiguity. Just as the ultimate meaning is intertwined with setting in *Lady Chatterley*, the ambiguous meaning of Joyce's egalitarian novel is in large measure due to the book's being set in the city. Joyce, one of the first urban novelists, depicts characters who are all city dwellers, not separated by caste or economic status but diversified by occupation and idiosyncrasy of habit. Bloom's urban livelihood as an advertising salesman depends on society, on people, as a service industry. His thoughts are largely preoccupied with social service, schemes for the betterment of mankind, or schemes for better ads. He is without a key to his own house and wanders all day a "competent keyless citizen." If there is a bower of bliss at No. 7, and if nature is identified with Molly, they are of a different variety from Lawrence's. Bloom's day is spent mostly in public. References to natural life, flowers and the like, are confined mostly to Bloom's memory of the rhododendrons on Howth. His younger counterpart in the novel, Stephen Dedalus, is also denied a key and even at the novel's end has no place to go. Their day is spent wandering, either in solitary thought or in the company of others. But as Joyce scholars have pointed out, the geography of the city, like the geography of the Mediterranean and Aegean in the *Odyssey*, provides the basis for the plot itself, a journey motif where people and places are part of the adventure. The Gardiner Street Church, the Ormond Bar, Barney Kiernan's, Davey Byrne's, the Mosque of the Baths, the cemetery, the hospital, the brothel, the cabman's shelter, and the detailed map of Ulysses-Bloom's wanderings are part of a novel of public behavior. Bloom's character is drawn in no small part through his interactions with others, and much of his stream of consciousness is associated with the geography in which he finds himself. The geography of the city is so all-pervasive that maps are available in every bookstore in Dublin for Joyce lovers to trace one or another of the Bloomsday paths. The odysseys of other characters such as Father Conmee are also recorded, rendering *Ulysses*, in effect, a topographical map of Dublin on June 16, 1904. When Bloom finally returns home and has to lower himself ignominiously over the area railings and climb through a basement window in order to get in, he is hardly in harmony with natural surroundings. Plumtree's ad comically emphasizes the difference between Mellors's Edenic bower and Bloom's city row house:

What is home without
Plumtree's potted meat?
Incomplete.
With it an abode of bliss. [U 75]

At day's end, Bloom finds flakes of Plumtree's meat in his bed—a tinned product of a packing plant, of society, a confinement metaphor, a death image, and a pun on Boylan's afternoon activities. The urban diversity leads to ambiguity of meaning and unresolved answers to unclear questions.

Lady Chatterley's Lover draws fixed meaning rather than ambiguity from place. As Mark Schorer poetically puts it, "In the background of this picture black machinery looms cruelly against a darkening sky; in the foreground, hemmed in and yet separate, stands a green wood; in the wood, two naked human beings dance."[9] The estate is divided spiritually and physically into two parts. Wragby Hall is the intellectual pole of rational discourse, achieving a relationship of economic determinism with the dingy village outside. The Edenic wood is the seat of passion and nature, scarred by the ravages of war when Clifford's father cut trench timbers. The wood contains the hut and the gamekeeper's cottage, twin bowers of bliss, the first where the initial knowledge is gained and the second—where knowledge is broadened—providing a transition from Edenic intimacy to the outside world. Julian Moynahan best summarizes the geography of this novel in terms of the sacred wood with its life mysteries, standing between the manor house and the village with their social and economic hostility and yet their joint worship of money, power, property, and the mechanistic organization of human affairs.[10]

In the wood all of nature complements the sex act, which is performed both outdoors and in: the raising of the game in the safety of Mellors's cages until it can be freed, the budding flowers, the changes of season, and the plethora of natural imagery which enhances the awareness of Connie and Mellors as they begin to commune with their surroundings. Yet Lawrence seems to realize that the lovers' participation in a transcendental life in the seclusion of their bower is but a moment in the life of Mellors and Connie, and that a permanent free existence has got to be gained in the world outside. If that world threatens the lovers in *Lady Chatterley*, it also provides a hope of salvation. Mellors, it seems, has found in farming the one vocation besides gamekeeping which provides gainful employment and interaction with nature. What hope there is for the couple's future is predicated on living outside the sacred wood. That hope is the difference between the book's being a tragedy of high, doomed emotion or a comedy that offers a chance for a satisfactory free life in an outside world still in harmony with nature. Mellors will certainly never be a public, Bloomian figure, but there is the hope that he may be able to exist in an uneasy truce with the rest of society. The question of whether the couple will live happily . . . is left in the air, but the issues are not ambiguous, thanks to their associations with the setting.

The war between nature and mechanized society is intertwined in Lawrence's didacticism with another force which militates against nature, the division of society into classes, and into the owners and the oppressed. If Clifford Chatterley can afford to maintain his sanctuary in Wragby Hall it is because he is separated by the woods from the encroachment of the grimy town and the collieries on which much of his income depends. In the days of "Merry olde England" the division between feudal lord and serf was not so destructive, because all classes lived in harmony with natural surroundings. But during the industrial revolution the classes all began to cooperate in destroying their natural surroundings by building collieries and the horrible towns surrounding them, or canals such as the one dividing the Brangwen property in *The Rainbow*. Both classes, while perpetuating the distinction between themselves in the new order, begin a ceaseless war with nature in which nature inevitably suffers. It is like the degradation of God. Clifford's failure as an artist is early revealed in his inability to write literature of a lasting value, presumably because it does not recognize the truths of nature, and his subsequent failure as a man is sealed by his embracing the new mechanization, which suits his paralyzed state and his twisted temperament.

The pattern begins with the inability of his mechanized wheelchair to operate in the woods and extends to his subsequent immersion in the mindless sounds of his radio. If to the town he achieves a kind of superior manhood through his inventions and his mechanical pervasion of nature, his inner soul and manhood crumble simultaneously into an infantile state in private life. Mrs. Bolton provides his last contact with the humanity of the town through her stories and pampering. The nurse too has known the joy of sexual fulfillment and detests Clifford at the same time she is compassionate toward him. At first she is overawed by his class position, but ultimately becomes scornful when she realizes that his inadequacies transcend class origins. Manhood cannot be defined through such arbitrary divisions. In a way her disgust and loyal service reflect the situation of an entire class of servants. Money makes slaves of all classes in the new society. Both Connie and Mellors reiterate repeatedly their condemnation of monetary greed as the principal preoccupation of all people rich and poor.

But Lawrence's novel is based primarily on the relation of sex to class distinction. It is, after all, about a love affair between a woman of the upper classes and her gamekeeper. The fact that their social positions are so divergent is a statement of the polemic and one possible resolution to the class struggle and social determinism that permeate all of Lawrence's novels about England. Had Connie indeed taken, as Clifford suggests, a lover of her own class for the father of her child, or had Mellors stuck with a wife of his own class or accepted another lover of his own class, there would, in effect, have been no point to the novel. Their sexual intercourse, which obliterates class distinction, is the novel's paradise, while mechanization and the industrial society, which impose a far harsher class determinism than the feudal system ever did, are the novel's hell. Clifford's literal descent into his own pit, his rejuvenation of the mines and industry, and ultimately his talent for enhancing the artificial class struggle, parallel his personal perversions in a satanic portrait.

Undoubtedly social class was linked with sexual tension in Lawrence's own life. The apparent disparity of his marriage to the daughter of a German baron and their search for sexual and intellectual values bridging the class distinction provided him with the basic dilemma of *Lady Chatterley's Lover* as well as a rationalization for his own marriage. The battle of sexes over economics, which is a primary source of lower-class marital discontent, was a part of Lawrence's youth, vividly portrayed in *Sons and Lovers* and closely intertwined in many of Lawrence's novels and short stories. But mere lovemaking is not the only resolution to the problem of class disparity. In *Lady Chatterley,* Connie's father and the gamekeeper reach a reciprocal respect transcending class origin by their mutual veneration of the physical. But Lawrence also seems to be retreating from the unrelenting sexual polemic of earlier works when he makes Mellors more gentlemanly in his natural demeanor than even the higher born or economically endowed: "Yet, she saw at once, he could go anywhere. He had a natural breeding which was really much nicer than the cut-to-pattern class thing" (*LCL* 342). Lawrence also emphasizes Mellors's gentility of speech gained in part at the tutelage of his army commander, so that Mellors's gentlemanliness has a learned aspect complementing its natural sources.

Joyce, on the other hand, was less concerned with social strata or the economic and social system than with intellect in determining the actions of the characters in *Ulysses.* His life with a former barmaid constituted less of a gap in social class than in intellectual ability for Joyce. Nora Barnacle was a primitive life force, a prototype for Molly Bloom, who is closer to nature than any other character and who unites the novel with her sensuality and vital energy. If Joyce felt inferior to Nora, it was like the situation in *Exiles,* where Richard Rowan feels inferior because of his wife Bertha's natural understanding of sexual security. The biggest difference between Stephen on the one hand and Bloom and Molly on the other is not that of age, class, or marital status, but of intellect. Half of the dilemmas of the novel are the products of Stephen's allusive intellectual nature. Where the intellect in *Ulysses* is important enough to be both hallowed and ridiculed, in Lawrence—at least in *Lady Chatterley's Lover*—it runs a poor second behind sensual experience. Leopold Bloom, the "allroundman," is partaker of both the intellectual processes and the experience of life. Class distinctions, such as they are, play little part in Molly's affair with Boylan, or Bloom's with Mrs. Breen, Gerty MacDowell, or Lizzie Twigg. Instead, sympathy, image, and intellect, all mental states, pervade these liaisons: Bloom's pity for Mrs. Breen, his romantic image of Gerty MacDowell, and his intellectual-artistic connections with Lizzie Twigg ("Young woman. . . . To aid gentleman in literary work," *U* 165). Art of another kind, vocal, is the basis of (or excuse for) the relationship between Molly and Blazes. The largely classless society of Irish literary and theatrical audiences obliterates social distinctions in art, and the general poverty in Roman Catholic Ireland obviates the need for economic distinctions as a basis for fiction.

It is perhaps in an examination of the characters that the most informative comparisons between the sensibilities of Joyce and Lawrence may be explored. Despite the title of Lawrence's novel, the central consciousness of the book is not Mellors but Connie Chatterley. As in *The Rainbow* and most of Lawrence's work, the development of the female character's awareness and perceptions constitutes the main interest of the story. The males exist as satellites of Connie Chatterley, as they shape her mind and decisions. This is not to say that Mellors does not learn anything or that his character remains static throughout the book; rather that our main interest remains with the mind of Connie Chatterley with whose history we are familiar long before we meet Mellors. *Ulysses* on the other hand is shaped largely by a male perspective. Of the three major characters in *Ulysses*, Bloom is clearly the predominant figure, both in the length of his narrative portion and in the detailed exploration of his mental outlook. The plain fact is that we do not know whether Bloom learns a great deal about himself or life, or in that sense whether there is a progression of action in the book. Most of us speculate that he has and that the action does progress. At any rate our interest is clearly with Bloom's dilemma, his problems, his answers, his sensibility throughout the day, much more than with Stephen's or Molly's. Molly, though the strongest advocate of a philosophical or life-position in *Ulysses*, is really, like Stephen Dedalus, a satellite of Bloom, and the females in the book, Mrs. Breen, Bella Cohen, and Gerty MacDowell, mere influences on his sensibility.

Bloom and Mellors are similar in a number of ways. Both are outside the establishment and the society in which they have to live. Both are identified as having female as well as male sensibilities. Bloom is called the "new womanly man" (*U* 493), while Mellors is similarly characterized: "They used to say I had too much of the woman in me," he says (*LCL* 344). Bloom possesses the same sort of gentility as Mellors; both have pretenses of knowledge as well as catholicity of reading. The terms in which Bloom is described by

Lenehan, as "a cultured allroundman" (*U* 235), could easily have been attributed to Mellors. Finally, both men are sensualists and both have a strong sexual instinct.

In the story line, however, Bloom's situation is much closer to Clifford's. The difference is that Lawrence is very careful not to allow Clifford's plight and paralysis to enlist the reader's sympathy, while Joyce opens the floodgates of pity and terror for Bloom's universal plight. Clifford is cuckolded, defeated, reduced to childishness in his inner life, while he achieves supermanhood in his external business dealings. Bloom's home and marital prerogatives are usurped, but he remains unbeaten. Clifford's literary and industrial victories likewise enable him to carry on. The difference is that Clifford's handicap is symbolic of his spirit, which forces him into a life of the outside world because of his shriveled personal life. Bloom, however, chooses of his own free will to face a hostile outside world, and the same spirit, love, and equanimity which he manifests in that world are brought to bear on his home life. On the other hand, Bloom is like Clifford in many ways, occasionally infantile, masochistic, and weak. But ironically from this he emerges stronger, his torments by the end of the day fended off mainly by the strength of his own personality. No one can say that Bloom is insensitive after being privy to his thoughts about his companions in "Hades" and his wife in "Lestrygonians" and "Sirens." But he never completely surrenders to suffering because he is better able to cope, self-sufficient from masturbation, and sympathetic to the plight of others.

On the literal level, Mellors and Boylan, his counterpart in *Ulysses*, represent male energy. While it is to Lawrence's credit not to succumb to the longitudinal fallacy of equating manhood entirely with penis size, Boylan's prodigious ability to produce sexual satisfaction is in direct proportion to his equipment. The jaunty jingling of Boylan's cart harnesses, his jaunty atmosphere of self-assurance, as described in "Sirens," is similar to Mellors's self-assured peacock pride in dealing with women. Here Mellors resembles both Molly and Boylan. Her sensuality and vitality are obvious to men, who generally see her in sexual terms. Her uninhibited espousal of sex almost as a political and religious cause closely allies her with Mellors, as do her innate self-assurance based on sexual principles and her ability to move in different classes (due to her artistry and sensual attractions). Mellors represents a way of life which is individualistic and, like Molly's, close to nature. Like her, he is a judgmental character who is set in his ways, and, in touch with a natural sexual reality, measures all people and things against that standard.

While Mellors and Clifford both, even in the most charitable eyes, exhibit a neuroticism born of past and present injustices, Connie, despite her past, is essentially as whole a person as Bloom and Molly. But Connie and Mellors both have pasts that so color their perspectives that their love assumes an attitude of desperation. It is in a sense Mellors's last stand (no pun intended) and Connie's discovery of life after the deadness of marriage and meaningless copulation. While Bloom and Molly have had a less-than-blissful marital history, neither one has been permanently disfigured, nor have their perspectives been substantially warped, though many shocked readers of "Circe" and "Penelope" may claim otherwise. An attitude of comedy, of universality, and of congenial and steadfast strength permeates their characters throughout the book. Mellors's alternating ecstasy and gloom lead him to focus on salvation. Only at the end of *Lady Chatterley* has his faith in life been restored enough for him to hope again for a happy existence with someone loving and caring. Mellors is a rebel hero. Like Molly, he has only his faith in sensuality to sustain him. That sexual base in nature provides what tentative resolutions there are in both books as the thoughts and judgments of Molly and Mellors close the novels.

Bloom of the womanly sensibility is like Connie Chatterley the discoverer. His poignant lovemaking with Molly on Howth among the rhododendrons is the turning point of his life, and influences his thoughts and actions during the day, providing him with a major buffer against self-derision and the slights of others. To both Bloom and Connie, offspring have great meaning. It is the coming of the child which shapes Connie's future more than any inner stasis or awareness of her own spiritual being. The pregnancy is a certainty. The possibility of having a child had been discussed by Connie and Clifford long before her pregnancy, but the impossibility of her continuing to live at Wragby Hall with the child after her consciousness is altered by Mellors leads to her leaving. The child is the hope for the future, the symbol of her union with Mellors and life, not to be stifled in the perversions of Wragby Hall. Mellors's earlier child with Bertha Coutts is for him dead. His future also lies in the birth of a new child. Likewise, Bloom's hope for a son in his future has, since the death of Rudy, never completely died. On this sixteenth day of June, Bloom's search for vicarious fatherhood goes on unabated. Will Stephen and Bloom become spiritual father and son? Stephen is only a parody of Telemachus, and there is certainly no indication that any permanent relationship will come to pass. Happiness in any tangible form such as the child represents is more likely to be the reward of Connie and Mellors than Molly and Bloom. In Joyce's world there are other compensations.

For Joyce's characters, art has always provided a means of salvation, personal as well as political. Bloom and Molly feel that Stephen could create great art in their company: Bloom's idea is that Molly would contribute to Stephen's musical education, and that Bloom could manage their joint concert tours, while Molly thinks that she will inspire Stephen to write great poetry, and that she would be preserved and enshrined in his art. For Joyce, art is the primary reason for being, and as such it is of paramount importance in his work.

The subject is less pervasive in Lawrence, though his great novels all have artists in them. Very often, like Will Brangwen, they are craftsmen rather than individuals gifted with the ability to create deathless art. Similarly, Clifford's artistic endeavors in *Lady Chatterley* bring the rewards of popularity to someone merely able to craft pleasingly. In both *Ulysses* and *Lady Chatterley's Lover* artists are often degraded as human beings. Stephen, who by the beginning of *Ulysses* has produced little other than the villanelle, is certainly not a particularly admirable figure, any more than Shem of *Finnegans Wake* or Richard Rowan of *Exiles.* They are as neurotic as Lawrence's Clifford and Duncan. Bloom, the would-be artist, seeing himself, like Philip Beaufoy, earning a guinea per column, defaces the artist's "maturer work," "Matchem's Master-stroke," by wiping his behind with it, as he thinks of the whole artistic enterprise principally in terms of its profit. He is not unlike Clifford and Michaelis in this regard. The theme running through both works is that artists use art as a rationalization for their own failings and psychological inadequacies.

Both Joyce and Lawrence as literary artists established credentials in another art form, though certainly Lawrence's painting has gained a greater notoriety and respect than Joyce's music. But both Joyce and Lawrence used the second art to enhance the first. Lawrence's visual imagery and Joyce's musical imagery are the sources of such memorable passages as Connie's first spring walk in the woods or the opening of the "Sirens" episode of *Ulysses*. While art provided stylistic devices and subject matter in the perfection of art and the imperfections of artistic people and would-be artists, both writers were careful to give art a realistic place in the actions, if not the minds, of their characters. None of Lawrence's artistic characters are deluded enough to see themselves as saviors of their race or nation, but Joyce's primary artist, Stephen Dedalus, will "go to encounter for the millionth time the reality of experience and to forge in the smithy of [his] . . . soul the uncreated conscience of [his] . . . race."[11] Stephen's preoccupation must not have been so different from Joyce's, when he wrote *Dubliners* and acknowledged his own messianic urges: "My intention was to write a chapter of the moral history of my country."[12] Whereas Joyce's treatment of Stephen in *Portrait* is ironic, by the time he wrote *Ulysses* Joyce had matured enough to be able to see genuine comedy in the artistic impulse, when he made artistic, civic-minded Bloom a parodied savior of Ireland. On the other hand, Lawrence never deviated from his own preoccupation with saving England from contemporary tawdriness. Lawrence finally kicked the traces of social didacticism and concentrated on the freedom of self in a human relationship, though tempered by the surrounding evil of a mechanized and money-grubbing society. The didacticism had merely shifted to a salvation stemming from an inner strength to ward off the encroachments of an increasingly meretricious world. Although Lawrence's characters do not find salvation revealed in art, and although Lawrence is not the reflexive novelist that Joyce is, still *Lady Chatterley* itself is a didactic work. At the end of his career Lawrence still maintained a serious messianic spirit, something the later Joyce heavily disguised, if indeed Joyce did not finally decide merely to reveal truth and let societal betterment go its own way.

The validity of this thesis may be tested by comparing the endings of the two novels. In *Lady Chatterley* Mellors is able to blend his love of nature and natural processes with the necessity of living in the world. While we do not know whether Clifford will divorce Connie or whether Connie and Mellors eventually will be married and happy, the lovers' determination to be together seems to presage a bright future. That optimism is reinforced by our wanting them to succeed without regard to the artistic merits of such a conclusion to the novel. They have enlisted our sympathy and we share the author's idea of what an ideal world should be.

Ulysses presents us with a different proposition. We make much of Molly's "yes" in the end, not only as an affirmation of life, but as her response to Bloom's request for breakfast the next morning. Has Bloom like his Greek precursor won the day and vanquished the suitors? Is Boylan to return no more? Is the citizen to throw no more biscuit tins? Is Bloom finally to publish to critical acclaim his experiences in a cabman's shelter, or does any of that really make any difference? It is difficult to find readers from whom Bloom has not elicited sympathy. It is equally difficult to find many who favor some sort of assertion of Bloom's will over Molly, or who seriously feel that Stephen would become a great artist if he would come to live with Bloom. The ending of *Ulysses* is ambiguous only if we wish to read a moral lesson in it; it is another slice of reality, as gripping and as poignant as any moment in Bloom's day. But its meaning goes beyond any lesson we may apply in practical terms to our own lives, any conception of good or evil. It is essentially a comic vision of life which plays a Sancho Panza to Lawrence's Quixote, the elemental contrast between the sensibilities of the two great figures in twentieth-century British fiction.

NOTES

1. Dorothy Brett, *Lawrence and Brett: A Friendship* (Philadelphia: J. B. Lippincott, 1933), p. 81.

2. *Letters of James Joyce*, vol. 1, ed. Stuart Gilbert (New York: Viking, 1957; rev. 1966), p. 309.

3. Strother B. Purdy, "On the Psychology of Erotic Literature," *Literature and Psychology* 20, no. 1 (1970): 28–29.

4. G. Wilson Knight, "Lawrence, Joyce and Powys," *Essays in Criticism* 11, no. 4 (1961): 413.

5. James Joyce, *Ulysses* (New York: Random House, 1961), p. 733; hereafter cited in the text as *U*.

6. Purdy, "On the Psychology of Erotic Literature," p. 29.

7. See F. R. Leavis, *D. H. Lawrence: Novelist* (Chicago: University of Chicago Press, 1955), p. 74, and Eliseo Vivas, *D. H. Lawrence: The Failure and the Triumph of Art* (Bloomington: Indiana University Press, 1960), pp. 144–47.

8. W. W. Robson, "Joyce and Lawrence," *Modern English Literature* (London: Oxford University Press, 1970), p. 91.

9. Mark Schorer, "On *Lady Chatterley's Lover*," *Modern British Fiction*, ed. Mark Schorer (London: Oxford University Press, 1961), pp. 298–99.

10. Julian Moynahan, *The Deed of Life: The Novels and Tales of D. H. Lawrence* (Princeton, N. J.: Princeton University Press, 1963), pp. 146–47.

11. James Joyce, *A Portrait of the Artist as a Young Man* (New York: Penguin, 1982), pp. 252–53.

12. James Joyce, *Letters of James Joyce*, vol. 2, ed. Richard Ellmann (New York: Viking, 1966), p. 134.

GAVRIEL BEN-EPHRAIM

The Achievement of Balance
in *Lady Chatterley's Lover*

The Lawrence of the essays seeks creative balance between man and woman. More than avoiding the sterile domination of one sex by the other, Lawrence combines integrity of self with profundity of union. In "Study of Thomas Hardy" he joins the two achievements through his concept of the "two-in-one" (*Phoenix* 515), the finding of pure maleness and pure femaleness within a larger creation: "clasped together with her, I know how perfectly she is not me, how perfectly I am not her, how utterly we are two, the light and the darkness, and how infinitely and eternally not-to-be-comprehended . . . is the surpassing One we make" (*Phoenix* 468). The paradox is that oneness can be found only in conjunction with the other; Lawrence does not describe the losing of the self to find it, but the finding it once only by finding it twice—first in its aloneness and, again, in its unity. The true source of vitality, thus, is relationship; man and woman create themselves when they create something new beyond themselves. The original creation is more than the sum of its parts; this third thing, the mysterious "two-in-one" which is neither two nor one, has its being in the man and woman, yet transcends them. It is the most elusive element in a strange Lawrencean trinity.

The third part of the triad is intangible, depicted typically in metaphors poised carefully between spirit and matter;[1] symbol as well as substance, the third thing is Lawrence's invisible and generative "Holy Ghost." He approaches his obscure subject through tropes that conflate the energy of conflict with an emblem of consummation. Writing of the "light" or "sun" born in the clash of "cosmic water upon the cosmic fire," or of the "spark" struck when the man is "fifty per-cent" and the woman "fifty per-cent," or of such related images as the "rainbow " or "crown," Lawrence refers to the graced resolution of a dialectic.[2]

But if Lawrence pursues his third thing through many of the major essays, its desirability preoccupying him to the point of obsession, in most of the novels balance and its productions remain no more than wishful intellectualizations. Only in *Lady Chatterley's Lover* does Lawrence's vision yield to fictional treatment.[3] The previous novels show imbalances on either side of the scale, the weight shifting as the disintegrative man of the early works gives way to the domineering male of the later. But since women retain their self-will throughout all the novels, the central problem from *Women in Love* through *The Plumed Serpent* is not one of imbalance but of incongruity. There is a fundamental incompatibility when the woman achieves *separateness*, the mind apart from its environment, while the man attains *singleness*, the spirit at one with nature. We might speak of deliberate "self" as opposed to instinctive "being," the former located in the conscious mind, the latter rooted deeply in the unconscious. The two modes can appear mutually exclusive, an inherently unstable combination that ends in the domination of one sex by the other. It is—in a mythic anomaly—as though Artemis and Hades were fatally united, their match to end in a shadowed moon or illumined underworld.

The prototype for such ill-suited union is the marriage, or "mismarriage," of Walter and Gertrude Morel in *Sons and Lovers.* The vitality of each denies the other, and their relationship leads to mutual erosion, the piteous spectacle of wasted potentialities. They exist for us less as a couple, however, than as the parents in a family triangle including their son, Paul. Moreover, as a fictional version of the young Lawrence, Paul provides the autobiographical background to the most important triangular relationship in Lawrence's fiction: that between the Lawrencean narrator and his two prototypical characters. The significance of the contrast goes beyond *Sons and Lovers*, providing background to the narrator's attitudes, when Paul's stances toward his parents are radically opposed. Overinvolvement marks his relationship with Gertrude, a damaging intimacy manifested by his erotic and emotional incapacities. Paul's merger with Gertrude is ritualized prenatally in a garden where moonlight ceremoniously binds unborn child, mother, and a white nature that reflects her mental-consciousness. In striking contrast, Paul is completely alienated from his father, who remains a foreign being from the otherworld of the coal-mines.

Paul's history helps clarify the point-counterpoint cycle of the novels: Lawrence grew increasingly hostile to the mental intimacy shared with his mother as his sympathy for his father's distant vitality grew. As early as *The Rainbow* Lawrence shows the fearfully destructive side of female assertion. That harpylike power also manifests itself in a moonlit setting: the glaring landscapes wherein Ursula "annihilates" Skrebensky. "Corrosive as the moonlight," Ursula consumes Skrebensky, burning him to "nothing." When she finally fastens upon him in a "hard and fierce" embrace, Skrebensky is circumscribed and dissolved in the circle of Ursula's stronger ego.

After *The Rainbow*, seemingly despairing of the independence of male consciousness, Lawrence turns to man's unconscious powers— the source of the "ineffable darkness and ineffable riches" that Birkin brings from "another world." Thereafter Lawrence's unapprehended father is reincarnated as a series of unknowable men whose dark instincts transcend the woman's domain of self. One example is *The Plumed Serpent*'s Cipriano, who unites with Kate, his Irish bride, in a blood-marriage that disdains her "repulsive" individuality. Although Lawrence intends to show a meeting on the level of passion, he actually denies Kate's strongest sexual instincts when Cipriano withdraws from her "seething, frictional, ecstatic" orgasm.[4] Lawrence may want to depict clitoral orgasm as the physical expression of self-will, but Cipriano's bringing Kate to the "volcanic deeps" while she lies passive and unchallenging subdues her to his will. They reach no equality, but rather reverse Ursula and Skrebensky when Cipriano stills the "flow" of Kate's womanhood.

Yet the "ineffable" power of dark men like Cipriano or *The Lost Girl*'s Ciccio or the Indians and gipsies of the shorter fiction is a weak element in Lawrence's work. Glorified in conception, the dark men tend to be one-dimensional in execution; as symbolic figures more appropriate to psychic mythology than realistic fiction, they are subject to a romanticization that becomes a diminishment. The paradox is dramatically evident during a passionate encounter between *The Lost Girl*'s Alvina and Ciccio: "She felt his heavy, muscular predominance. So he took her in both arms, powerful, mysterious, horrible in the pitch dark. Yet the sense of the unknown beauty of him weighed her down like some force. . . . the spell was on her, of his darkness and unfathomed handsomeness. And he killed her. He simply took her and assassinated her. How she suffered no one can tell. . . . He intended her to be his slave, she knew. And he seemed to throw her down and suffocate her like a wave. And she could have fought, if only the sense of his dark, rich handsomeness had not numbed her like a venom."[5] The passage's cumulative repetitions describe Alvina's extinction by stages in a variety of passionate deaths. Ciccio is her assassin but also her deliverer, since the death of consciousness can lead to the life of the unconscious. The ignorant troupe-performer becomes a demon murdering the woman into birth, a wizard drowning her in a vital darkness as the "sense" of him overwhelms her in unknown feeling.

But on a deeper level it is Ciccio who is encompassed by Alvina. For the scene is ultimately a phenomenological study, an examination of how an object comes to represent what the mind discovers about itself. Focusing on Alvina, the passage is about an internal process; with no voice of his own, Ciccio is most convincing as an externalization of Alvina's uncovered inner darkness, the weapon with which she murders herself. Indeed, he is a kind of anti-self extending the range of her self-knowledge, his projective function resembling that of a Jungian shadow or reversed Blakean emanation.[6] Despite his fluid vitality, Ciccio's is an instrumental role, resembling that "huge peak" in *The Prelude* which leads the receiving consciousness into "unknown modes of being" (I. 378, 393). In Wordsworth's poem and Lawrence's novel the importance of the natural man or object finds a context in the sensibility it naturalizes, and that sensibility is the central concern of the narrative voice. Ostensibly dominated by Ciccio, the scene negates itself when structured by a consciousness purportedly overwhelmed. That consciousness, albeit in changed form, remains at the heart of a passage devoted to its annihilation.

Thus, in a reversal typical of the late works, the novel's vision of splendid manhood reveals itself as something of a mirage, to be apprehended vicariously through the stubbornly central medium of woman's perception. Before Mellors, no Lawrencean dark man is narrated from the inside, and it is as a genuine counter to the more subtle form of female domination that the gamekeeper's three-dimensional characterization is so significant. Bridging narrator and instinctual male to alleviate the narrator's hostility to his female protagonist, Lawrence's last novel moves toward a final equilibrium.

In the earlier sections of *Lady Chatterley's Lover*, Lawrence destroys the interferences with that equilibrium by rejecting both woman's presumptuous ego and man's aggressive helplessness in ego-based relationships. Accordingly, the novel opens with a sardonic view of womanly self-sufficiency. Achieving their "beautiful pure freedom" is the chief concern of Connie and Hilda Reid, young women liberated in the modern (circa 1910) fashion. The sexual explicitness of *Lady Chatterley's Lover* (replacing the earlier metaphorical obscurity) focuses on their method for maintaining a spiritual independence in the midst of erotic experience: "a woman could yield to a man without yielding her inner, free self. . . . For she only had to hold herself back in sexual intercourse, and let him finish and expend himself without herself coming to the crisis: and then she could prolong the connection and achieve her orgasm and her crisis while he was merely her tool" (*LCL* 40). The sisters view the overwhelming pleasure of mutual climax as a threat to the supremacy of the self, while sequential orgasm protects the mind's priority by denying the autonomy of the body. Similarly, when physical sensation is transformed into intellectual function, sex is subordinated to the word, the "thrill" of language preceding the "thrill" of the flesh, and the lapsed moments of passion reduced to a punctuational "row of asterisks" that end a paragraph or break a theme (*LCL* 41). This forced mentalizing of sensuality suggests the domination of the self-imprisoning ego described in "The Crown." The sisters remain in "the tight-shut shell" as the mind mechanically ensures the self's repetitive experience of itself.

The narrator's animus to Connie and Hilda is frank throughout his exposition, viewing their early sexuality as experiments in the power of will. He becomes more sympathetic in his description of Connie's connection with Michaelis. Their sequential orgasm is the consequence of the playwright's frail manhood. "The physical desire he did not satisfy in her; he was always come and finished so quickly. . . . But then she soon learnt to hold him, to keep him there inside her when his crisis was over. And there he was generous and curiously potent; he stayed firm inside her, given to her, while she was active" (*LCL* 65). Yet both partners salvage gratification from near-disaster. They welcome sustained isolation because each thereby protects the experience within the safety of consciousness. Sex threatens to reduce Michaelis to a child deprived of his "defenses," whereas rapid orgasm assures the expeditious return of his "effrontery," a crafty self-consciousness that restores his manhood.[7] Connie's satisfaction also increases her separateness; granting a "mechanical confidence in her own powers," sexuality intensifies her impervious "self-assurance, something blind and . . . arrogant" (*LCL* 66). Her blind self-satisfaction makes her insensitive to Michaelis's humiliating role, goading him into an outburst at her indifference and his own incapacity: "You couldn't go off at the same time as a man, could you? You'd have to bring yourself off! You'd have to run the show!" (*LCL* 93). Michaelis's separate satisfaction here turns to frustration and a sense of futility.

The playwright leads Connie's husband, Clifford Chatterley, toward a different kind of anticlimax by instructing him in the dynamics of literary fame. For Michaelis, having tamed "the bitch-Goddess . . . success" and mastered her handmaiden "publicity," arouses the interest of an aristocrat-turned-writer whose career is motivated by the "blind, imperious instinct to become known." Clifford, crippled below the waist and literally limited to mental experience, is anxious to become a name (a word) to that "vast amorphous world he did not himself know" (*LCL* 56). This is the clue to the function of the bitch-Goddess for Clifford. To be known without knowing is a way to expand the self without challenging it, fame creating an audience that is a great X in an unrestricted algebra of egoism. The nature of Clifford's writing is relevant here, for he is the author of cerebral, "very personal stories about people he had known. Clever, rather spiteful, and yet, in some mysterious way, meaningless. The observation was extraordinary and peculiar. But there was no touch, no actual contact. It was as if the whole thing took place in a vacuum" (*LCL* 50). The "vacuum" would be the tedious repetitions of consciousness, the fearful, predictable enclosure of a mind taking only itself as object and therefore turning all objects into subject. The ego existing only in-itself, breaking down all personalities and ideas to its own "spiteful" terms, creates a circular emptiness, an eternal return to the starting-point as the mind distorts the world to a mirror of the self. Through fame the mind increases the number of mirrors to solidify the reflected image.

The isolation that Connie and Michaelis feel with one another reaches a terrible perfection in Clifford. Apparently containing nothing within himself except self-consciousness, he suffocates Connie with the boredom of "his endless treadmill obsession with himself, and his own words" (*LCL* 137). His language is not a bridge for communication with another but a fortress for the self, simultaneously extending and protecting the ego. Through words his frightened psyche substitutes itself for sensory reality, but this makes him impotent as a writer as well as a man, disabled as a maker of fiction, when he can only iterate in art that "treadmill" already deathly repetitive in experience.

His turning language into a cul-de-sac eventually rebounds against Clifford, for he is "gradually dying" in the mental-life. What he seeks in language is compensation for physical and psychic paralysis. Looking to counter the sense of helplessness, he replaces the vague acquisitions of fame with the harsh satisfactions of power. Clifford finds industry superior to art as a way of imposing himself upon the mass of men. As a mining industrialist he feels the "new sense of power flowing through him: power over all these men. . . . He simply felt life rush into him out of the coal, out of the pit. The very stale air of the colliery was better than oxygen to him" (*LCL* 154). Mechanization serves Clifford as a weapon against the organic world—internal and external—from which he is divorced. Monstrous efficiency results when he intuitively grasps the advantages of increased reliance on the machine, implementing automatic systems that make men obsolete and nature desolate. Yet in the process he hastens his own dehumanization, so that cold machinery replaces self-absorbed language as the instrument and reflection of will.

The paradox is that while "life" rushes into Clifford in the activity of power, death is perpetuated within and around him. Beneath the apparent strengthening, he finds a more energetic, objectified way to die. This recalls "the retrogression to death" discussed in "The Crown" and touches on a central idea of Freud's "Beyond the Pleasure

Principle."[8] (*Lady Chatterley's Lover* raises some inescapable connections between these two extraordinary essays.) One of the seminal points in Freud's essay is that the ego's final purpose is death; this destiny is fulfilled when the individual organism seeks peace in its inorganic origin—the process Freud refers to when he says, *"the aim of all life is death"* ("BPP" 38). Insofar as man knows himself separate (the very function of the ego), he knows himself as something that will die. The will toward self-extinction is intrinsic to the ego, and it is to ensure the resolutional achievement of death that the ego-instincts become the death-instincts.

This is a universal pattern, but Clifford's self-mechanization is a specific enactment of the dictum that every "organism wishes to die . . . in its own fashion" ("BPP" 39). Clifford embodies the death-instinct only; indeed, wishing to make his marriage a long round of familiar "habit," he demonstrates the compulsion to repeat that inspired the very notion of a death-instinct ("BPP" 35–36). The matter goes beyond the individual when Clifford, as a master of the blighting collieries, helps convert Thanatos into England's national destiny. The mechanical England blotting out the organic is a macrocosm of the ego blotting out the body in human beings.

Strangely, the other side of Clifford's industrial tyranny is an infantile dependency that would appear to be its polar opposite. His childishness toward Connie is felt throughout, but is grotesquely climaxed by the gratification he feels when kissing Mrs. Bolton's breasts, finding "the exaltation of perversity, of being a child when he was a man. . . . While she was the Magna Mater, full of power and potency, having the great blond child-man under her will" (*LCL* 362). Contrary as Clifford's two aspects seem, they are profoundly related when the industrial tyrant compensates for the regressions of the man-child at the breast. Both roles complete psychologically that annihilation of manhood which the war had begun physically. He evades human responsibility by perversely distorting himself to a machinelike thing or reducing himself to an infant. This duality is most vividly captured when Lawrence speaks of Clifford as "one of the . . . invertebrates of the crustacean order, with shells of steel, like machines, and inner bodies of soft pulp" (*LCL* 156). The unity behind the division becomes clear if the "shell" is understood as Clifford's thing-like insentience, his inability to recognize anyone else, while the "soft pulp" captures his equally strong need to be recognized and merged with a self stronger than his own.

The nature of that stronger self is indicated by Mrs. Bolton's transformation into a physical Magna Mater, with Clifford finding peace as the child she enfolds. More significant is the psychic image beyond her, the mother in the mind, surely connected to Connie's strange spiritual meaning for him. If we see Clifford as a "broken-off fragment of a woman,"[9] a man who is incomplete because of a lingering subservience to an internalized figure, we can understand the primitive emotions revealed when he worships Connie "with a queer, craven idolatry, like a savage, a worship based on enormous fear, and even hate of the power of the idol, the dread idol" (*LCL* 157). Such passages indicate the etiology of Clifford's fragmentation, the cause of his partial being. Beyond his disability, Clifford cannot attain manhood because he remains a child psychically. The consequence of his fixation is a character as devoid of natural life as his body. A relevant characteristic of the crustacean is that it borders on being inorganic, part mineral-like object, part formless mass—these the metaphors for two opposed but complementary states of total, blind self-involvement. Incompletely separated from the mother, Clifford can neither attain wholeness within himself nor hold a woman in balance.

For Connie, the result of being unseen and untouched is a depletion of vitality, Clifford draining her like "a bulb stuck parasitic on her tree of life." Despite his often repeated respect for her individuality, he strangles her separate existence: "It was as if thousands and thousands of little roots and threads of consciousness in him and her had grown together into a tangled mass, till they could crowd no more, and the plant was dying" (*LCL* 126.) The culprit of the extended simile is not Clifford but consciousness itself, as though mental-relationships inevitably choked organic life. Indeed, Connie's "separateness" is the mirror of Clifford's and hence not recognized, for when the ego identifies with another self-consciousness, the other becomes the self. The antithesis—as we learn from Connie's involvement with Mellors—is the experience of the body wherein even the self becomes other. As much as by his actual invalidism, Clifford is deprived of bodily life by the Magna Mater who cripples him in her continuing psychic domination.

Drawing Connie into the mental life, he matches the actual woman to the psychic image, merging her in his own freakish egocentricity to separate Connie from natural patterns. In the end, Clifford is an organism that creates nothing, whose only natural activity can be to die; he remains a decaying child who will never father, Thanatos unbalanced by Eros.

Conversely, Connie saves herself in the vital reality that escapes Clifford's rigid ego. In a central irony, the maternal instinct ultimately leads her toward life, the "dread idol" becoming a spontaneous creature. The engulfing Magna Mater becomes a creative force in equal union with a strong male. Hence the centrality of Mellors, whose role for Connie begins in a vision of a man bathing in a wood. Her strongest impression of that experience is of Mellors's joyful intimacy with his body, an energetic and unselfconscious physicality: "his white slim back was curved over a big bowl of soapy water, in which he ducked his head . . . with a queer, quick little motion, lifting his slender white arms, and pressing the soapy water from his ears, quick, subtle as a weasel playing with water, and utterly alone. . . . Perfect, white, solitary nudity of a creature that lives alone. . . . And beyond that, a certain beauty of a pure creature . . . revealing itself in contours that one might touch: a body!" (*LCL* 107). In a novel partly about people who disdain physicality, the contrast struck by Mellors's vital animation is enormous. Compressing pleasure, grace, and skill into a simple activity, he unifies spirit and body. Equally striking is his pure aloneness, not to be confused with isolation, for his seclusion is of a creature in nature and his independent vitality is connected to the landscapes beyond the cottage. Withal, he contains a wholeness of controlled energy imaged by "the warm, white flame" that will intensify when he goes beyond oneness to union.

Connie's response to this sight, however, is divided: "Connie had received the shock of vision in her womb. . . . But with her mind she was inclined to ridicule" (*LCL* 107). This is precisely the self-division she later feels in their lovemaking, the mind mocking the physical revelation of her deepest interiority, her womb. In her fierce inner battle, the mind actively resists diminishment of its sovereignty over being. The harm that sovereignty causes is shown when Connie looks at her own naked figure: "Her body was going meaningless, going full and opaque, so much insignificant substance. . . . She was old . . . with no gleam and sparkle in the flesh. Old through neglect and denial, yes denial" (*LCL* 111). Beyond Clifford's "denial" she comprehends the depth of her cruel self-neglect. She is dismayed by sudden awareness of her wasted femininity, of a body whose borders go "flat, slack, meaningless" because she fails to inhabit them, her life proceeding elsewhere. The opacity of flesh and "flattening" of outline are metaphors for the way self-consciousness blurs physical awareness. Having seen Mellors's "contours that one might touch," she revealingly perceives herself in a mirror-image that cannot be touched.

This dual vision begins Connie's singling herself from Clifford, her divesting herself in "cold indignation" of "his writings and his talk": yet inward change is equally essential for Mellors. She may be "withered" in the flesh, but he attains vital wholeness only to show how unsatisfactory the achievement of oneness is. When Connie encounters him, he is motivated by a despairing aversion to mankind: "He felt if he could not be alone, and if he could not be left alone, he would die. His recoil away from the outer world was complete; his last refuge was this wood; to hide himself there!" (*LCL* 131). He hides from women primarily, his "big wound from old contacts" inflicted by their avoidance or over-assertion of sex, and by his refusing to be frustrated or dominated. Hence the resistance Connie initially meets, as in his wariness about sharing the key to his hut, is a fear of vulnerability as well as a sexual self-guarding. He keeps his male being jealously about him as a defense or weapon; these stances are taken in other late works of Lawrence, but *Lady Chatterley's Lover* acknowledges their frightened barrenness. Mellors's most serious wound is the self-infliction of exile, his paradoxical uniting of singleness and sterility.

Connie and Mellors share a fear of intimacy, but this is overcome in a setting that dramatizes their cowardice. Connie is shamed into awareness when she visits the keeper's hut and feels envy toward the hens in their nearby coops. The hens' "soft nestling ponderosity of the female urge, the female nature" saddens her into knowledge that she has been "forlorn and unused, not a female at all, just a mere thing of terrors" (*LCL* 160). Her "unused" womanhood leaves a vacuum filled by neurosis; she has recapitulated Clifford's anxiety and isolation.

Despair at being unable to identify with the generating creatures, however, begins the identification. Their primitive maternal instinct poses a counterforce to ego as their "heat" pierces to her neglected female being. Connie's slow involvement with the hens helps restore that femaleness, gradually returning her to the organic world. The birth of a "tiny, tiny perky chicken" betokens the rebirth of nature in the woman, though she initially realizes only the contrast between its "fearless new life" and her own fearful avoidances. Yet the restitution of naturalness starts in the pain of its absence; her "agony" leads to a form of tragic recognition, bringing the tears that compel a response from Mellors: "He glanced apprehensively at her. Her face was averted, and she was crying blindly, in all the anguish of her generation's forlornness. His heart melted suddenly, like a drop of fire" (*LCL* 163).

Her generation has imposed "forlornness" on itself by abandoning natural touch and feeling, but her tears signal the drowning of the will and the cleansing of self-consciousness. Not quite a baptism into organic being, her grief does suspend her conscious ego; at this tender moment it is as though the obstruction of self falls away from her, leaving a pure living creature that arouses Mellors's withheld instincts. If her transformation is by water, his is by fire, both elements speaking of fundamental change, of being taking new forms. Mellors, indeed, is both melted and burned away in a "drop of fire," an oxymoron that expresses the intimate relation of compassion and passion.

The passion between Connie and Mellors, progressing through the remainder of the novel, begins with this scene. Yet it is worth pausing here to note the striking correspondence between the above event and the introduction of Paul to Miriam in *Sons and Lovers* (chapter 6). That similarly placed meeting shows Paul reassuring a Miriam whose alienation from physical experience also is represented by fear of a pecking hen. The occurrence, though it has obvious sexual implications, is ironic rather than prophetic, since neither Paul nor Miriam is able to fulfull a sensual relationship.

It would be an exaggeration to say that Lawrence returns to the British Midlands (the location of his more successful novels) to have Mellors realize Paul's unkept promise. Still, the gamekeeper needs to be understood in relation to both Paul and Walter Morel. Mellors's portrait contains deliberate references to the two autobiographical figures, combining Paul's intuitive sensitivity and Walter's vital manliness in a complex, fully apprehended character. (The similarities to Walter include Mellors's occasional use of dialect and the pleasure he takes during the epiphanic washing-scene.) Conflating Walter and Paul, Lawrence presents his character in depth—often through internal narrative that directly communicates thoughts and feelings—but presents him in psychic and physical wholeness. Creating a whole man, Lawrence finally integrates the image of the father into a male protagonist, an achievement that signals the integration of the father into the narrator and into Lawrence himself.[10] The synthesis is necessary to a narrator who becomes one with *both* his protagonists. Finding his way to the father, the narrator frees himself from the female domination that vexes tale and teller in most of the novels; excising the image of the Magna Mater from the pond of his fiction,[11] the narrator generates language that flows into "the *passional* secret places of life" (*LCL* 146). The narrator who operates beyond the personal ego directly opposes Clifford. Indeed, Clifford, prohibited by an internalized presence from entering the secret "places," is the shadow or inversion of the Lawrencean narrator.

Having raised the father, to find balance the narrator must dissolve the mother, devoting major passages to the "melting" of Connie's ego. Her continuing rigidity is manifested in the self-consciousness that separates Connie from her first intimacy with Mellors—an experience that brings a one-sided fulfillment to the man completed by the other sex: "It was the moment of pure peace for him, the entry into the body of the woman" (*LCL* 164). Wholeness is a mystery resolved in the other's physicality; but if the "peace" is consummated in her body, it is restricted to his soul. Wholeness escapes Connie as she continues her mental examinations, turning the mind into a voyeur of touch: "Her tormented modern-woman's brain still had no rest. . . . The man lay in a mysterious stillness. What was he feeling? What was he thinking?" A familiar image represents the mind that keeps itself apart and intense, refusing the dark unknown of indeterminable sensuality: the "very brilliant little moon shining above the afterglow" (*LCL* 164) symbolizes the consciousness that observes closeness from a sometimes mocking height. "If you were a woman,

and apart in all the business, surely that thrusting of the man's buttocks was supremely ridiculous" (*LCL* 174). More than being "apart"
from Mellors, she abandons her own instinctive self.

Maternal feeling helps unify Connie's divided being. An emotional meeting with a young girl, whose "unconscious cheeky little
legs" and "fearless" nature recall the courage of the tiny chick, makes
Connie long to have her own child, and the profound desire for a
"baby" precedes her first experience of sexual self-loss. That union
feels like a "rippling, . . . a flapping overlapping of soft flames, soft as
feathers, running to points of brilliance . . . and melting her all
molten inside," a merging of fire, water, and self into another substance. The trope of melting is a romantic conceit indicating the
dissolution of mind into body and self into being.[12] But the melting is
more than intrapsychic when the woman's receptivity becomes oneness with the man: "all her womb was open and soft . . . like a
sea-anemone under the tide, clamoring for him to come in again and
make a fulfillment for her." No longer keeping herself apart from the
"tide" in moonlike independence, she is completed by its inchoate
power, by the man who unites her in sound that liquefies and dis-
solves: "The voice out of the uttermost night, the life! The man heard
it beneath him with a kind of awe, as his life sprang out into her. And
as it subsided, he subsided too and lay utterly still, unknowing"(*LCL*
183–84). The long synesthetic description of their passion culminates
in a "concentric fluid of feeling" centered in her womb, the human
organ of generation and a microcosm of the oceanic source of life.
Transformed from a distinct self to a vessel of conception, she anticipates her actual child when she feels freshly created herself. Such
overwhelming experience turns her to a flowing receiver of "new life";
the old identity breaks down in "adoration" of the man and their
future creation: "In her womb and bowels she was flowing and alive
now and vulnerable, and helpless in adoration of him as the most
naive woman.—It feels like a child, she said to herself; it feels like a
child in me" (*LCL* 185). Water, simultaneously lethal and generative,
drowns the old self as it conceives the new; Connie is born a woman
when ready to bear a child. But Mellors is equally transcendent when
both partners join the universal generation that goes beyond individual being. Participating in procreative process, they are the human

embodiments of Eros, representing the creative force that counters the machine-Thanatos of Clifford's "evil electric lights and diabolical . . . engines." *Lady Chatterley's Lover* becomes a parable of life against death, an ecological fable with Connie and Mellors an endangered species threatened by "mechanised greed."

Freudian Eros is relevant here because it subsumes sexuality to the reproductive drive of the life-principle. Freud's Eros is contingent on union, the life-seeking "germ-cell" achieving its function only "if it coalesces with another cell similar to itself and yet differing from it" ("BPP" 40). Life is the going beyond the organism, death the staying within: Freudian coalescence like Lawrencean liquefaction is indebted to Aristophanes' notion, in Plato's *Symposium*, that male and female become complete only when they join together—but Freud and Lawrence add that the union is truly accomplished when two creatures unite to create another. To be sure, through most of his career Lawrence would hardly have subscribed to such a formulation. Nevertheless, in Eros Connie and Mellors unite with the surrounding propagative surge, with the novel's celandines and bluebells, with a living nature where coming into being and bringing into being are the same. Lawrence's Eros is self-creation through the creation of another: with the child and its making suffusing through their veins, Connie and Mellors escape the disintegrating mechanical world.

But *Lady Chatterley's Lover* does not altogether resolve itself in a clear Freudian dichotomy. Mellors creates tension by resisting subordination to Eros. Nor is the narrator entirely approving when Connie finds herself in a "satisfying and stupefying" daze of actual conception. This dulled state recalls her banal thoughts about the "warm" and "fulfilling" advantages of pregnancy. Without undercutting procreation as a *sine qua non* of deepest intimacy, the narrator's diction hints at maternal complacency, the generation of the child eclipsing regeneration in the adult.[13] Mellors, wary of being exploited as a mere begetter of children, is more intent on the state of creation than its products and concentrates on the renewal of flesh and spirit in "healthy human sensuality, that warms the blood and freshens the whole being" (*LCL* 112). The threat in the late sections of the novel is that Connie will reduce generation to an aspect of her ego instead of losing her ego in generation, that she will thus reestablish the Magna

Mater by considering reproduction merely an enhancement of her female self.

Mellors initiates the "burning out" of shame to continue the salutary breaking down of that self. When he smelts "the heaviest ore of the body into purity," anal intercourse is strongly suggested by the language of the encounter (*LCL* 311–13); and the male "fire of sheer sensuality" saves Mellors from drowning in an intimacy on female terms. In a strategy familiar from *Women in Love,* Mellors presses Connie to acknowledge corruption as well as creation and accept forms of gratification not predicated on conception.[14] Mellors protects the phallic mystery by bringing Connie to the "jungle of herself," but above all he keeps their relationship exploratory, balanced in an irresolution of power.

That balance is disturbed when their "awful sensuality" is therapeutic only for Connie. Glorified as a "reckless devil" and "wild animal," Mellors is also simplified into a one-dimensional figure, causing change in the woman without needing it in himself. The scene, accordingly, depicts Connie's self-transformation in the hunting-out of shame, while Mellors, superior in ultimate shamelessness, is kept at a mythic distance. The over-assertion of maleness nearly turns Mellors into a Ciccio-like "demonic" character. Yet the events of that night are perhaps best understood as a redressing of Mellors's increasing inferiority before Connie's social standing; its advantages become glaringly apparent as she handles the details of divorce, childbirth, and remarriage: "The money is yours, the position is yours, the decisions will lie with you," he tells her. "I'm not just my lady's fucker, after all" (*LCL* 345). Their "sensual passion" follows Mellors's exposure to Hilda's withering contempt, the class-consciousness of her sister signifying Connie's sometimes-discarded self. Mellors's reactions to Connie's social power involve the mask of dialect, the hiding of personal need in revolutionary rhetoric, and the folding of Eros into Thanatos in the "extravagances of sensuality" that bring her "a poignant, marvellous death" (*LCL* 312).

A potentially serious clash between self and being emerges toward the end of the novel, but the imbalances of Lawrence's other works fail to crystallize. The main difference is that *Lady Chatterley's Lover* never becomes a fantasia on the death of the ego. Neither lost in the

Abruzzi Mountains nor isolated beside a Mexican lake, Connie and Mellors remain in England. The geographical reality frames a psychological realism, the search for "a small farm of their own" striking a compromise between natural escape and social necessity. In parallel fashion, the struggle between self and being will not cease; each character, like all of us, will follow a private path to death. Each will take a separate refuge, but for Connie and Mellors the separating instinct will be balanced by a stronger instinct still, by the merciful drive toward "the creative act which is far more than procreative."

NOTES

1. Thus my remarks are a variation, not a revision, of the dualistic approach to Lawrence. In H. M. Daleski's formulation, Lawrence's scheme sees all levels of reality—the self, human relations, even inanimate nature—as involving the interaction of the male and female "principles." See *The Forked Flame: A Study of D. H. Lawrence* (Evanston, Ill.: Northwestern University Press, 1965), pp. 18–41.

2. The "light" and "sun" images are from "The Two Principles" (*Phoenix II* 231); the "spark" is from "Him with his Tail in His Mouth" (*Phoenix II* 434–35); the "rainbow" and the "Holy Ghost" images are used frequently in "Study of Thomas Hardy" (*Phoenix* 398–516), while "the crown" has a central role in the essay by that name (*Phoenix II* 365–415).

3. The problem of balance between Ursula and Birkin in *Women in Love* is discussed in my book *The Moon's Dominion: Narrative Dichotomy and Female Dominance in Lawrence's Earlier Novels* (East Brunswick, N.J.: Fairleigh Dickinson University Press, 1981), pp. 202–32.

4. D. H. Lawrence, *The Plumed Serpent* (New York: Vintage Books, 1959), p. 463.

5. D. H. Lawrence, *The Lost Girl* (Harmondsworth, Middlesex: Penguin, 1982), p. 244.

6. Myra Glazer Schotz describes Blake's "emanation" as the "female correspondent" of male "faculties—intellection, intuition, sensation, feeling— . . . [her] ideal function is to nurture, sustain, support, enrich, and ennoble." There is no male emanation, however, because Blake "mostly portrays the female only as an aspect or extension of the male. His is, appropriately, a male psychology designed, like Lawrence's, to invoke the struggles besetting the psyche of a male artist." Yet Schotz's point is dubious in relation to Lawrence, since the female psyche is at least as central in his work as the male. See Schotz's "For the Sexes: Blake's Hermaphrodite in *Lady Chatterley's Lover*," *Bucknell Review* 24, no. 1 (1978): 19.

7. Mark Spilka gets at the underlying emotional issue: "Michaelis . . . climaxes quickly out of some unexpressed fear of giving himself up to the act with real generos-

ity of feeling." See Spilka's "On Lawrence's Hostility to Wilful Women: The Chatterley Solution," in *Lawrence and Women*, ed. Anne Smith (New York: Barnes and Noble, 1978), p. 203.

8. Sigmund Freud, "Beyond the Pleasure Principle," in *The Standard Edition of the Complete Psychological Works of Sigmund Freud*, ed. and trans. James Strachey (London: Hogarth Press, 1955), 18: 7–66. Subsequent references to this edition of "Beyond the Pleasure Principle" will be indicated parenthetically in the text by the abbreviation "BPP."

9. See D. H. Lawrence, *Women in Love*, ed. Charles L. Ross (Harmondsworth, Middlesex: Penguin, 1982), p. 271.

10. Schotz's points about the role of androgyny in *Lady Chatterley's Lover* seem more pertinent to the narrator than to Connie and Mellors. See "For the Sexes: Blake's Hermaphrodite in *Lady Chatterley's Lover*," p. 25.

11. The reference is to the well-known scene from *Women in Love*, pp. 322–25.

12. The centrality of the image to romantic tradition, and to Lawrence, is developed at length in Colin Clarke, *River of Dissolution: D. H. Lawrence and English Romanticism* (London: Routledge and Kegan Paul, 1969).

13. Kingsley Widmer comments: "Children are significant in the novels only . . . in a projected, but necessarily incomplete and uncertain, pastoral-utopian flight from society—the pregnancy endings to *The Lost Girl* and *Lady Chatterley's Lover*. . . . The death of god and the father gives primacy, in the whole direction of Lawrence's work, to regeneration over generation." See Widmer's *The Art of Perversity: D. H. Lawrence's Shorter Fictions* (Seattle: University of Washington Press, 1962), pp. 26–27. Widmer's statements are persuasive when applied to most of Lawrence's work (including *The Lost Girl*, largely about the "death" of the old Alvina); but in relation to *Lady Chatterley's Lover* his account omits the significant birth of the father.

14. See *Women in Love*, pp. 395–97, and *The Moon's Dominion*, pp. 228–32.

KEITH CUSHMAN

The Virgin and the Gipsy and the Lady and the Gamekeeper

D. H. Lawrence wrote *The Virgin and the Gipsy* while living at the Villa Bernarda in Spotorno in January 1926. Frieda's daughter Barbara Weekley was staying nearby, and her stories about growing up in a household ruled by her grandmother and aunt, where it was forbidden to mention her mother's name, helped provide the genesis of the novella.

No one is certain why *The Virgin and the Gipsy* was not published during the last four years of Lawrence's life. The office of Martin Secker, Lawrence's English publisher, prepared a typescript of the work early in 1926, but Secker decided not to publish it. He had read some of the novella while visiting the Lawrences in Spotorno, but he must not have liked the complete work. A plan to include it in a projected three-novella volume was dropped, and the book did not appear until Pino Orioli brought it out in his Lungarno Series shortly after Lawrence's death.

F. R. Leavis called *The Virgin and the Gipsy* "one of Lawrence's finest things"[1] and devoted ten enthusiastic pages to it in *D. H. Lawrence: Novelist.* But few critics have shared Leavis's enthusiasm, and even now its status in the Lawrence canon remains ambiguous. However, the novella is commonly regarded as having an important bearing on *Lady Chatterley's Lover,* the novel Lawrence was to complete two years later. In his introduction to the Grove Press edition of *Lady Chatterley,* Mark Schorer describes *The Virgin and the Gipsy* as "preparatory to" the later novel.[2] Harry Moore similarly calls it a "prelude to *Lady Chatterley's Lover,*"[3] and more recently Donald Gutierrez has commented on the tendency to regard the work as "a dry run for *Lady Chatterley's Lover.*"[4] Nevertheless, though the relationship between novella and novel is regularly assumed, it has never been explored in detail. I propose in this essay to examine in what ways *The Virgin and the Gipsy* is indeed a significant prelude to *Lady Chatterley*—and in what ways it is not.[5]

Both works were written in the last phase of Lawrence's career, following his near-fatal illness in Mexico in February 1925 and his final return to Europe. For the first time he had also been forced to confront the fact that the disease he suffered from was tuberculosis. *The Virgin and the Gipsy* and *Lady Chatterley* both partake of the twilight quality of Lawrence's last creative years. The urgency, intensity, and turbulence of his greatest novels are absent from these works. Though he still yearns to remake the world after his own fiery heart's desire, he possesses a new recognition of human limitation. If as usual Lawrence uses his fiction as a vehicle for his compulsive search for clarity and self-resolution, his mood in this search is now more subdued and less urgent. Facing death and rendered sexually impotent, he writes fablelike fictions of renewal and regeneration, preparing his own little ark in which to escape the coming annihilation.

In rough outline much is similar between the two works. Each makes use of one of Lawrence's most habitual fairy-tale plots, that of the Sleeping Beauty, for in each work a dormant English heroine is awakened by a potent outsider. The vicar's daughter, Yvette Saywell, "that tender look of sleep"[6] on her face, is passionately attracted to the gipsy, Joe Boswell. He saves her life during the flood at the end of the novella by taking her to the top floor of the house, rubbing her dry with a towel, and clasping her in his arms through the night. Connie Chatterley, trapped in a moribund marriage, is also ready for awakening: "a new phase was going to begin in her life" (*LCL* 127). She is restored to life by Sir Clifford's gamekeeper, Oliver Mellors, in the famous encounters in the woods near Wragby Hall. In each work salvation is to be found in the flesh. Furthermore, in each work fable is blended with satire and social commentary.

The unfinished story called "The Flying Fish," dating from March 1925, points toward *The Virgin and the Gipsy* and *Lady Chatterley's Lover* in that its protagonist, recovering from a serious illness in Mexico, recognizes that the rebirth he seeks can be achieved only in his native England. It is hardly surprising that Lawrence, so close to death, would yearn to end his exile and return to England. In "The

Flying Fish" Gethin Day reflects that "it did not matter that England was small and tight and over-furnished. . . . He wanted to go home" (*Phoenix* 783). Lawrence returned to Europe in September 1925. *The Virgin and the Gipsy* and *Lady Chatterley's Lover* both present English characters in an English setting, and in a sense they are parables of return as well as parables of regeneration. Once more Lawrence was exploring the possibility of renewal in an expressly English context. Novella and novel constitute a homecoming for him.

Both draw on actual visits Lawrence made to his native Midlands. In October 1925 he went north to visit his sisters, a trip that included a motor tour of Derbyshire, the setting of *The Virgin and the Gipsy*. Lawrence called Derbyshire "one of the most interesting counties in England" but felt he was unable to "look at the body of my past, the spirit seems to have flown" (*CL* 859). His final visit to England came a year later. Though he was distressed about the effects of the coal strike, he experienced a renewed hopefulness about his native land: "Curiously, I like England again, now I am up in my own regions. It braces me up: and there seems a queer, odd sort of potentiality in the people, especially the common people. One feels in them some odd, unaccustomed sort of plasm twinkling and nascent. They are not finished" (*CL* 933). Lawrence's feelings about England would never be more than ambivalent. But in *The Virgin and the Gipsy* and *Lady Chatterley* he sought to end his long self-exile, to explore imaginatively England and the English.

There is no evidence that Lawrence was thinking about *The Virgin and the Gipsy* when he first embarked upon *Lady Chatterley* in October 1926, but many details from the novella show up strikingly in the novel. Each heroine has an older sister—in each case two years older—to serve as her foil. The elopement of the vicar's wife "with a young and penniless man" (*VG* 1) echoes the Frieda-Lawrence-Weekley circumstance, and so does Clifford's refusal to give Connie a divorce at the end of *Lady Chatterley*. The motor trip Yvette and her friends take through the "grim villages" (*VG* 22) seems to anticipate Connie's bleak motor trip to Uthwaite. Each novel ends with a letter from the male protagonist to the heroine. Yvette's suitors are "dog-like" (*VG* 62); Connie's lover Michaelis has a "hang-dog expression" and is a "real dog among dogs" (*LCL* 63). Similarly the vicar has a "snarling, doggish look" (*VG* 37), and Clifford too is "so doggy" (*LCL* 313). (Michaelis and the suitors are doglike in being overly domesticated. The dogginess of the vicar and Clifford seems associated with the intrusion of mental consciousness into sensuality.[7])

Furthermore, the vicar is a minor man of letters, a "clever writer" (*VG* 75), "somewhat distinguished as an essayist and a controversialist" (*VG* 1). The vicar's secondary career is appropriate enough to a character named Saywell. This motif figures more prominently in *Lady Chatterley*, in which both Clifford and Michaelis are minor but successful writers. The tyranny of "ready-made words and phrases, sucking all the life-sap out of living things" (*LCL* 137), rather undeveloped in *The Virgin and the Gipsy*, becomes a central theme of *Lady Chatterley's Lover*.

The key scene in which Connie encounters Mellors at work making pheasant coops is drawn directly from the novella. Yvette goes out cycling among the "vast maze of stone fences," feeling as if she has "climbed on to another level": the language suggests the transcendent revelation that is to be granted her. She finds the gipsy, "seated on the ground with his back to the cart-shaft, hammering a copper bowl. . . . The only sound was the rapid, ringing tap-tap-tap of the small hammer on the dull copper" (*VG* 66). This scene is matched in *Lady Chatterley* (*LCL* 130–32) when Connie, walking in the woods, happens upon the "secret little clearing, and a secret little hut made of rustic poles." "The keeper in his shirt-sleeves was kneeling, hammering," hard at work on pheasant coops. Like Yvette, Connie listens "to the tapping of the man's hammer." The gipsy "looked up at once" at Yvette; Mellors "lifted his face suddenly and saw" Connie. Each scene is constructed pictorially, and the meaning of the pictures is easily interpreted. The two men are poised, absorbed in their male work, and proud and isolated in their maleness. The hammering has a latent sexual meaning, especially the gipsy's hammering of the bowl. The two young women are intruders; Connie herself perceives that "here was a trespass on his privacy." The sight of the men, cut off and enrapt in their work and somehow vulnerable, produces a powerful feeling of attraction in the women. Yvette is immediately "aware of *him*, as a dark, complete power," and she is "gone in his will" (*VG* 70). Connie watches Mellors "fixedly," and "it was the stillness, and the timeless sort of patience, in a man impatient and passionate, that touched Connie's womb."

Lawrence also borrowed one other plot situation for *Lady Chatterley*, and that is the gipsy's experience in World War I. World War I was the first modern technological war, but both Joe Boswell and Oliver Mellors are throwbacks, for both were "connected with horses" (*LCL* 135). The gipsy served under Major Eastwood and was "one of our grooms, A.I. man with horses" (*VG* 75). In the army Mellors also worked with horses, "a clever fellow that way." The gipsy-Eastwood relationship is enlarged in *Lady Chatterley* into the relationship between Mellors and the colonel who "took a fancy to him" and made him a lieutenant. Ultimately Mellors had grown tired of the "blind, thoughtless life with the horses" and resigned from the military. But the significant feature of this parallel history is the association of both men with an archetypal image of maleness and with an earlier heroic tradition of combat that has been destroyed by modern industrialism. Furthermore, the vague suggestion of male bonding between Boswell and the major grows in *Lady Chatterley* into Mellors's past with "the colonel who had loved him and whom he had loved" (*LCL* 192), a relationship that also draws on "The Prussian Officer" at the beginning of Lawrence's career.

The parallels extend even further. In an overtly symbolic detail, Major Eastwood is a "resurrected man," for he was "buried for twenty hours under snow" until his rescue. Eastwood's counterpart, the colonel in *Lady Chatterley*, was not so fortunate, for he died of pneumonia. Both Boswell and Mellors have also almost died from pneumonia. The gipsy is qualified to bring Yvette to life, for "he's a resurrected man" (*VG* 88) himself, and Mellors observes that he has "died once or twice already . . . [yet] here I am, pegging on" (*LCL* 277). Of course in both instances the pneumonia is a deflected version of Lawrence's tuberculosis. More importantly, the resurrection motif, with its religious overtones, is central to Lawrence's powerful vision of human renewal and the life of the body. As in *The Escaped Cock*, resurrection must be of the flesh.[8]

At the least these parallels demonstrate Lawrence's economical use of his fictional materials. Certain scenes and paradigms appear and reappear throughout his fiction, revised, reworked, and presented in various shapes and sizes. However, something more is involved in the relationship between *The Virgin and the Gipsy* and *Lady Chatterley*. Lawrence began the first version of *Lady Chatterley* the same year that he wrote *The Virgin and the Gipsy*. The novella offered an appropriate myth and a convenient scaffolding on which to build. *The Virgin and the Gipsy* is a prelude to *Lady Chatterley's Lover* in the sense that the novella provided a starting-point. But beginning from that starting-point, Lawrence proceeded to construct a novel very different in most key respects.

Perhaps the most obvious difference between *The Virgin and the Gipsy* and *Lady Chatterley's Lover* is that of scale and ambitiousness. Lawrence wrote the novella quite rapidly in January 1926. The narrative, direct and spontaneous, flows along relatively unburdened by authorial commentary. The fable, rather offhand in manner, is sufficient unto itself, and if anything, the novella is somewhat underdeveloped. In contrast *Lady Chatterley* is a major fictional undertaking whose three separate versions occupied Lawrence for over sixteen months. He must have suspected that the book might be his last full-scale novel, for he seems eager—sometimes too eager—to make a definitive statement about the condition of the modern world. It would seem likely that the difference in scope between the two works has an effect on some of Lawrence's artistic choices.

Lady Chatterley's Lover is filled with detailed sexual encounters whereas the virgin and the gipsy do no more than rub each other dry with towels and huddle together for warmth during the night of the flood. Indeed, one of the purposes of the novel is to violate literary taboo and present uncensored sexuality within a serious work of fiction. In this respect *Lady Chatterley* is a culmination of Hardy's attempt in *Jude the Obscure* to write a novel that does fuller justice to human experience than was allowed by Mrs. Grundy.

A more surprising difference between novel and novella is the treatment of nature. *Lady Chatterley's Lover* is, among other things, a version of pastoral. The woods near Wragby Hall are sacred, and the coming together of Connie and Mellors partakes of the harmony of nature. One would expect nature to figure in the same way in the simplified world of *The Virgin and the Gipsy*, especially since Lawrence had written "Sun," which presents its heroine's regeneration as part of the process of nature, just a month before he wrote the novella. But nature is not an important element in *The Virgin and the Gipsy*. During the outing in chapter 3 that ultimately takes the young people to the gipsy-camp, Yvette insists they stop at Lady Louth's deer park, where the deer nestle "in the gloom of the afternoon under the oaks by the road." The hart with his antlers and the doe with "her spotted flanks" point to the meeting of the gipsy and Yvette, but these are tame deer that seem to desire the "stimulus of human company" (VG 22). The brief deer-park episode suggests the thematic possibilities of nature's involvement in the human cycle, but these possibilities are not developed. *Lady Chatterley* is a richer work of fiction partly because the relationship between the two lovers and the natural world is so impressively achieved.

Scott Sanders has commented that *The Virgin and the Gipsy* "lacks the overt social message of *Lady Chatterley's Lover*."[9] This is something of an overstatement, for *The Virgin and the Gipsy* contains an acid portrait of bourgeois English life. "The bleak stone streets" of Papplewick, its "old stone cottonmills," and the "rather ugly stone house" of the vicar and his family all define the oppressiveness of middle-class England. Yvette is stifled by the "dank air of that middle-class, degenerated comfort" (VG 10). Life at the rectory is filled with pretentiousness, false spirituality, and a blind allegiance to social convention. It offers a "complete stability, in which one could perish safely" (VG 5). The rector and his family are cut off from life, a condition Yvette finds unendurable. The grotesque old Mater may even be intended as a symbol of the dead weight of the Victorian past.

The "young rebels" of Yvette's set offer no alternative. Through them Lawrence comments on the emptiness of the postwar generation. Yvette's friends are frivolous and lacking in direction. Though "the keys of their lives were in their own hands," the keys "dangled inert" (VG 21). Yvette is caught between her constricting family and the aimless new generation. Even the Eastwoods, who live outside the rules and regulations of society, offer no real alternative, for the "little Jewess" remains "intensely moral, so moral" (VG 79), and her rebellion is willful and self-conscious.

But if *The Virgin and the Gipsy* does have a strong moral message, that message is not as front-and-center nor as fully articulated as the social commentary of *Lady Chatterley's Lover*. *Lady Chatterley*, the most didactic and schematic of Lawrence's novels, sometimes seems perilously close to a fictionalized sermon. Chapter 11, in which Connie motors to Tevershall and into the countryside on the way to Uthwaite, is an extended setpiece illustrating the "grey, gritty hopelessness" (*LCL* 206) of modern industrial society.[10] Unlike *The Virgin and the Gipsy*, *Lady Chatterley's Lover* features a social critic within the novel, for that is one of the roles played by Oliver Mellors. More dubiously, the novel has a second built-in preacher in Tommy Dukes, Connie's "oracle" (*LCL* 95), whose function is to expound the officially sanctioned Lawrencean lessons. Dukes is just one of the devices through which Lawrence recapitulates several of his indictments against modern civilization: the failure of the English aristocracy and intelligentsia and the failure of modern manhood, the substitution of empty words for human experience, the despoliation of the English countryside and community by the industrial machine. In writing what was apt to be his last full-scale novel, Lawrence wanted to make sure that his message was loud and clear. Sometimes his message is louder—and more overt—than it needs to be.

Yvette and Connie have much the same function in their respective fictions, for both are versions of the Sleeping Beauty, poised on the brink of awakening. Yvette is "tangled and tied up" (*VG* 10), but she is also "like the Lady of Shalott" (*VG* 51), waiting to be rescued. Her virginity, insisted upon in the title, is emphasized throughout the novella. She seems "so virginal" (*VG* 63), and she talks with "soft, virgin, heedless candour" (*VG* 61). She is above all virgin in the sense that she is living in potentiality, ready to be brought to life. Connie's unawakened quality is also emphasized. As she looks at herself naked in the mirror, she observes that "her body was going meaningless, going full and opaque" (*LCL* 111). Yvette has yet to enter life while Connie is fading before her time. Both are in need of the quickening they receive.

Yvette doesn't belong with her frivolous friends, for her blitheness, her generous spirit, and her independence set her apart. Nevertheless Lawrence places her squarely in the new generation as she wisely rejects the moribund values of her family but finds it difficult to know where to turn for direction. Chronologically Connie is part of the same generation, and, on a higher social plane, she and her sister have had the appropriate aimless experiences: time spent in Germany enjoying the feeling of freedom, talking endlessly about philosophy, sociology, and art, tramping "off to the forests with sturdy youths bearing guitars," and having "their tentative love-affairs by the time they were eighteen" (*LCL* 39). But while Yvette faces the future, in many ways Connie faces the past. She is a character who has been supplied with a large dose of Lawrence's conservative sexual politics.

Connie is misplaced in her modern generation and rather displaced as an aristocrat as well. She is a nostalgic throwback to an idealized earlier era of manly men and womanly women. Lawrence feels that the blurring of sexual identity is both a symptom and a cause of the sickness of modern times, but Connie Chatterley, unknown to herself, is an old-fashioned woman. The Saywell sisters, avatars of the new generation with slightly ambiguous sexuality, are "tall" and "slender" (*VG* 10) and have "bobbed hair and young-manly, deuce-take-it manners" (*VG* 8). In contrast Connie is a "ruddy, country-looking girl with soft brown hair and sturdy body" (*LCL* 38). The "female roundness" of her figure is now "out of fashion: a little too female, not enough like an adolescent boy." But though her body is "disappointed of its real womanhood, it had not succeeded in becoming boyish" (*LCL* 110–11).

While modern women have buttocks "like two collar studs" (*LCL* 77), Connie has the "nicest woman's arse as is." She is "not one o' them button-arsed lasses as should be lads." Even Mellors's touching of Connie's "two secret openings" (*LCL* 284) is by way of celebrating her abiding femaleness. In contrast the aggressive Bertha Coutts is one of those modern women with "beaks between their legs, and they tear at you with it till you're sick" (*LCL* 261). Such women are threatening to a man's malehood, but Connie knows how to be properly receptive in achieving her sexual pleasure. She follows Mellors's directions "with a queer obedience," and during intercourse she lies "quite still, in a sort of sleep" (*LCL* 163). Sleeping Beauty is not a threatening archetype.

There is something deeply conservative about Lawrence's vision of human renewal in *Lady Chatterley's Lover,* for the hope of the future is to be found in the past. Connie has a "tormented modern-woman's brain" (*LCL* 164). Her experience with Mellors shows her how to be less modern, and in the process the torment disappears. Presumably she becomes the right sort of woman to dwell in the pseudo-medieval Neverland that Mellors conjures up, where men "sing in a mass and dance the old group dances, and carve the stools they sit on, and embroider their own emblems," where "they wouldn't need money" and the "industrial problem" (*LCL* 372) is solved.

Another of Connie's old-fashioned qualities is rarely observed: her frustrated maternal feelings. This is a major aspect of her character, made clear by her concern over her unborn child, her delight in Mrs. Flint's baby daughter, her response to the pheasant chicks. When Mellors says that it seems "wrong and bitter . . . to bring a child into this world," Connie, "shocked," responds, "Then you *can't* ever really want me!" (*LCL* 279). Her fulfillment as a woman will not be complete until she has become a mother. Throughout, the portrait of Connie Chatterley is extremely traditional.

Thus a myth of sexual identity is at the heart of both *The Virgin and the Gipsy* and *Lady Chatterley's Lover.* A man should be male and a woman female, but in the modern world men and women have become more and more like one another. People once said that Mellors "had too much of the woman" (*LCL* 313) in him, but his relationship with Connie helps him clarify and assert his maleness. Yvette's young male friends dress with "effeminate discretion" (*VG* 62), and Tommy Dukes complains that modern love consists of "fellows with swaying waists fucking little jazz girls with small boy buttocks" (*LCL* 77). It is hard to take this analysis of what ails modern civilization very seriously, but convincing or not, it is a notion basic to both works. Lawrence's conservative conception of sexual identity is much more developed in the character of Connie than it is in Yvette. In Yvette he attempts a young woman of the postwar generation, striving for emancipation but caught between the old and the new. In the more considered statement that is *Lady Chatterley,* Lawrence creates a woman closer to his own heart's desire, a character shaped by his nostalgia for traditional sexual roles.

The myth of sexual identity also bears significantly on the characterization of the gipsy and the gamekeeper. One of the most quoted of Lawrence's letters is the one he wrote Witter Bynner in March 1928, repudiating the search for an ethos of male leadership that had occupied him in *Aaron's Rod, Kangaroo,* and *The Plumed Serpent.* The letter neatly articulates Lawrence's passage from the ideal of power to his new ideal of tenderness: "The hero is obsolete, and the leader of men is a back number. . . . [T]he leader-cum-follower relationship is a bore. And the new relationship will be some sort of tenderness, sensitive, between men and men and men and women." The contrast between novella and novel also seems to dramatize Lawrence's abandonment of the "one up one down, lead on I follow, *ich dien* sort of business" (*CL* 1045), particularly in the characters of Boswell and Mellors and the relationships they form with the heroines. This contrast demonstrates that *The Virgin and the Gipsy* was a transitional work for Lawrence. Yvette's gipsy, at least until the end of the novella, is a full-blown rendition of the fantasy Lawrence entertained about male domination during the leadership period. The gipsy, a one-dimensional icon of male prowess, is in sharp contrast to the fully humanized Mellors. Interestingly, however, our changed perspective on the gipsy at the conclusion of the novella seems to indicate Lawrence's own criticism of his ideal of power.

The gipsy is a figure of fantasy, concocted from the cultural myth of the darkly powerful, highly sexualized outsider. He is colorfully dressed and altogether glamorous, poised and handsome with "big, bold eyes" (*VG* 43) and "fine, quick hips" (*VG* 62). As in pulp romantic fiction, when Yvette sees him, she melts: "He stood on his limber legs, casually looking down on the group, as if from a distance, his long black lashes lifted from his full, conceited, impudent black eyes. There was something peculiarly transfusing in his stare. Yvette felt it, felt it in her knees" (*VG* 29). One of her first reflections is, "He is stronger than I am!" (*VG* 27). It is hard to find a more unadulterated embodiment of machismo in Lawrence's fiction.

The gipsy is able to "insinuate . . . a subtle suggestion of submission into his male bearing." When he speaks to Yvette, "he [looks] back into her eyes for a second, with that naked suggestion of desire which acted on her like a spell, and robbed her of her will" (*VG* 55). She is "aware of *him,* as a dark, complete power" (*VG* 70). There is no question but that this relationship (if that is the right word) is endorsed: Yvette wants "somebody, or something to have power over her" (*VG* 56).

This portrayal of the spell the gipsy casts over Yvette is highly unconvincing, not to say laughable. The central relationship is reduced to the level of pulp romantic fiction in a way that seems unworthy of a novelist capable of treating human love and sexuality with such complex understanding. It is pleasing to speculate that one of the reasons Lawrence apparently made so little effort to get the book into print might have been his subsequent rejection of such a vulgar depiction of sexual allure. At any rate, at the end of the novella Lawrence seems to back away from the vulgarity of this depiction, and in doing so he points toward Oliver Mellors.

Though the gipsy is heroic and in a real sense Yvette's savior, during the cataclysm of the flood he is scaled down to human size (*VG* 107–14). All his glamor is gone when Yvette is "aware of the sodden gipsy, in paroxysms of coughing at the head of the stairs, his cap gone, his black hair over his eyes, peering between his washed-down hair." His face is alternately "green-white" and "livid," and his teeth go "snap-snap-snap-snap, in great snaps, cutting off his words." Yvette and her gipsy wind up naked in bed together, but the encounter is not romantic or even sexual. Though it is an experience of touch, it is also an experience of "shock" and terror.

The gipsy is scaled down even further at the very end when Yvette receives his letter. The prose is commonplace and uneducated, and it is signed "Your obdt. servant Joe Boswell" (*VG* 120). This is the first time she even knows his name. The darkly handsome, romantic, mysterious unnamed gipsy has been transformed into a rather drab obedient servant with a very ordinary English name. The experience with the gipsy has brought Yvette into contact with her essential self and pointed out the direction of her own independent path. Boswell is no less revitalizing for turning out to be a flesh-and-blood human being. It is as if the flood allows Yvette to see beneath the fantasy figure. Boswell the human being, not the glamorous gipsy, brings new life to her.

Mellors's first appearance in *Lady Chatterley's Lover* is sinister and threatening. "A man with a gun strode swiftly, softly out after the dog, facing their way as if about to attack them" (*LCL* 84). But soon after Mellors makes this entrance as a latter-day Natty Bumppo, we learn that he is beleaguered and vulnerable. Unlike the gipsy, Mellors, despite his sexual potency, is never simply presented as an embodiment of male power and mystery.

The gamekeeper is only a closet proletarian. He can speak the King's English and is "a reader after all" with "books about bolshevist Russia, books of travel, a volume about the atom and the electron" (*LCL* 273) by his bedside. But what makes him an effective character— and in the process goes a long way toward making *Lady Chatterley* a moving novel—is the fact that he is not darkly mysterious and idealized but is instead vulnerable and more than a little broken. The gipsy is presented as a magic healer who casts a spell over Yvette and begins her renewal. The parable of regeneration is much more satisfying in *Lady Chatterley's Lover*, for Mellors is no less in need of rejuvenation than Connie. If he has the power to awaken her, she does no less for him.

Mellors's "narrow escape from death" and "his damaged health" (*LCL* 192) are insisted upon. The pneumonia "left my heart not so strong and the lungs not so elastic," and he is "not to make violent physical efforts" (*LCL* 254). Though he says that his cough is "nothing" (*LCL* 159), Connie and the reader know better. Like so many of Lawrence's protagonists, Mellors has a strong streak of "noli me tangere." He dreads "with a repulsion almost of death, any further close human contact." He does not want to subject himself to Connie's "female will" or her "modern female insistency" (*LCL* 132). It is as if he is an ailing organism, busily engaged in preparing himself for death, and dreading the intrusion of any further contact with the living. Indeed he is cousin-german to the man who died. But how poignant and meaningful it is that Mellors overcomes his dread and reenters the community of human tenderness. At the end of the novel Mellors is truly a resurrected man: he is learning to farm, he has fathered a child (yet unborn), and he has a strong bond with a vital young woman.

The affirmations of *Lady Chatterley's Lover* are muted and even melancholy. The novel celebrates life in the teeth of death. Tenderness and loving human contact have no enduring effect against the ubiquitous forces of annihilation. It would be simpler just to give in and die. The fact that Mellors allows himself to be awakened by touch back into life is a triumph, of the body and of the spirit as well. The handsome, aloof gipsy with his "straight nose, . . . slender mobile lips, and the level, significant stare of the black eyes" (*VG* 62) is coarse and unconvincing by contrast.

When Yvette wakes up after the flood, "her gipsy of this world's-end night" (*VG* 117) is gone. Though in her heart she moans that she loves him, "her young soul knew the wisdom of" his disappearance (*VG* 120). The novella ends openly and rather abruptly. In *The Virgin and the Gipsy* it is easy for Lawrence to present the renewal that comes with touch and passion, but it seems less easy for him to work beyond that to imagine his heroine in an ongoing, life-giving marital relationship.

The fortune-teller's prophecies of "a dark man who means good luck" and "a death in the family" come true, so we are meant to believe that Yvette will "marry when I'm twenty-three, and have heaps of money and heaps of love, and two children" (*VG* 35). The suggestion is that after her awakening through the gipsy, she will be able to find her own way within the confines of society. But Lawrence leaves this happy ending in the realm of vague prophecy, perhaps because it does sound so much like a fairy-tale ending.

And this is a final significant way in which *Lady Chatterley's Lover* diverges from *The Virgin and the Gipsy*. *Lady Chatterley* dramatizes the same myth of renewal through the flesh, but it also attempts something more difficult. *Lady Chatterley* is a story not only of passion but also of love and commitment. The future is ambiguous, and the novel ends with the lovers separated. Clifford has refused to grant a divorce. Mellors writes his long, impassioned letter (*LCL* 370–75) declaring that he loves "chastity now." "There's a bad time coming" and the world is filled with "Cliffords and Berthas, colliery companies and governments and the money-mass of people."

But as gray and destructive as people and institutions are, "all the bad times that ever have been, haven't been able to blow the crocus out." As uncertain as the future of the lovers must be, they are committed to being with each other whatever the future brings. Because of what has passed between them, "a great deal of us is together" even when they are apart. And perhaps above all there is the unborn child as a promise and living bond between them. "Her womb, that had always been shut, had opened and filled with new life" (*LCL* 185). Ursula loses Skrebensky's child at the end of *The Rainbow* and waits, more determined than ever, for the son of God who will come to her. Connie is carrying Mellors's child, and somehow the lady and the gamekeeper—no son of God but a frail, vulnerable human being— will find a way to make their future together.

Lady Chatterley's Lover is famous for its explicit sex, but the sex is not what the novel is all about. Lawrence, beleaguered and close to death himself, is in the end able to place his faith not only in the revitalizing power of sexuality but also—and more importantly—in the redemptive force of love and tenderness. *The Virgin and the Gipsy* is a stylish, modern fairy tale. *Lady Chatterley's Lover,* with its celebration of love in a world inimical to love, is a rare act of hopefulness and courage. The sex between the lady and the gamekeeper seems earnest and antiquated today, but the tenderness remains more powerful than any of the gipsy's dark glances at his English virgin.

NOTES

1. F. R. Leavis, *D. H. Lawrence: Novelist* (New York: Knopf, 1956), p. 362.

2. Mark Schorer, Introduction to *Lady Chatterley's Lover,* by D. H. Lawrence (New York: Grove [Revised Black Cat Edition], 1982), p. 16.

3. Harry T. Moore, *The Priest of Love: A Life of D. H. Lawrence* (Carbondale and Edwardsville: Southern Illinois University Press, 1974), p. 416.

4. Donald Gutierrez, *Lapsing Out: Embodiments of Death and Rebirth in the Last Writings of D. H. Lawrence* (Rutherford, N. J.: Fairleigh Dickinson University Press, 1980), p. 55.

5. I have chosen to concentrate on the novella and the final version of *Lady Chatterley.* An interesting developmental argument could be constructed, tracing important elements of *The Virgin and the Gipsy* through the three separate versions of *Lady Chatterley.* Among other things, such an argument might show how Parkin in *The First Lady Chatterley* is an intermediary between the gipsy and Mellors.

6. D. H. Lawrence, *The Virgin and the Gipsy* (New York: Bantam, 1968), p. 69; hereafter cited in the text as VG.

7. Lawrence's fullest account of doggishness is found in his "John Galsworthy" essay (*Phoenix* 539–50), which dates from the same period.

8. Resurrection of the body is discussed at length in *John Thomas and Lady Jane* (see *JTLJ* 61–65).

9. Scott Sanders, *D. H. Lawrence: The World of the Five Major Novels* (New York: Viking, 1974), p. 177.

10. Tevershall is an "underworld" with "something uncanny and underground about it all" (*LCL* 205). The motor trip is Connie's heroic journey to the underworld, preparatory to her rebirth. Cf. Dennis Jackson, "The 'Old Pagan Vision': Myth and Ritual in *Lady Chatterley's Lover*," *D. H. Lawrence Review* 11, no. 3 (Fall 1978): 261–62.

DENNIS JACKSON

Literary Allusions in
Lady Chatterley's Lover

Allusion in D. H. Lawrence's fiction is never the innovative, virtuoso performance it is in the works of Joyce, Pound, and Eliot. But Lawrence was throughout his life a voracious reader—Jessie Chambers recalls that he "seemed to read everything"—and his own writings are often filled with ideas and expressions gathered from other authors. His last novel, *Lady Chatterley's Lover,* is saturated with allusions to the Bible, hymns, popular songs, classical myths, and other literary works from Plato to Proust. These references typify Lawrence's analogical method, becoming a primary means by which he defines characters and themes and creates dramatic irony. Frequently he uses allusions to guide the reader's response to the antithetical philosophical worlds between which his heroine moves—the unvital realm of Wragby Hall, where the "life of the mind" and spiritual consciousness are paramount, and the vital Pan world of Wragby Wood, where the "life of the body" and intuitive consciousness reign. In the novel's thematic structure the use of allusion helps create a philosophic subtext that awakens the reader to the larger implications of the lovers' sexual and psychic regeneration. In this essay I shall focus on the pattern of allusion that creates this subtext: the allusions characterizing Sir Clifford Chatterley and his Wragby Hall circle. With these allusions Lawrence discredits certain well-entrenched philosophical concepts ranging from Platonic idealism to modern scientific materialism.

Allusions characterize the failing relationship of Clifford and his wife, and even figure prominently in Connie's ultimate rejection of him; she reacts bitterly to his reading tastes (his liking for Proust makes him seem "very dead, really") and to his tendency to "[turn] everything into words." When Clifford responds to forest flowers with two quotations, "Sweeter than the lids of Juno's eyes" and "Thou still unravished bride of quietness," Connie despairs: "How she hated words, always coming between her and life: they did the ravishing . . . ready-made words and phrases, sucking all the life-sap out of living things" (*LCL* 135–37). Clifford has quoted first from Shakespeare's *The Winter's Tale* and then from Keats's "Ode on a Grecian Urn." Perdita invokes Proserpina to supply her with spring flowers—among them "violets dim, / But sweeter than the lids of Juno's eyes / Or Cytherea's breath" (IV. iv. 120–22). Connie objects, however, that she sees no "connection" between Clifford's quotation and the "actual violets." In Keats's ode, the speaker looks on the urn and projects himself into its "flowery tale." Conversely, Clifford looks at the real flowers and tries to translate them into art. His response is neither immediate nor vital, but indirect, literary, and cerebral; typically, he substitutes words for feelings. Connie's later remark about Proust—"He doesn't have feelings, he only has streams of words about feelings" (*LCL* 252)—reflects the way she comes to feel about her husband.

The opposition between words and experience also informs the scene where Clifford reads Racine to Connie soon after her third sexual encounter with Mellors. She sits, "gone in her own soft rapture," the keeper "in all her veins," while "the noise" of Clifford's reading continues; "of the Racine she heard not one syllable." There is exquisite irony here. "One gets all one wants out of Racine," Clifford declares. "Emotions that are ordered and given shape are more important than disorderly emotions." Connie, fulfilled by the ecstatic "after-humming" of her own disorderly emotions, leaves without kissing her husband goodnight; upset, he thinks that "even if the kiss was but a formality, it was on such formalities that life depends" (*LCL* 188–90). Insisting as he does on "formalities," on "order" in life (*LCL* 366), on reason, Clifford feels a natural affinity for Racine, and his defense of the playwright reveals much about his own personality.

After Connie exits, Clifford's dread of "annihilation" comes upon him. Alone at night he feels "lifeless," but desperately stays awake, "as if he were triumphing over life in spite of life. 'Who knoweth the mysteries of the will—for it can triumph even against the angels—' " (*LCL* 190). Lawrence alludes to the epigraph to Poe's "Ligeia": "Who knoweth the mysteries of the will, with its vigor? For God is but a great will pervading all things by nature of its intentness. Man doth not yield himself to the angels, nor unto death utterly, save only through the weakness of his feeble will." Ligeia, who dies reciting part of this quotation from Joseph Glanvill,[1] never yields herself "unto death utterly"; with her "gigantic volition" she overcomes death and returns to her lover by supernaturally usurping the body of his second wife. Lawrence once called Poe's tale "a ghastly story of the assertion of the human will . . . against death itself,"[2] while condemning the two lovers in "Ligeia" for shaping their "spiritual, nervous love" into a destructive "battle of wills" (SCAL 68–69). In *Lady Chatterley* he appropriates Poe's story for his own analogical purposes, using the allusion to define the way Clifford uses his own "gigantic volition" to resist death and the great "bruise" of the war. Two pages earlier, Lady Chatterley thinks of her husband in terms as applicable to Poe's heroine as to Clifford: "What a strange creature. . . . One of those creatures of the afterwards, that have no soul, but an extra-alert will" (*LCL* 189). Both Connie and Clifford's relationship and that of Ligeia and her husband are characterized by a struggle of "wills."[3] Connie is repulsed by her husband's "cold, inflexible will"; he in turn denounces the fact that "the lady loves her will" (*LCL* 189–90), recalling the last line of a traditional four-line song called "The Four Loves": "The Hart he loves the high-wood, / the Hare he loves the hill, / The Knight he loves his bright sword, / the Lady loves her will."[4] Moreover, Ligeia and her mate, like the Chatterleys, avidly pursue "the mental life." Ligeia, a woman of "immense" knowledge, joins her husband in "metaphysical investigation," just as Connie collaborates on Clifford's stories. But whereas Ligeia submits to "the vampire of her husband's consciousness" (SCAL 69), Connie does not. Though Clifford thinks of his wife as "embedded in his will" (*LCL* 365), she finally frustrates him by fleeing Wragby. The "Ligeia" allusion thus yields a richer, fuller text for the reader who recognizes Lawrence's source and activates the two texts simultaneously.

Moreso than the other characters in *Lady Chatterley*, Clifford is characterized by allusions, which serve to enhance the ironies of his character and to associate him with what Lawrence regarded as the twin evils of modern life—the "mental life" and scientific materialism. Clifford is made the living image of much that his creator detested in Western civilization, the chief angel of a fallen world resulting from man's over-reliance on "mental-spiritual" modes of consciousness. This fallen world and its potential redemption are the focus of a number of statements made by Clifford's friend Tommy Dukes, a chief spokesman for Lawrence. Dukes's declarations are often informed by the myth of the Fall and by the Christian belief in the Resurrection. He prophesies a "resurrection of the body," a "democracy of touch" that will come after men have "shoved the cerebral stone away a bit" (*LCL* 117), alluding to passages in the Synoptic gospels which describe the removal of the stone before Christ's sepulcher; but the entombed body is not just Christ's—it is that of all men entombed by the "stone" of spiritual-mental consciousness. Dukes similarly uses images of the Fall when he tells the Wragby intellectuals: "[W]hile you *live* your life, you are in some way an organic whole with all life. But once you start the mental life you pluck the apple. You've severed the connection between the apple and the tree: the organic connection . . . you've fallen off the tree" (*LCL* 75). In Lawrence's view man fell from grace in ancient Greece, when he "ate the apple and became endowed with . . . mental consciousness" (*Phoenix II* 624) in the age of Platonic/Socratic rationalism. Plato, insisting that man's nature is essentially spiritual and that man should subjugate his dark "lower" faculties in order to give ascendancy to the "light of reason," was a natural enemy to Lawrence, and the frequent allusions to the *Dialogues* in all three versions of *Lady Chatterley* reflect the way Lawrence regarded his novel as an assault on the tradition of scientific rationalism which Socrates and Plato had initiated.

Dukes's speech on "fallen" man is a direct response to Plato's epistemology expressed in the *Theaetetus.* In arguing that "real knowledge comes out of the whole corpus of the consciousness; out of your belly and your penis as much as out of your . . . mind and . . . reason" (*LCL* 74–75), Dukes is countering Socrates' assertion that "knowledge . . . is not to be found in the sensations we undergo, but in our thought about them; it is only by the latter that we make contact with experience and truth" (*Theaetetus* 186 D).[5] Here and elsewhere in the *Dialogues* (for instance, in *The Republic* Book VII and in the *Phaedo* 79–80), Socrates asserts that sensation deceives man, yielding an unworthy copy of ultimate reality, and argues that real knowledge can be derived only through "properly mental activity" (*Theaetetus* 187 A), which acts upon reports of the sense organs. Dukes's refutation echoes Lawrence's own earlier statements about "blood-knowledge" and about Plato. For instance, in a 1915 letter to Bertrand Russell he had observed that our collective tragedy "is that the mental and nerve consciousness exerts a tyranny over the blood-consciousness. . . . Plato was the same" (*CL* 393).

Clifford's identification with Platonism is most obvious in *The First Lady Chatterley.* His wife thinks of him as "the speculative spaniel of Plato" (*FLC* 62), and the Chatterleys often converse in the "symbols of Plato's myths" (*FLC* 20), on one occasion thoroughly dissecting the Phaedrus myth. Eventually, however, Constance rebels against Platonism, just as she does in version three, and concludes that Clifford's "heaven of the pure abstraction" is but a "prison" (*FLC* 22) and that her own preference is for the "immortality of the flesh" (*FLC* 48). The Platonic allusions in version three, though less insistent, remain a major vehicle by which Lawrence explores his philosophic concerns and characterizes Chatterley and his friends. The attack on Socrates and Plato is launched early, when Lawrence recounts several of the "famous evenings" at Wragby Hall. During one typical gathering, the issues of love, sex, and marriage are debated by two-dimensional characters who represent antithetical philosophies: to Hammond, marriage means "a comfortable house" for the "life of the mind"; to May, sex is merely an "interchange of sensations" (*LCL* 69); and for neither is sex a vital act. This after-dinner disputation on "the sexual problem" (*LCL* 68–78) forms a rough parallel to Plato's *Symposium,* where, after a dinner party, Socrates and his circle discuss the general question, "What is Love?"[6] The Wragby guests display the same "mental friction" (as Dukes labels it) that characterizes Plato's urbane but ironic disputants, and Lawrence unquestionably has the *Dialogues* in mind as he describes Clifford and his friends. After remarking on the Wragby intellectuals' "spiteful" talk, Dukes says: "[T]he mental life seems to flourish with its roots in spite. . . . Always has been so! Look at Socrates, in Plato, and his bunch around him! The sheer . . . joy in pulling somebody else to bits. . . . Protagoras, or whoever it was! And Alcibiades, and all the other little disciple dogs joining in the fray!" (*LCL* 73–74). (*Protagoras* and *Alcibiades* are titles of other *Dialogues,* and Alcibiades, a Greek general, participates in the *Symposium.*)

Clifford is especially linked with Platonic thought in the last half of *Lady Chatterley.* In chapter 13 Connie accompanies her husband and his motorized wheelchair into Wragby Wood:

> "I ride upon the achievements of the mind of man [brags Clifford], and that beats a horse."
>
> "I suppose it does. And the souls in Plato riding up to heaven in a two-horse chariot would go in a Ford car now," she said.
>
> "Or a Rolls-Royce. Plato was an aristocrat!"
>
> "Quite! No more black horse to thrash and maltreat. Plato never thought we'd go one better than his black steed and his white steed, and have no steeds at all, only an engine!" [*LCL* 235]

The irony appears later in the scene, when the chair stalls amid bluebells, rendering Clifford a helpless prisoner. He pits his mind against the chair, trying to will it to move, but ultimately he is forced to summon the gamekeeper, whose bodily strength frees the chair. Such a symbolic opposition of mind and body is seen also throughout the *Phaedrus,* which the Chatterleys allude to. Plato's argument concerns the reasons why a philosopher should welcome release from the body, in the certainty that the soul is immortal. By introducing the *Phaedrus* myth into *The First Lady Chatterley,* Lawrence indicates how much Clifford's mentality has been shaped by the *Dialogue:* in the baronet's mind, he and his wife are, in their sexless marriage, "like two souls free from the body and all its weariness, two souls going hand in hand along the upper road that skirts the heaven of perfection" (*FLC* 18). Socrates in the *Phaedrus* (253 D–254 E) describes the nature of man's soul in terms of two winged horses, a "good" white one and a "bad" black one, drawing a charioteer (man) toward the heavenly fields of light where truth, goodness, and beauty exist. When the charioteer sees a "vision of love," the black steed surges wildly toward the beloved, but is restrained. Once subjugated, the black horse follows the charioteer's will and they reach the heavenly fields. All of this is meant to illustrate Socrates' idea of the conflict between those forces of the psyche that urge an individual to seek gratification and those that urge caution and restraint. The obedient white horse represents those idealistic impulses of the psyche that cause man to be ruled by fear and shame and the love of honor, while the dark horse is, as Constance explains, a symbol of "the body straining after the goal of its own gratifications" (*FLC* 21). According to Socrates, and to his many European followers, the best men restrain the steed of passion.

But of course Lawrence disagreed, and in *The First Lady Chatterley* (*FLC* 18–22) full sympathy is given to the black horse. Clifford accepts the imagery of "the two horses that draw the chariot of the soul," but his wife vigorously declares that she will let her own dark horse "run right to his goal." The Phaedrus myth thus accentuates the opposed philosophies of the Chatterleys and illuminates the heroine's internal struggle: like the soul in the Socratic mythos, Constance must decide whether to follow the dictates of her "white horse of pure yearning" (and remain faithful to the ideal of her marriage) or to follow the instinctive urges of her "black horse" (leading her to union with the keeper). In *John Thomas and Lady Jane,* the *Phaedrus* material is pared to less than two pages (*JTLJ* 80–81), and though it is reduced even further in *Lady Chatterley's Lover* to the brief conversation I quoted earlier, that minimal allusion to the myth of the two horses still affords Lawrence maximum symbolic effect as he treats the passion/reason dichotomy. In the final version, he uses the Phaedrus myth to voice his complaints that, for passionless modern man, there is "no more black horse to . . . maltreat" (*LCL* 235) and that the "engine" has replaced the "steed" in men's lives and imaginations (later, in *Apocalypse,* he complains that his contemporaries have "lost the horse," the "symbol of surging potency," in their psyches[7]).

After the Chatterleys' brief discussion of the Phaedran charioteer, the baronet's chair stalls and Mellors subsequently joins with Connie to push Clifford out of the forest, in what amounts to a rite of expulsion. Throughout this important chapter, allusions—to the Bible, to Juvenal, to British and American poems, to Proust, and especially to Plato's *Republic*—are expressive components of Lawrence's art. It is here that Connie most emphatically rejects her husband, and the allusions help reveal her reasons. Throughout the wheelchair scene she and Clifford debate the justice of a British economic system wherein one class are "rulers" and the other "servers," leading her to recognize and reject the inhumanity of her husband's ruthless paternalism. His truculence is on display throughout chapter 13, especially when he and the keeper contend over the stalled chair. But Clifford loses the battle with Mellors, who in effect succeeds to the kingdom. Connie herself views the clash between the two men as a contest for power, for the right to "rule." Throughout the chapter, she and Clifford lengthily discuss the issue of "ruling," and she ultimately protests to him, "You don't rule. . . . You only bully with your money" (*LCL* 252–53). By that time she has realized for the first time that she "definitely hated Clifford" and that she cannot "go on living with him." Thus usurped, Clifford suffers a symbolic death, as his wife suddenly wishes him "obliterated" and thinks of him as a cold "skeleton," a man "very dead" (*LCL* 250–53).

Clifford's attitudes toward political power and business ethics are well elucidated by references to Plato's *Republic*. Chapter 13, more vividly than any other passage in Lawrence's fiction, indicates the influence of the Platonic dialogues. The influence is not limited to ideas borrowed and personified in a character for purposes of refutation. It bears directly on the form of *Lady Chatterley*. In his 1923 essay "Surgery for the Novel—or a Bomb," pondering the death of modern "self-conscious" fiction in Proust and Joyce, Lawrence had written:

> If you wish to look into the past for what-next books, you can go back to the Greek philosophers. Plato's Dialogues are queer little novels. It seems to me it was the greatest pity in the world, when philosophy and fiction got split. They used to be one, right from the days of myth. Then they went and parted. . . . The two should come together again—in the novel. [*Phoenix* 520]

In passages like the wheelchair scene Lawrence was making his own attempt to bring fiction and philosophy "together again." More directly than the earlier Wragby Hall scenes recall the *Symposium*, the discussion in the wheelchair scene parallels that in Book I of the *Republic*. That book records a Socratic conversation on the question "what is justice?" and on the related topics of political power and the "function" of the individual in society; Socrates and his acquaintances debate whether justice can be identified with business morality and whether might makes right. These are precisely the issues disputed by the Chatterleys during their visit to Wragby Wood.

When Connie laments the rancor that exists between British ruling and serving classes, and wonders if there could be "a mutual understanding," her husband responds, "Absolutely: when they [the workers] realize that the industry comes before the individual" (*LCL* 236). His comment recalls the Platonic ideal community ("larger than an individual," formed "to satisfy our many varied needs") delineated in Book II of the *Republic* (368 E–369 C). Clifford then defends the ownership of property: "The point is *not*: take all thou hast and give to the poor, but use all thou hast to encourage the industry and give work to the poor" (*LCL* 237). He reverses Luke 18:22, where Christ tells the rich man to "sell all that thou hast, and distribute to the poor" in order to "have treasure in heaven." Clifford's Tory paternalism, as Connie realizes, is no benevolent, New Testament sort of Charity, but rather a harsh economic tyranny. The disparity between masters and masses, he argues, is the result of fate: somebody must be "boss of the show," and industrial owners are the ones "fated" to live up to the "responsibility of their own boss-ship." The aristocratic Wragbys and Shipleys have given the colliers political liberty, education, and everything "worth having" (*LCL* 237).

Such ideas of "boss-ship" come straight from Book I of the *Republic*, where Socrates declares that the "true" ruler is the honest man who reluctantly assumes political power because no one else is capable, and who rules always with the interests of the masses in mind. Socrates' remarks are in reply to the cynical sophist Thrasymachus, who has argued that "justice is nothing else than the interest of the stronger," that in any state the governing party makes the moral code and legislates to maintain its domination and its own interest. This is the justice of nature and of the strong, and the supreme embodiment of this ideal is the successful tyrant—just such a tyrant as Clifford shows himself to be in this chapter. He argues that the industrial captains, possessed of superior wisdom, have generously assumed power over the helpless workers "for their own good." But Connie disagrees. "All the things you mention now [political liberty, etc.], Wragby and Shipley *sell* them to the people, at a good profit," she complains. "You don't give one heart-beat of real sympathy. And besides, who has . . . given them this industrial horror?" (*LCL* 236, 238). Clifford counters that the workers themselves are to blame, that they are "animals" little different from "Nero's mine slaves." "The masses are unalterable," he declares. "*Panem et circenses!* Only today education is one of the bad substitutes for a circus" (*LCL* 239). He is alluding to Juvenal's tirade, in the tenth satire, against "the mob of Remus," who compass their own destruction by misguided wishes for only two things: bread and circuses.[8] The masses, being what they are, will need ruling till time ends, Clifford argues, and he proclaims arrogantly: "I can do my share of ruling . . . and give me a son, and he will be able to rule his portion after me." When Connie reminds him that such a son may not be his own, of his own "ruling class," Clifford again directly echoes the *Republic:* "It is not who begets us that mat- ters, but where fate places us. Place any child among the ruling classes, and he will grow up, to his own extent, a ruler. . . . It is the overwhelming pressure of environment." In Plato's Commonwealth, environment is more important than heredity; and people become specialized (and "class"-ified) according to their ability to fulfill a particular "function" (*Republic*, Book III). Clifford, thinking of Plato, tells Connie: "Aristocracy is a function, a part of fate. And the masses are a functioning of another part of fate. The individual hardly mat- ters. It is a question of which function you are brought up to and adapted to. . . . When it comes to expressive or executive function- ing, I believe there is a gulf and an absolute one, between the ruling and the serving classes. The two functions are opposed. And the function determines the individual" (*LCL* 239–40).

Similarly, Gerald Crich in *Women in Love* believes that "position and authority" are "the right thing" because they are "functionally necessary."[9] "What mattered was the pure instrumentality of the indi- vidual. As a man as of a knife: does it cut well? Nothing else mattered. Everything in the world has its function, and is good or not good in so far as it fulfils this function. . . . Gerald himself, who was responsible for all this industry, was he a good director? If he were, he had fulfilled his life" (*WL* 295–96). Gerald refers to a passage in Book I of the *Republic* (353 A),[10] where Socrates and Thrasymachus agree that cer- tain things have a "function"—an eye for seeing, an ear for hearing, a knife for cutting. The "function" of a thing, Socrates says, is the work that it alone can do. Its specific virtue is the quality essential to the right performance of its function. Man's virtue is to perform his "function" well. This concept relates to the question "what is justice?" that informs this book of the *Republic:* since no man can do all tasks equally well, there must be a specialization of labor resulting in a form of "justice," each man performing the "single job for which he is naturally fitted" (*Republic* 370 C). Thus both Chatterley and Crich, arguing for the "instrumentality of the individual," follow Platonic concepts.

Lady Chatterley perceives the cruel dishonesty in her husband's economic attitudes and the irony in his statements on "boss-ship": "You don't rule," she tells him bitterly. "You have only got more than your share of the money, and make people work for you . . . or threaten them with starvation" (*LCL* 251–52). In the *Republic* Thrasymachus loses the argument to Socrates over the question of whether might makes right, but in Clifford's economic world, the sophist's philosophy prevails. The baronet mouths Socrates' ethical and political theories, but practices Thrasymachus's philosophy; "justice" in the Midlands is just what Clifford and other industrial captains say it is.

Several other allusions in the wheelchair scene characterize Clifford. When the baronet's wheelchair rolls downhill through a patch of blue hyacinths, the narrator exclaims: "Oh last of all ships, through the hyacinthian shallows! Oh pinnace on the last wild waters, sailing in the last voyage of our civilisation! Whither, Oh weird wheeled ship, your slow course steering! . . . Clifford sat at the wheel of adventure. . . . Oh captain, my Captain, our splendid trip is done!" (*LCL* 241). Lawrence has spent the previous paragraphs preparing for this extended metaphor, which makes Clifford the "Captain" of the chair-"ship" that steers a "channel" through a flowery sea. The mock grandeur of the scene is established by the author's repeated Whitmanesque apostrophe to the chair ("Oh last of all ships . . . Oh pinnace . . . Oh weird wheeled ship"), by the suggested Homeric epithet "hyacinthine," and by allusions to poems by Robert Bridges and Walt Whitman. "Whither, Oh weird wheeled ship, your slow course steering!" roughly reproduces the opening of Bridges's "A Passer-By," which addresses a magnificent sailing ship: "Whither, O splendid ship, thy white sails crowding . . . / Whither away, fair rover, and what thy quest?" Lawrence's allusion, in reference to Clifford's chair, yields trenchant irony: the vessel in "A

Passer-By" is a "stately" ship moving in accord with nature, propelled by the wind, but Clifford's own "wheeled ship" is a weird, ignoble machine jolting over flowers.

Similar irony prevails in the line "Oh captain, my Captain, our splendid trip is done," which echoes the opening of Whitman's "O Captain! my Captain! our fearful trip is done." That lyric, in the "Memories of President Lincoln" section of *Leaves of Grass*, laments a captain who brings his ship to port but arrives there "Fallen cold and dead" (line 8). Similarly at the conclusion of his own "voyage" through Wragby forest, Clifford seems to Connie "cold" and "dead" (*LCL* 252–53). Whitman portrays Lincoln as a wise, sensitive leader, the sort of just ruler Socrates describes in the *Republic.* But Clifford is hardly Lincoln-like as a "captain" of the industrial state, and consequently suffers diminution in the comparison implicit in the Whitman allusion. The baronet has entered the forest playfully portraying himself as a questing knight, "Sir Clifford on his foaming steed," and then seriously as a stalwart "boss" of industry, but he is deflated as the scene progresses: immediately after the apostrophe is made to him and his chair, his wife surreptitiously arranges a rendezvous with the keeper, and the "Captain" and his "wheeled ship" founder helplessly in a sea of hyacinths. The irony is conclusive. Moments earlier Clifford, following Socrates, has asserted that "the function determines the individual," only to suffer a ludicrous failure of "leadership." His machine ceases to work, he tries but fails to will the chair into motion, and he is finally a "prisoner," wholly at the mercy of his "serving class" gamekeeper. The impotence of his engine also reflects his inability to "function" as a sexual mate for his wife, whereas the keeper's act of pushing the chair through Wragby Wood suggests the other way he supplements his employer's power, through his phallic union with Connie.

Shortly after the wheelchair incident, Connie finds Clifford reading Proust and says of that author: "He bores me: all that sophistication! He doesn't have feelings, he only has streams of words about feelings" (*LCL* 252). Lawrence shared her attitude. "*Proust* too much water-jelly," he wrote in 1927. "I can't read him" (*CL* 991). For Lawrence, Proust was a "grand pervert" who tried to "intellectualise and so utterly falsify the phallic consciousness" (*CL* 1049). In *Lady*

Chatterley the association of Clifford with Proust illuminates the baronet's character. Proust may have been in Lawrence's mind when he described how Clifford's fictional "analysis of people and motives . . . leaves everything in bits at the end" (*LCL* 89–90)—a description strikingly like that made of Proust's art in "Surgery for the Novel" (*Phoenix* 517–18). Lady Chatterley's criticism of Proust is leveled at not only Clifford's reading tastes but his attitudes as well. When she complains of Proust's "streams of words about feelings," she is clearly recalling Clifford's own recent words about the ruling class taking "responsibility" for helping the masses and his subsequent "stupidly insentient" treatment of the keeper. Further, her weariness over Proust's "self-important mentalities" obliquely rejects Clifford's afternoon discourse on Platonic concepts and Wragby's "mental life" in general. Finally, the exchange about Proust reinforces the idea of Clifford's symbolic death at the end of this chapter: his reading of Proust makes him seem "very dead" to Connie (*LCL* 253). From this death-in-life at Wragby she flees, as the chapter closes, slipping into the wood for her assignation at the keeper's cottage, where she will make another bold step toward a vitalistic life.

Later in the novel another complex of allusions, again involving one of Plato's dialogues, reveals the extent to which Clifford has become aware of his wife's affair. In the second letter that he writes to Connie while she vacations in Venice, Clifford alludes to the *Phaedo*, Cellini's *Autobiography*, Rabelais, the Marquis de Sade, and a couple of lyrics. His letter describes the scandal caused by the return of Bertha, who charges Mellors with "unspeakable things" during their marriage and with "keeping" women at his cottage. Reporting the local gossip, Clifford writes: "I have been to the depths of the muddy lives of the Bertha Couttses of this world, and when, released from the current of gossip, I slowly rise to the surface again, I look at the daylight in wonder that it ever should be." He then extends the water metaphor:

> ". . .[O]ur world, which appears to us the surface of all things, is really the *bottom* of a deep ocean. . . . Only occasionally the soul rises gasping . . . up to the surface of the ether, where there is true

air. . . . [T]he air we normally breathe is a kind of water, and men and women are a species of fish.

". . . It is our mortal destiny . . . to prey upon the ghastly subaqueous life of our fellow-men. . . . But our immortal destiny is to escape, once we have swallowed our swimmy catch, up again into the bright ether, bursting out from the surface of Old Ocean into real light. Then one realises one's eternal nature.

". . . Carnal appetite makes one seize a beakful of prey: then up, up again . . . from the wet into the dry." [*LCL* 334]

This passage follows the story of the "hollows" in Plato's *Phaedo*, wherein Socrates pictures the destiny of souls, using an ostensibly scientific account of the earth. The earth is round, he says, but men do not live on its surface, rather in certain wet "hollows" that they mistake for the "actual earth" above. "We . . . imagine ourselves to be living on its surface; and we call the air the heaven. . . . [But] if one of us could get to [the air] . . . or acquire wings and fly aloft, then just as a fish which gets his head above water in this everyday world can see its sights, he would behold the sights of the world above; and . . . realize that *there* was the real heaven, the genuine daylight" (*Phaedo* 108 E–110 A).

Obviously Clifford's letter has been informed by this fanciful myth. His diction and imagery closely echo Plato's, and he is clearly following Socrates as he metaphorically envisions men as "fish" who may emerge from their watery world into the "dry" realm of "real light." Most important, Clifford's letter follows the *Phaedo* myth in separating flesh from spirit. Socrates argues that man should make a daily effort to separate body from soul in order to live in a world of pure ideas and to prepare for the inevitability of death, when the discarnate soul of "righteous" men, "delivered from the prison-house" of earth, will live in the "world above" the "hollows" (*Phaedo* 114 B–C). But Socrates has personal reasons for exploring his subject—in prison at Athens, he is only a few hours away from death by hemlock. We subsequently discover that Clifford, too, on the occasion of his writing to Connie, has special personal reasons for being fascinated by the notion of an ethereal "actual earth" of discarnate beings. His *Phaedo* allusions are part of a concentrated effort to deal with his discovery that his wife has been implicated in a crude scandal. As

Connie realizes upon receiving his letter, Clifford is "evidently upset." In this context, the impotent husband's expression of disdain for the flesh, for what he calls "carnal appetite," explains his attraction to the Platonic story of the "hollows," with its contrast of earthly misery and heavenly bliss.

Clifford's earlier letter to Connie had dealt casually with the "local excitement" caused by Bertha's return. That letter had seemed detached and, in its allusions, lightly mocking, as Clifford recounted how the "manhandled Venus" had returned to her "Apollo" (*LCL* 328). By the time he writes again, knowing that his own wife has been "manhandled" by this Apollo, a new intensity marks his correspondence. Still, we have to read yet another letter, from Mellors to Connie, before we can be certain how much Clifford *knows* about his wife's affair. The keeper's blunt letter is an ironic gloss on his employer's correspondence. "The cat is out of the bag," Mellors announces directly; Bertha has identified Lady Chatterley as his "paramour," and Clifford has consequently brought an injunction against Bertha and has fired the keeper (*LCL* 337). Mellors's letter is short and to the point. Clifford's, by contrast, is long, and though it persistently circles "the scandal," it avoids mentioning that Lady Chatterley herself has been implicated. "The cat" never quite gets "out of the bag" in Clifford's correspondence.

Mellors reports that during his interview with Clifford, the baronet had "talked around things" (*LCL* 338). That is precisely what Chatterley is doing in his second letter to Connie—*talking around things*, and using allusions to the *Phaedo* and other works to do so. For example, he reports Bertha's accusations that Mellors had done "beastly things" to her during their conjugal life, and though Clifford never explicates those "unspeakable things," his allusions show that he believes Mellors guilty of anal copulation. After reporting Bertha's accusations, Clifford writes: "Humanity has always had a strange avidity for unusual sexual postures, and if a man likes to use his wife, as Benvenuto Cellini says, 'in the Italian way,' well that is a matter of taste. But I had hardly expected our game-keeper to be up to so many tricks" (*LCL* 335). Clifford has undoubtedly considered that the keeper may have performed such "beastly" acts on Connie too. Certainly the Cellini allusion provides evidence that Lawrence had buggery in mind while narrating the "night of sensual passion," wherein Connie experiences "rather awful sensuality" (*LCL* 311–13). Some of the most meaningful hints that the "arse" or "tail" (to use Lawrence's words) has been involved in Mellors's sex acts with Bertha—and, by implication, Connie—come from allusions in Clifford's letter. In *The Autobiography of Benvenuto Cellini,* the artist recounts how he had been accused in an Italian court of having performed a "filthy practice" with his former model and mistress, Caterina, who had claimed that "I had used her in the Italian fashion, that is to say, unnaturally, like a sodomite."[11] The judge had clarified Caterina's meaning: "She means that you did it by another way than the way for begetting children." Thus when Clifford refers to the "unusual sexual postures" used by Mellors and Bertha, and alludes to Cellini, he is likely thinking of anal intercourse.

Two other allusions further suggest that Clifford is associating Mellors's sexual acts with anal copulation. In his letter Clifford writes:

> [Mellors] goes about as usual, with his Miller-of-the-Dee air, I care for nobody, no not I, if nobody cares for me! Nevertheless, I shrewdly suspect he feels like a dog with a tin can tied to its tail. . . . [In] the village the women call away their children if he is passing, as if he were the Marquis de Sade in person. He goes on with a certain impudence, but I am afraid the tin can is firmly tied to his tail, and that inwardly he repeats, like Don Rodrigo in the Spanish ballad: "Ah, now it bites me where I most have sinned!" [*LCL* 336]

Clifford first quotes Isaac Bickerstaff's ballad "The Miller of the Dee," whose refrain is, "I care for nobody, no, not I / If nobody cares for me."[12] The other allusions here tell us considerably more about Clifford's attitudes toward the keeper. Sade and Rodrigo are both associated in the minds of students of literature with animalistic sexuality. Sade, because his books and plays depict various sexual perversities, has become a figure of monstrous sexual fantasy, but of more significance to *Lady Chatterley* is the fact that, of all literary figures, he is the one that readers stereotypically associate with sodomy. Buggery clearly appealed to him more than normal intercourse (as Anthony Burgess observes, Sade "abhors the womb, and therefore sodomy . . . rules all desire" for him[13]), and he expressed this preference in one book after another, especially *Juliette, Justine, 120 Days of Sodom,* and *Philosophy in the Boudoir*. It seems no accident that Clifford, just after recalling Cellini's passage on sex performed "in the Italian fashion," would think to compare Mellors with Sade.

The exclamation, "Ah, now it bites me where I most have sinned!" is Lawrence's rendering of a passage from "The Penitence of Don Roderick," a Spanish ballad that recounts the downfall of a medieval monarchy. Don Roderick (Rodrigo), the last of the Visigothic kings, was blamed for allowing the Moors into Spain, allegedly because of his involvement in an adulterous affair. Lawrence probably knew the story as it appeared in J. G. Lockhart's translation of *Ancient Spanish Ballads* (1823), which had been reprinted frequently through the nineteenth century. According to these ballads, Roderick became fatally enamored of Alcava, the daughter of one of his nobles; in her father's absence, the king, who was married, forced her into a sexual affair. In retaliation, her father helped the Moors enter Spain. In "The Penitence of Don Roderick," the deposed king flees to a holy man who reveals that, for penance, the king must make his bed in a tomb that holds a two-headed serpent. The snake eats the king's genitals with one head and his heart with the other, and, in the passage that Clifford alludes to, the king tells the eremite: "He eats me now, he eats me now, I feel the adder's bite, / The part that was most sinning my bedfellow doth rend" (lines 50–51). Although Don Roderick is never charged with having forced Alcava into anal intercourse, Clifford uses "The Penitence of Don Roderick" to hint that Mellors, having engaged in sodomy, is now paying for it. As G. Wilson Knight has pointed out, the word "tail" is used in *Lady Chatterley* as a synonym for "rump,"[14] and the paragraph in which Clifford mentions Don Rodrigo has a "rump" orientation: besides the reference to Sade, there is the repeated simile comparing Mellors to a dog with a can tied to his "tail," suggesting that the posterior is the place where the keeper most has "sinned." Like the *Phaedo*, the story of Rodrigo, demonstrating that carnality leads to ruin, naturally appeals to Clifford when he writes to Connie.

Clearly, Clifford aims to defile the image of the gamekeeper. He identifies Mellors with Cellini, Rabelais, Sade, Rodrigo—sexual sinners all—and simultaneously imagines his adversary punished for offending "common decency" (*LCL* 335). Of course Mellors certainly is not suffering for his adulterous acts, and neither does Connie accept the vision of the keeper—as a Sade-istic figure of erotic abandon—that Clifford is trying to create with the allusions. Yet these allusions are successful, in the way they help Clifford cope with his domestic trials. By casting Mellors as a *literary* figure, Clifford in effect removes him from the reality of his own existence at Wragby and translates him into an abstraction. Though Clifford assures his wife that, with the keeper's departure, "the place will soon become normal again," he is "evidently upset" and doubtful of the future, and in the very act of writing his letter to Connie, he is steeling himself against the inevitability of her desertion of him. As he closes, he returns to the undersea imagery he had initiated in alluding to the *Phaedo:* "So you see, we are deep-sea monsters, and when the lobster walks on mud, he stirs it up for everybody. We must perforce take it philosophically" (*LCL* 337). That last sentence provides a clue to the motivation behind his allusions to the *Phaedo* and the other literary sources: in constructing his letter, the cuckolded husband has "perforce" tried to take his adversary—and the threat Mellors poses to life at Wragby—"philosophically." He has sought relief and compensation in the only resource available to him, his imagination, through which he projects the Platonic "actual earth" where one is not troubled by the "carnal appetites" of the Cellinis, the Sades, the Rodrigos, the "deep-sea monsters" around him.

Clifford also advocates ideas of Alfred North Whitehead, whose metaphysics developed from Plato's. Like his Cambridge colleague Bertrand Russell, with whom he collaborated on *Principia Mathematica,* Whitehead was a "Philosophic—and Mathematics man," to use Lawrence's phrase describing Russell (*CL* 314). Such books as *Science and the Modern World* (1926) and *Religion in the Making* (1926) had brought Whitehead recognition as the leading metaphysical thinker of his day. An allusion in *Lady Chatterley* indicates that Lawrence knew at least one Whitehead book. One evening Clifford reads aloud from "one of the latest scientific-religious books":

> "The universe shows us two aspects: on one side it is physically wasting, on the other it is spiritually ascending. . . . It is thus slowly passing, with a slowness inconceivable in our measures of time, to

new creative conditions, amid which the physical world, as we at present know it, will be represented by a ripple barely to be distinguished from nonentity. . . . The present type of order in the world has risen from an unimaginable past, and will find its grave in an unimaginable future. There remains the inexhaustive realm of abstract forms, and creativity with its shifting character ever determined afresh by its own creatures, and God, upon whose wisdom all forms of order depend. . . ." [*LCL* 296–97]

Clifford never mentions the title or author of this popular book, but he is quoting directly from the last page of *Religion in the Making*,[15] Whitehead's short book on the interdependence of science, philosophy, and religion.[16] Connie labels the philosopher a "famous wind-machine" and dismisses his argument as "silly hocus-pocus." "It only means *he's* a physical failure on the earth, so he wants to make the whole universe a physical failure," she responds. Victor Lowe contends, in his book on Whitehead, that the philosopher never meant to predict a nonphysical order of nature and that Lawrence misreads Whitehead's conception of the creative advance of the universe.[17] At any rate, Lawrence obviously views Whitehead as another perpetuator of escapist metaphysics, another despiser of the body, and the conclusion of *Religion in the Making* is made to seem in *Lady Chatterley* an amplification of what Connie has heard the "mental-lifers" saying earlier about how men could improve their own nature by "forgetting" the "physical side" of life and becoming mere "spirit" (*LCL* 116).

Moreover, the Whitehead quotation triggers a fresh debate over the "life of the mind" and the "life of the body" (*LCL* 297–98) which establishes a philosophical framework by which we can measure Connie's affair with Mellors, especially her experiences during the upcoming "night of sensual passion." Clifford, defending Whitehead's theories, calls the physique an "encumbrance" and asserts that "whatever God there is is slowly eliminating the guts and alimentary system from the human being, to evolve a higher, more spiritual being." He thus rationalizes his own paralysis into a spiritual advantage. But Connie argues that "whatever God there is has at last wakened up in my guts." For Lawrence, her physical awakening has been indeed "religion in the making."

The excerpt Clifford reads from this "scientific-religious" book thus further sharpens the philosophic issues in *Lady Chatterley* and stresses Lawrence's belief that both Whitehead and Chatterley are successors to Plato, minor "priests" continuing the "crucifixion of the procreative body for the glorification of the spirit, the mental consciousness" (*Phoenix* 569). Connie extends her attack on Whitehead to a broad assault on Platonism and Christianity: "The human body is only just coming to real life. With the Greeks it gave a lovely flicker, then Plato and Aristotle killed it, and Jesus finished it off. But now the body is . . . rising from the tomb" (*LCL* 298). Frequently in late works such as *Etruscan Places, Apocalypse,* and "A Propos of *Lady Chatterley's Lover,*" Lawrence praises the way ancient peoples led lives untainted by doctrinal "thought-forms" like those proposed in the *Dialogues,* the way they had spontaneously perceived the wonder of life through their senses. In *Lady Chatterley* he urges reaccommodation with the spirit of the ancients—with their animistic conception of an earth that was alive and sacred, and especially with their attitude toward sexuality. To render this "old pagan vision" of life (*CL* 1205), Lawrence laces his narrative realism with suggestions of primitive myth and ritual—the archetypes of the underworld descent, the dying-reviving god, the restoration of the powers of fertility, and the hierogamy of sun and earth.[18]

The ancient nature cults appealed to Lawrence because they celebrated the vital phallic relation of man and woman, and offered psychic and physical revitalization for an impotent modern civilization. Throughout *Lady Chatterley* Lawrence emphatically ascribes the problem of impotence directly to Socrates and Plato. In *The First Lady Chatterley* the narrator blames "science and Socrates" for "murdering" the penis in order to exalt the intellect (*FLC* 137), a concept dramatically rendered in *Lady Chatterley's Lover* in the persons of Clifford and Dukes. Lamenting that his penis "never lifts its head up," Dukes complains: "God! when one can only talk! Another torture added to Hades! And Socrates started it" (*LCL* 77). Moreover, because of Clifford's strong identification with the tradition of scientific rationalism, the reader is led to conclude that the baronet's own impotence (war wound or not) is also somehow attributable to "science and Socrates." Because he and Dukes have set their "mind and . . . reason to cock it" (*LCL* 75) over their psyches, each man has lost the phallic power which "connects us with the stars and the sea and everything"

(*JTLJ* 307), that "organic connection" of which Dukes speaks in narrating man's Fall.

Most allusions examined so far have pertained to Clifford's relationship with his wife. Another meaningful set of literary references relates to his increasing intimacy with nurse Bolton and to his concomitant infatuation with the "science of industry." Mrs. Bolton's talk about the failing collieries inspires him to seek "the bitch goddess of success" through industrial production, to become "the new Achilles" of mining technology (*LCL* 152, 155).[19] This allusion to the Greek hero ultimately becomes part of the process of diminution to which Clifford is subjected, as "the new Achilles" becomes at last a whimpering "child-man" before the woman who has inspired his "man's victory" in industry. Clifford is not the first of Lawrence's industrial magnates to conceive of himself as a Greek warrior. In organizing the mines in *Women in Love* Gerald Crich similarly takes as his ideal "the days of Homer, when a man was chief of an army of heroes" (*WL* 294). He further believes that any man able to subjugate Matter to his will is "the arch-god of earth," the "God of the machine" (*WL* 296, 301). Clifford considers himself similarly godlike in his application of modern technology to the mining of coal. In the "technical science of industry," he finds, "men were like gods, or demons, inspired to discoveries, and fighting to carry them out" (*LCL* 154). He alludes to H. G. Wells's utopian romance *Men Like Gods* (1923), a fictional disquisition on the happy, inevitable ascent of technology.[20] An earlier reference to *Men Like Gods* occurs when Dukes extends his condemnation of Socrates to a related attack on modern scientific intellectuality and the "industrial ideal" that would make each individual "a machine-part" submerged in the great social productive machine: "We're all as . . . passionless as idiots," he declares. "We think we're gods . . . men like gods! . . . One has to be human, and have a heart and a penis, if one is going to escape being . . . a god" (*LCL* 77).

He thus opposes the substitution of the "mechanical" principle of life for the "organic" ideal, and his remarks reflect Lawrence's own bias against the scientific rationalism of Wells's romances and utopias. *Men Like Gods* describes a superior race of men in Utopia, a "world of vast intellectual activities" where life has evolved three thousand years ahead of ours. Utopia, without a central government, has only functional experts doing their jobs scientifically and rationally. *Men Like Gods* conveys what Lawrence condemns: optimism about the scientific reorganization of society, hope for material progress, and acceptance of the machine. Lawrence agreed that men could come to be like "gods," but fiercely disagreed with Wells over what *sort* of gods men should strive to be like. As I have indicated, the author in *Lady Chatterley* is in effect proposing his own version of a world of "men like gods," in the way the experiences of his lovers form a pattern of mythic regeneration analogous to the death-and-resurrection arche-type found in the myths of the old vegetation gods. He directly mentions such year gods—"Apollo, and Attis, Demeter, Persephone"—as he pursues his complaint against science and Socrates in "A Propos of *Lady Chatterley's Lover*": "We've got to get them back, for they are the world our soul, our greater consciousness, lives in. The world of reason and science, the moon, a dead lump of earth, the sun, so much gas with spots: this is the dry and sterile little world the abstracted mind inhabits." He argues that modern men can regain their "magic connection" with nature by seeking these old nature gods again through the imagination (*Phoenix II* 511–12). He thus once more champions man's "religious and poetic" modes of "knowing" over what he views as the destructive "mental, rational, scientific" modes instituted among men by Plato and perpetuated by writers such as Alfred North Whitehead and H. G. Wells.

Once Lady Chatterley has announced her intention to leave Wragby, Lawrence withdraws the reader's sympathies from the cuck-olded husband through the use of several allusions that record Clifford's reaction to the news and that reflect his consequent intimacy with Mrs. Bolton. The first describes Mrs. Bolton's strategy for handling his "male hysteria" over Connie's behavior: "The only thing was to release his self-pity. Like the lady in Tennyson, he must weep or he must die" (*LCL* 361). For the reader who recognizes this reference to one of the intercalary songs of *The Princess*, there is a double-edged irony. The song, which prefaces section 6, opens: "Home they brought her warrior dead: / She nor swooned, nor uttered cry: / All her maidens, watching, said, / 'She must weep, or she will die.' " She cries, finally, when a nurse places the dead warrior's child upon its mother's knee. Weeping, the lady declares, "my child, I live for thee." But Clifford's nurse will place no child upon his knee—his wife is pregnant, but by another man; she will leave no heir in the Chatterley cradle. Clifford does at last weep, but it is "for himself" (*LCL* 361), not for any lost mate or for the heir she might have left him. The Tennyson line recalled by Mrs. Bolton thus comments ironically on Clifford's response to losing his wife.

Two other allusions, to a nineteenth-century French play and to the Old Testament, serve similarly to characterize Clifford's response. When Connie declares her love for the keeper, Clifford cries, "You're one of those half-insane, perverted women who must run after depravity, the *nostalgie de la boue*" (*LCL* 368). "*Nostalgie de la boue*," or "*homesickness for the mud*," is an expression used in a key passage of Émile Augier's *Le Mariage d'Olympe* (1855), and Lawrence may have this play in mind as he records Chatterley's moralistic condemnation of Connie's "beastly lowness."[21] It seems reasonable that Clifford would recall Augier on this occasion, for the Frenchman was particularly well known for his social dramas that exalted home, family, marital fidelity, and the moral standards of the middle class. *Le Mariage d'Olympe* is an explicit indictment of illicit love. In the first scene, characters discuss a notorious Parisian courtesan, and one of them wonders if a fallen woman could ever again be happy with a "vie calm et pure." This exchange follows:

> LE MARQUIS DE PUYGIRON: Mettez un canard sur un lac au milieu des cygnes, vous verrez qu'il regrettera sa mare et finira par y retourner.
> BARON DE MONTRICHARD: La nostalgie de la boue![22]

Thus Augier states his theme in *Le Mariage d'Olympe*. His heroine Pauline, an ex-courtesan, tricks a wealthy count into marriage, and for a time lives respectably with his noble family; soon bored, she begins to feel "la nostalgie de la boue" and takes a lover. When she tries to blackmail her husband's family into granting her an "amicable separation" that would allow her to keep the family name and money, she is killed. Augier thus does to Pauline what Clifford can only wish to do to his own unfaithful wife—to have her "wiped off the face of the earth!" (*LCL* 367). With its brutal dispensation of justice to an adulterous woman about to desert her husband, *Le Mariage d'Olympe* would understandably appeal to Clifford on the occasion of his final meeting with Connie. If indeed he is thinking of Augier's play as he identifies his wife with "perverted women who must run after depravity, the *nostalgie de la boue*," then he is simply doing what we have seen him doing often before, translating his domestic situation into literary terms, "turning everything into words," as Connie has earlier charged.

Clifford soon becomes "wistfully moral, seeing himself the incarnation of good, and people like Mellors and Connie the incarnation of mud, of evil" (*LCL* 368). Such self-righteous behavior shows how aptly Mellors characterizes him as a vengeful Jehovah. Clifford, writes Mellors to Connie, "will want to get rid of you at last, to cast you out . . . to spew you out as the abominable thing" (*LCL* 375). Mellors's words, "cast . . . out," "spew . . . out," "abominable thing," echo diction of several Old Testament chapters—Leviticus 18, Isaiah 65, and Jeremiah 16—which report Jehovah's threats to the Israelites who have defiled his land with "abominable things." Jehovah threatens to punish his rebellious people for their ingratitude and acts of immorality—precisely the transgressions the "wistfully moral" Clifford feels his wife and his gamekeeper have committed against him. The allusion to Chatterley as an angry and judgmental Old Testament God serves as another means by which Clifford is unsympathetically drawn in the closing pages of *Lady Chatterley*.

Lawrence's ultimate dismissal of Clifford is conveyed through two allusions, one biblical, one mythical, describing the baronet's "intimacy of perversity" with Mrs. Bolton. With Connie gone, Clifford regresses into the position of a suckling child, gazing on his nurse with "wonderment, that looked almost like a religious exaltation: the perverse and literal rendering of 'except ye become again as a little child'—While she was the Magna Mater, full of power and potency . . . " (*LCL* 362). Lawrence alludes first to Luke 18:17, where Jesus tells the ruler, "whosoever shall not receive the kingdom of God as a little child shall in no wise enter therein"; and the effect of this allusion and Lawrence's reference to "madonna-worship" is to make Clifford's relationship with Mrs. Bolton seem all the more perverse. In mentioning the Magna Mater, Lawrence recalls the myths of the ancient Asiatic deity involving incestuous mother-love (precursors of the Oedipal story),[23] and the allusion nicely characterizes Clifford's involvement with the nurse, his "half-mistress, half foster-mother" (*LCL* 158). Lawrence thus once again loads the dice against Clifford, leaving him bound in perverse infantility, but it is just another part of the calculated process of reduction to which Chatterley—and all he represents on a philosophical level—has been steadily exposed throughout the novel.

Some of Lawrence's allusions in *Lady Chatterley* pose problems for even the most alert reader. As I have illustrated, Lawrence occasionally paraphrases, condenses, or simply misquotes material he is appropriating from other writers. Moreover, some allusions (for example, those to *Men Like Gods*) are submerged in his narrative with no overt indication—beyond the semantic markers or direct verbal echoes themselves—that any outside text is being referred to. Even when transparent markers (such as the mention of Tennyson or the quotation marks around passages from "Ligeia" and *Religion in the Making*) signal an external source, much is yet left for the reader to fill in, in order to complete the allusion's unstated significance. Yet Lawrence was writing to the same literate audience to which Joyce and Eliot were directing their own esoteric allusions, and he was asking no more of his readers than those authors were. In general, his allusive technique is a complex and successful component of his art in *Lady Chatterley*. The allusions I have examined are particularly valuable for the way they encourage the reader to take the story "philosophically," to see the broader implications of Clifford's adherence to "the mental life." These allusions to classical writings, to Plato's *Dialogues*, to the Bible, and to works by various British, American, and continental writers—in effect to literature echoing the entire span of Western culture—allow Lawrence to bring past and present into collocation, and to extend the meaning of his "novel contrasting the mental consciousness with the phallic consciousness" (*CL* 1047) far beyond the confines of Wragby Hall and Wragby Wood. By paralleling Clifford Chatterley and other characters with figures from the literature of the past, Lawrence surrounds them with clusters of associations which endow their individual experiences with universal human significance.

NOTES

1. Edgar Allan Poe, "Ligeia," *Complete Stories and Poems of Edgar Allan Poe* (Garden City, N.Y.: Doubleday, 1966), p. 97. Glanvill was a seventeenth-century English moralist associated with the Cambridge Platonists. The quotation has never been located in his works, and it is believed that Poe fabricated the passage to serve his purposes in "Ligeia." I am indebted to J. A. Leo Lemay for information on the Glanvill epigraph.

2. D. H. Lawrence, *Studies in Classic American Literature* (New York: Viking, 1964), p. 75; hereafter cited in the text as *SCAL*.

3. Lawrence thinks of the Chatterleys' relationship in terms of another Poe tale in *The First Lady Chatterley*, p. 22. Clifford's Platonism seems to Constance a "prison: like the white-hot steel walls of a Poe story"—a reference to "The Pit and the Pendulum," where the narrator suffers "Inquisitorial vengeance" in Spain and is tortured in a dungeon where burning iron walls close in on him.

4. Words and music of "The Four Loves" appear in *The Oxford Song Book*, vol. 2, ed. Thomas Wood (London: Oxford University Press, 1936), p. 126.

5. After each quotation from Plato, I indicate its location, by page and (if applicable) column number, in the standard Greek text of Henricus Stephanus (Paris, 1578 edition).

6. The *Symposium* is never mentioned in *Lady Chatterley's Lover*, but in *John Thomas and Lady Jane* (p. 296) Connie alludes to Aristophanes' humorous and fantastical concept of love (developed in *Symposium* 189–192).

7. D. H. Lawrence, *Apocalypse* (New York: Viking, 1967), p. 98.

8. See Juvenal, *Satires*, X, ll. 77–81: ". . . *duas tantum res anxius optat, / panem et circenses*" (". . . limits its [the Roman people's] anxious longings to two things only, / bread, and the games of the circus").

9. D. H. Lawrence, *Women in Love*, ed. Charles L. Ross (Harmondsworth, Middlesex: Penguin, 1982), p. 300; hereafter cited in the text as *WL*.

10. T. A. Smailes comments on Lawrence's allusions to *The Republic* in *Women in Love*, in "Plato's 'Great Lie of Ideals': Function in *Women in Love*," in *Generous Converse*, ed. Brian Green (Cape Town: Oxford University Press, 1980), pp. 133–35.

11. Benvenuto Cellini, *The Autobiography of Benvenuto Cellini*, trans. George Bull (Baltimore: Penguin, 1961), pp. 280–82.

12. "The Miller of the Dee" first appeared in Bickerstaff's ballad opera *Love in a Village* (1762). See *The Oxford Song Book*, vol. 1, ed. Sir Percy C. Buck (London: Oxford University Press, 1916), pp. 138–39.

13. Anthony Burgess, "Our Bedfellow, The Marquis de Sade," in *The Perverse Imagination*, ed. Irving Buchen (New York: New York University Press, 1970), p. 45. Sade's preference for sodomy is also treated in John Atkins, *Sex in Literature* (London: Calder and Boyars, 1973), vol. 2, pp. 255–61.

14. G. Wilson Knight, "Lawrence, Joyce and Powys," *Essays in Criticism* 11, no. 4 (1961): 404. Knight identifies "The Penitence of Don Roderick" as the source for Lawrence's quotation in *Lady Chatterley*.

15. See Victor Lowe, *Understanding Whitehead* (Baltimore: Johns Hopkins University Press, 1962), p. 106. See also Roland Hall, "D. H. Lawrence and A. N. Whitehead," *Notes and Queries*, May 1962, p. 188.

16. Alfred North Whitehead, *Religion in the Making* (New York: Macmillan, 1926), p. 160.

17. Lowe, *Understanding Whitehead*, p. 106.

18. I discuss mythic patterns in the novel in "The 'Old Pagan Vision': Myth and Ritual in *Lady Chatterley's Lover*," *D. H. Lawrence Review* 11, no. 3 (Fall 1978): 260–71.

19. Frequent references are made in *Lady Chatterley* to this "bitch-goddess Success," and on one occasion the narrator says the phrase is "after Henry James" (p. 69). It is, rather, after William James, from an 11 September 1906 letter to H. G. Wells. See *The Letters of William James*, ed. Henry James (Boston: Atlantic Monthly Press, 1920), vol. 2, p. 260.

20. H. G. Wells, *Men Like Gods* (London: Cassell, 1923). Lawrence alludes to this book also in *The First Lady Chatterley*. When Clifford urges his wife to take a lover, he says, "It's all awfully like an H. G. Wells novel, where prize specimen human males are raised on a sort of antiseptic stud farm, and led round to the passive females at the proper season" (*FLC* 66). In *Men Like Gods*, when the Earthling Father Amerton discovers that the Utopians "*regulate* increase" among their women, he is scandalized: "The human stud farm!" he gasps. "Refusing to create souls! The *wickedness* of it!" (p. 63). Lawrence also uses "Men Like Gods" as titles of two of his poems in *More Pansies*. Wells and his ideas were undoubtedly on Lawrence's mind during the time he wrote all three versions of *Lady Chatterley*. In addition to the allusion to *Men Like Gods*, there is in *The First Lady Chatterley* (p. 61) a mention of a Wells "catchword"—"race-urge"—from *The World of William Clissold* (1926), which Lawrence reviewed shortly before he began writing his novel. There is also a disparaging reference in *John Thomas and Lady Jane* to "scientific-materialistic Wellsian ideas" (p. 56).

21. *Le Mariage d'Olympe* [Olympe's Marriage], produced in 1855, was published in Augier's *Théâtre Complet*, 7 vols. (Paris, 1877–1878), and in *Four Plays of Émile Augier*, trans. B. H. Clark (New York: Knopf, 1915). Clark's translation of the play also appeared in *Drama* 5, no. 19 (August 1915): 358–439.

22. Émile Augier, *Le Mariage d'Olympe*, in *Nineteenth Century French Plays*, ed. J. L. Borgerhoff (New York: Appleton, 1931), p. 486. In English, these lines read:

> MARQUIS DE PUYGIRON: Put a duck on a lake among swans, and you will observe that the duck misses its mire, and will end by returning there.
>
> BARON DE MONTRICHARD: Homesickness for the mud!

23. On the Magna Mater myth see Edith Weigert-Vowinkel, "The Cult and Mythology of the Magna Mater from the Standpoint of Psychoanalysis," *Psychiatry* 1, no. 3 (August 1938): 347–78.

EVELYN J. HINZ
AND JOHN J. TEUNISSEN

War, Love, and Industrialism: The Ares/Aphrodite/Hephaestus Complex in *Lady Chatterley's Lover*

*What would you say again to the tale . . . of how Hephaestus, because of
similar goings on, cast a chain around Ares and Aphrodite?*
—Plato, *The Republic*

An underlying assumption of much criticism of *Lady Chatterley's Lover* is that its mythic dimension is to be found in its Frazerian motifs and accordingly that the work's "redemptive" value has to do with Lawrence's attempts to revitalize ancient fertility rituals. Though he himself is partly responsible for the situation—in terms of some of his comments in "A Propos of *Lady Chatterley's Lover*"—Lawrence has elsewhere also made clear that the qualities of a truly mythic modern work are of a very different kind.

Specifically, in his review of Frederick Carter's *Dragon of the Apocalyse*, Lawrence defines myth as a *story* about a fundamental truth of the human condition: "Myth is an attempt to narrate a whole human experience . . . a profound experience of the human body and soul, an experience which is never exhausted and never will be exhausted, for it is being felt and suffered now, and it will be felt and suffered while man remains man." The modern scientific world, however, has tried to "explain the myths away," ignoring their phenomenality and splitting their original integration of the cosmic and the psychic into two abstract and theoretical parts: either myths are regarded as psychological paradigms or they are treated as allegories about the operations of the universe. The consequence of this loss of ancient humanistic history is that modern man thinks his experiences are unique, and it is in countering this egocentricity by illustrating that history repeats itself that the real "redemptive" value of modern mythic work resides. For to be ignorant of the myth one is in "only means [that] you go on suffering blindly, stupidly, 'in the unconscious,' instead of healthily and with the imaginative comprehension playing upon the suffering" (*Phoenix* 295–96).

This is not to suggest, however, that the artist sets out to write a mythic work; indeed, if this is the case then the end result will be not "mythic literature" but "literature about myth"—literature which is characterized by nostalgia or by the deliberate manipulation of parallels between the past and the present.[1] Mythic literature, in contrast, originates in the artist's *discovery* that the modern story he is telling is an old one, just as it is because the story is an archetypal one that the symbolism of the myth invariably manifests itself in the realistic details. Thus if we begin this study with a consideration of the extent to which *Lady Chatterley's Lover* has precedents, our purpose is not to imply that these are the sources that Lawrence consulted and refashioned; rather we draw attention to these artifacts merely as a strategy for bringing to consciousness the modern reader's intuitive recognition that there is something eternal about Lawrence's lovers and their situation. Furthermore, having provided this context, we will then examine the genesis of *Lady Chatterley's Lover* with a view toward demonstrating that in the initial phases of its composition, far from wanting to realize the mythic dimensions of his material, Lawrence struggled against the recognition.

Stripped to its essentials, *Lady Chatterley's Lover* is the story of the love between the wife of a crippled industrialist and an erstwhile soldier and of the humiliation they experience and the entanglements that ensue when their relationship is exposed. As such, this story of love, war, and industrialism is also the same in kind as that told by Homer over three thousand years ago, when the blind bard Demodocus sang of the love of Ares and Aphrodite and of the revenge of Hephaestus.

As redacted in the Greek epic, Ares (the god of war) was the clandestine paramour of Aphrodite (the goddess of love), their meetings taking place within the wronged husband's domain. Aphrodite's husband was the lame smith-god Hephaestus, who was finally informed of his cuckoldry by the all-seeing Sun. Instead of taking immediate or direct action, Hephaestus fashioned a gossamer-sheer bronze net and suspended it over the bed where the lovers were wont to have their trysts. Upon their next encounter, the adulterous pair were thus ensnared, and Hephaestus called the other gods to witness his dishonor and to adjudicate his rights—complaining, however, not about the blow to his masculinity but about the violation of the marriage contract. Focusing upon the enchained condition of Ares, one of the gods moralized that here was a case of the triumph of the mental and the mechanical over the physical; focusing upon the beauty of Aphrodite, Hermes concluded that her love was worth any price one might have to pay.

Nor, paradoxically, does the sense of *déjà vu* diminish when one notes that Mellors is as much a "god of the woods" as a "god of war," or that Clifford is as much associated with the "upper" as with the "nether" regions. On the contrary, these seeming disparities serve to emphasize the fact that mythic expression always takes the form of *"eadem, sed aliter"*[2] and that to discover both what is constant and the forms which this constant can take one must examine a variety of "signatures." Thus it is that in the Roman counterparts of the Greek trio—Mars, Venus, and Vulcan—one finds the elements "missing" in the Homeric version: Mars was an agricultural deity as well as a military god;[3] Vulcan's abode was the "volcano," and as a patron of crafts he was regarded as an agent of civilization.

In turn, much that seems missing from the Roman "signature" is to be found in the articulations provided by various Renaissance painters. In *Venus and Mars*, for example, Botticelli "anticipates" the triumph of the feminine when he depicts Mars as lying in a defenseless sleep of exhaustion while satyrs play with his weapons and Venus looks on with a bemused smile. The humiliation of both lovers is the theme of Tintoretto's *Venus and Mars Surprised by Vulcan*, wherein the almost naked Venus is subjected to a degrading inspection by her suspicious husband, while his little dog (think ahead to the role of "Flossie") barks to attract attention to Mars, who is half-hidden beneath draped furniture. Jan Brueghel's contribution in *Venus at the*

Forge of Vulcan lies in his evocation of the clank and clutter that Connie experiences when she drives through the industrial Midlands. Nor does one fail to find depictions of those quieter and more gentle aspects of the myth which occasioned Lawrence to consider entitling his novel "Tenderness": in Veronese's painting of *Mars and Venus United by Love* a compassionate Venus has placed her hand on Mars's shoulder, while he sits in a meditative mood and holds a piece of drapery to preserve her modesty; an added touch of innocence and domesticity is provided by a small Cupid who is holding up a bunch of flowers, while in the background, beneath a tree, a horse waits patiently.

To move ahead a couple of centuries—to the work of François Boucher—is similarly to find paintings that could serve as illustrations of key themes and situations in *Lady Chatterley's Lover*. In *Venus and Vulcan*, for example, in Boucher's depiction of a "crude" Vulcan looking up from his work in supplication to a "lovely" Venus who looks down listlessly, one finds the pictorial equivalent of Lawrence's dramatization of the fear and idolatry that accompany Clifford's recognition of the incompatibility of his relationship with Connie. In *Venus Consoling Love*, wherein two fledgling doves play at her feet while Venus tries to restrain and comfort her little son, Cupid, one finds a conflation of the two episodes which Lawrence uses to illustrate Connie's maternal instinct: her quieting of Mellors's child over the shot "pussy" and her own weeping over the "cheekiness" of the pheasant chicks. In *Mars and Venus Caught by Vulcan*, the flight and fright of birds and babes is used to highlight the terror of exposure, with the latter involving the substitution of a snare for a canopy and with the specifically Lawrencean dimension lying in the paradoxically ominous and hierogamous nature of the thunderstorm that serves as the background for Boucher's painting.

Compelling as such general evidence is, furthermore, the shock of recognition becomes even greater when one examines the way in which the symbolism of the myth pervades the texture and diction of *Lady Chatterley's Lover*. What, for example, could be more evocative of the sounds and smells of Hephaestus at his forge than Lawrence's description of "the rattle-rattle of the screens at the pit, the puff of the winding-engine, the clink-clink of shunting trucks, and the hoarse

Venus at the Forge of Vulcan, by Jan Breughel.
Courtesy of the John Woodman Higgins Armory Museum.

Mars and Venus United by Love, by Paolo Veronese.
Courtesy of the Metropolitan Museum of Art, Kennedy Fund, 1910.

Detail of *Venus and Mars Surprized by Vulcan,* by François Boucher.
Courtesy of the Wallace Collection.

little whistle of the colliery locomotives. . . . The air always smelt of something under-earth: sulphur, iron, coal, or acid" (*LCL* 47). Similarly, the visual atmosphere of the god who served as craftsman for the other Greek deities (as well as his "volcanic" dimension in Roman mythology) emerges unmistakably from Lawrence's long-range view of the area: "The vast plumes of smoke and vapour rose from . . . the great 'works', which are the modern Olympia with temples to all the gods. . . . And Uthwaite, on a damp day, was sending up a whole array of smoke plumes and steam, to whatever gods there be" (*LCL* 207). As for the crippled smith god himself, his essential lineaments are well embodied in Clifford Chatterley, whose "shoulders were very broad and strong, his hands were very strong"; "he was very strong and agile with his arms" (*LCL* 38, 87). Mentally, as well, Clifford perfectly embodies the qualities of Hephaestus, amazing Connie with "his shrewd insight into things, his power, his uncanny material power over what is called practical men" (*LCL* 157). Like Hephaestus, too, Clifford is a proponent of technology, thrilling to "the ingenuity and the almost uncanny cleverness of the modern technical mind, [it was] as if really the devil himself had lent fiend's wits to the technical scientists of industry" (*LCL* 153–54). In particular, furthermore, Hephaestus invented two objects—a mechanical chair and a self-powered table on wheels—which are conflated in Clifford's major prop: his motorized wheelchair. And just as Clifford is presented as an emotional cripple before he becomes a physical one, so there are two stories concerning the origin of Hephaestus's lameness: in the *Odyssey* he complains that he was born that way, whereas in the *Iliad* he explains that he was crippled when he was hurled from Olympus by Zeus for taking his mother's side in a domestic dispute.

In his characterization of Mellors, Lawrence seems to incline more toward Roman than toward Greek mythology, emphasizing the "agricultural deity" side of the Ares figure. At the same time, however, his "god of war" dimension is never lost sight of, and significantly it is in this guise that he makes his first appearance in the novel: "A man with a gun strode swiftly . . . , facing their way as if about to attack them," a man with "a red face and red moustache" who "saluted with a quick little gesture, a soldier!" (*LCL* 84). It is also as a man of violence that Connie first encounters Mellors on her own (when he shoots a poaching cat and ill treats his child), and he comes to admit to Connie that anger is a key component of his constitution: "But why are you in a bad temper? . . . Do you mean you are *always* in a bad temper?" she asks, to which he replies, "Pretty well. . . . I don't quite digest my bile" (*LCL* 222). Instead of disliking Mellors's anger, however, Connie feels that it "gave him a peculiar handsomeness, an inwardness and glisten that thrilled her," and during their "night of sensual passion" she voices a preference for his aggressiveness: "she was a little startled and almost unwilling: yet pierced again with piercing thrills of sensuality, different, sharper, more terrible than the thrills of tenderness, but, at the moment, more desirable" (*LCL* 311–12). As for Mellors's gentler side, Mars had one too, and thus even in their night of tender love the Ares/Mars symbolism is not absent. But this episode is best dealt with later; for the present, one should draw attention to the way in which Sir Malcolm's Hermes-like admiration of Mellors evokes the central "cuckolding" action of the myth: "A gamekeeper, eh, my boy! Bloody good poacher, if you ask me. . . . I'll bet you've a good cod on you; oh, you're a bantam, I can see that. You're a fighter. Game-keeper! Ha-ha, by crikey, I wouldn't trust my game to you!" (*LCL* 353).

Whereas Clifford and Mellors thus incarnate their prototypes from the very beginning, as it were, Connie must be awakened to her identity as Aphrodite, and accordingly Lawrence's first evocation of the goddess of love takes the inverted form of a quotation from Swinburne in which the poet evokes "the Cytherean" in the course of lamenting her demise (*LCL* 128). For the same reason, when Connie does experience her apotheosis as a woman born to love, she at first sees Mellors/Ares as an agent of destruction: "She felt his penis risen against her with silent amazing force and assertion. . . . She quivered again at the potent inexorable entry inside her, so strange and terrible. It might come with the thrust of a sword in her softly-opened body, and that would be death" (*LCL* 229). Instead of death, of course, what Connie experiences is her rebirth as Aphrodite. Too long to quote in its entirety, the passage begins with a simile, "And it seemed she was like the sea, nothing but dark waves rising and heaving," and then moves into metaphor—"and she was the ocean rolling"—and after progressing through a description of the parting of the deeps, concludes with her "soft, shuddering convulsion, the quick of all her plasm was touched . . . the consummation was upon her, and she was gone. She was gone, she was not, and she was born: a woman. Ah, too lovely, too lovely! In the ebbing she realised all the loveliness" (*LCL* 229). As the Botticelli nature of this description also suggests, if Clifford has a distinctively "Greek" cast and Mellors a distinctively "Roman" one, Connie is most allied with "Renaissance" signatures.

It is not, therefore, surprising that in Lawrence's description of the sexual encounters of Connie and Mellors a certain amount of "Renaissance" softness casts a romantic glow over the classical evocations of Ares and Aphrodite. Thus Connie leaves for her first night with Mellors "with a certain anger and rebellion burning in her heart. It was not the right sort of heart to take to a love-meeting. But à la guerre comme à la guerre!" (*LCL* 253). And after Mellors has outlined the cruelty of his previous sexual experiences, Connie observes: "We *are* a couple of battered warriors." "Are you battered too?" he laughs. "And here we are returning to the fray!" (*LCL* 264)—which is what they do in terms of the quarrel they have concerning the nature of love, until tenderness overcomes their fighting and they go to sleep in each other's arms. In the morning, however, it is the classical Ares/ Mars who is evoked in the description of Mellors's "erect phallos rising darkish and hot-looking from the little cloud of vivid gold-red hair" and whose appearance leaves Connie feeling "startled and afraid": "How strange he stands there! So big! and so dark and cock-sure!" Nor can the fact that Mellors is frail and consumptive prevent this manifestation: "Between the slim breasts the hair was dark, almost black. But at the root of the belly, where the phallos rose thick and arching, it was gold-red, vivid in a little cloud." So that Connie's reiterated response is, "So proud! . . . And so lordly! . . . A bit terrifying! . . . No wonder men have always been afraid of him! . . . He's rather terrible" (*LCL* 270–71).

To the same effect, for all their nakedness in the famous thunderstorm scene, their lovemaking is not unclothed of Ares/Aphrodite symbolism; just as they lay on "a brown soldier's blanket" when they first made love (*LCL* 163), so when they come in out of the rain, they wrap themselves in Mellors's "army" blankets and he threads "flowers in the fine brown fleece of [her] mount of Venus" (*LCL* 284–85).

Connie's "mount of Venus" is also the focus during the scene of their reunion in London—upon her return from the seaside resort of "Venice"—and it causes Mellors's face to soften, "losing its armour," while conversely it makes him determined to do "battle against the money, and the machine, and the insentient ideal monkeyishness of the world" (*LCL* 348).

Perhaps what brings the Ares/Aphrodite/Hephaestus complex into clearest focus, however, is the recurrent net and chain symbolism. Pervasive in Lawrence's description of the industrial world—where the "steel threads of the railways" link town to town (*LCL* 208)—the symbolism comes especially to identify the plight of lovers trapped in this world and in their legally binding marriages. In fact, the plot of the novel begins when Clifford explains to Connie that he wants a son because "one is only a link in a chain" and that he does not care if it should be fathered by another man, since he and Connie are "interwoven in a marriage." Not being very "keen on chains," Connie thinks to herself: "Was it actually her destiny to go on weaving herself into his life. . . . She was to be content to weave a steady life with him. . . . How could one say Yes? for years and years? . . . Why should one be pinned down by that butterfly word?" (*LCL* 81–84). Her struggle to be free of Clifford is similarly registered in her "unravelling the tangle of his consciousness and hers, breaking the threads gently, one by one, with patience and impatience to get clear." But as Lawrence then ominously goes on to suggest, "the bonds of such love are more ill to loose even than most bonds" (*LCL* 126), and thus Clifford's reaction to her request to be freed is to feel that "she was as it were embedded in his will. How dared she now go back on him, and destroy the fabric of his daily existence" (*LCL* 365–66).

Conversely, Mellors's initial reluctance to enter into a relationship with Connie is based upon his dread of such nets: "The connection between them was growing closer. He could see the day when it would clinch up and they would have to make a life together. 'For the bonds of love are ill to loose!' . . . Must he entangle this woman? Must he have the horrible broil with her lame husband?" (*LCL* 193). And although he comes to feel positively about his relationship with Connie—to the point of sanctioning the marriage of John Thomas and Lady Jane with the phrase, "Blest be the tie that binds our hearts in kindred love" (*LCL* 271)—when Connie explains that she is going to have a child, "she saw a certain exultance spring up in him. But it was netted down by things she could not understand" (*LCL* 344).

But, of course, the episode which is most explicitly directive in its use of "net" symbolism is the one wherein Duncan Forbes agrees to "pose" as the father of Connie's child on the condition that she "pose" as a model for him. For when Forbes states his condition, Mellors's response is: "Better have me as a model at the same time. . . . Better do us in a group, Vulcan and Venus under the net of art" (*LCL* 357).

"*Vulcan* and Venus"? Thus no sooner does the myth come into sharp focus than everything begins to seem confused. For although Mellors has the right iconographic configuration, it is Mars not Vulcan who was ensnared with Venus and accordingly it is with the former that he should identify. Nor can the "mistake" be dismissed as a slip on Lawrence's part, since he has Mellors go on to explain, "I used to be a blacksmith." But what, then, is Lawrence's point?

One possible answer would seem to lie again in Lawrence's distinction between myth and allegory—specifically in his observation that mythic figures always have a "Janus" aspect and that mythic works always have a dialectical nature: not *a* "meaning" or even "meaning *within* meaning: but rather, meaning against meaning" (*Phoenix* 295). For the fact that Mellors was a blacksmith is not the only point of affinity between him and Vulcan. It is, after all, the sound of his "hammering" that brings Connie to his hut, and his occupation as gamekeeper is to set traps. Most important, not only do he and Connie christen themselves as "Knight of the Burning Pestle" and "Lady of the Red Hot Mortar," but their "night of sensual passion" is pervaded with smelting metaphors: "It was sensuality sharp and searing as fire, burning the soul to tinder. Burning out the shames, the deepest, oldest shames, in the most secret places. . . . And necessary, forever necessary, to burn out false shames and smelt out the heaviest ore of the body into purity" (*LCL* 312).

Furthermore, balancing the Hephaestus/Vulcan side of Mellors is the Ares/Mars side of Clifford. Before he became an industrialist, Clifford was a soldier, and military metaphors continue to characterize his new vocation: in the field of technology, as he sees it, "men were like gods, or demons, inspired to discoveries, and fighting to carry them out." The "new Achilles in him" has also developed its own kind of armor: "a hard, efficient shell . . . shells of steel" (*LCL* 154–56). In his concern with the preservation of the "wood" he also has an "agricultural" side.

The more one thinks about it, however, the more one realizes that instead of serving to *qualify* his Hephaestus/Vulcan side, Clifford's Ares/Mars qualities are so different from those of Mellors that they serve rather to *emphasize* his Hephaestus/Vulcan side, and the same holds even truer—in reverse—for Mellors. Accordingly, though Lawrence's "composite" mode of characterization does add an element of complexity which prevents *Lady Chatterley's Lover* from being an allegory, Mellors's identification of himself with Vulcan cannot be justified in this way and so must be regarded as a mistake that Lawrence deliberately has Mellors make.

As for the significance of the mistake, here the explanation is to be found in the extent to which Mellors's recourse to an explicit and "literary" allusion is totally "out of character" and contrary to the entire direction of the novel thus far. Such literariness, that is, is something that characterized Connie at the outset of *Lady Chatterley's Lover*, but it is something of which she was "cured" by her contact with Mellors. Thus when she enters the wood, in the "key" chapter, "endless phrases swept through her consciousness"—allusions to Milton and the New Testament, references to "Persephone" and "Absalom"; but after coming in contact with Mellors and his "vernacular," she returns home to criticize Clifford for his continual use of "poetic" language: "Violets were Juno's eyelids, and windflowers were unravished brides. How she hated words, always coming between her and life . . . ready-made words and phrases sucking all the life-sap out of living things" (*LCL* 137). In turn, when Connie comes to a realization of her mythic identity as Aphrodite, she does so in a totally *evocative* manner: "She was her sensual self, naked and unashamed. She felt a triumph, almost a vainglory. So! That was how it was! That was life! That was how oneself really was! . . . She saw her own nakedness in his eyes, immediate knowledge of her. . . . Oh, how voluptuous and lovely it was to have limbs and body half-asleep, heavy and suffused with passion!" (*LCL* 312–13). Mellors's *invocation* of "Vulcan and Venus under the net of art" is therefore in itself indicative that something is wrong, that he does not have a sure sense of his mythological identity.

Supporting such an interpretation, furthermore, is the fact that leading up to the faulty recognition scene there is a conversation between Mellors and Connie concerning his true nature, a conversation in which he admits to being confused at the same time that Lawrence himself subtly evokes his Ares/Mars qualities: "I can feel something inside me, all mixed up with a lot of rage. But what it really amounts to, I don't know" (*LCL* 345–46). Connie knows, however, and by explaining that he has "the courage of [his] own tenderness" she unobtrusively identifies the combination of strength and softness which is symbolized by the union of Ares and Aphrodite.

If Ares and Aphrodite symbolize this ideal fusion, however, Vulcan and Venus are husband and wife, and herein lies a related way of accounting for Mellors's mistake: namely, as a kind of wish fulfillment, as a recasting of himself in a role that will make for a happy outcome for him and Connie. For according to mythology, upon being released from the net, Aphrodite blithely left Ares to return first to her native abode but ultimately to return to Hephaestus, who "had no real intention of divorcing her."[4] If Mellors can see himself as Hephaestus, in short, then he can rest assured that in due time Connie—who has also returned to her native land, Scotland—will come back to him. And this dream of reunion, of course, is the motivating force behind Mellors's concluding "hopeful" letter to Connie, and accounts for his further attempts to identify with Vulcan. Thus he resorts to fire imagery to describe their love—"We fucked a flame into being"—and specifically rejects the Ares/Mars type as a "Don Juan" who is "impotent ever to fuck [himself] into peace" (*LCL* 374). Vulcan, however, was too impotent to "fuck" at all; his marriage to Venus was an asexual union which produced no offspring and which was responsible for her affair with Mars (which resulted in the birth of Amor/Cupid, the "god of love"—just as Connie's affair with Mellors has resulted in her pregnancy). To be true to the character of Vulcan, therefore, Mellors—who has awakened Connie sexually—finds himself in the paradoxical situation of having not merely to champion "chastity" but also of having to dismiss the child as "a side issue."

What makes his attempt so desperate, furthermore, is the teller *vs.*

tale nature of his letter—the extent to which everything about his situation unmistakably identifies him as an Ares/Mars figure who is caught in a Hephaestus system: like Mars the agricultural deity, Mellors is on a "farm," having obtained the assistance of a man he knew in the "army"; getting this position involved "a bit of contriving," and he now lives in the cottage of "an engine-driver" in a "colliery district" named "Engine Row"; the farm is owned by a colliery company, and the couple with whom he lodges have "lost their only son in the war"; and just as Aphrodite had a calming effect upon her militant lover, so compensating for the fact that the miners do not have "enough of the old fighting-cock in them" is Mellors's contact with cows who "are very female" and "have a soothing effect on me. When I sit with my head in her side, milking, I feel very solaced" (*LCL* 370–71).

If *Lady Chatterley's Lover* has a moral, therefore, it is that mythic configurations inexorably shape our lives and that a failure to realize where one fits in the cosmic scheme is the real cause of modern man's anxiety. For it is not the fact that he is away from Connie that bothers Mellors as much as a general sense of alienation; his total investment in their love, indeed, is the result of a feeling that he has no other connections. Although in theory he knows that a man must "trust in something beyond himself" and that "a higher mystery" controls events, in practice his frame of reference is limited to "the little flame between us. For me now, it's the only thing in the world. I've got no friends, not inward friends. Only you" (*LCL* 373). As such, Mellors is a perfect example of the alienated type that Lawrence describes in *Apocalypse*: "When I hear modern people complain of being lonely then I know what has happened. They have lost the cosmos.—It is nothing human and personal that we are short of."[5] What this loss of the cosmos also entails, as Lawrence explains in his review of Carter's *Dragon*, is a shift from an immediate enjoyment of life to a view of fulfillment in the future: "While life itself is fascinating, fortune is completely uninteresting, and the idea of fate does not enter. When men become poor in life then they become anxious about their fortune and frightened about their fate. By the time of Jesus, men had become so anxious about their fortunes and so frightened about their fates, that they put up the grand declaration that life was one long misery and you couldn't expect your fortune till you got to heaven; that is, till after you were dead" (*Phoenix* 299). Mellors, of course, does not go quite so far. He repeatedly tells Connie not to worry, but his assertions are undermined by the equal repetition of "Patience, always patience" and "Wait." Even more ironic is his long polemic on the subject of "living" *vs.* "spending" and his advocacy of "old group dances" as a solution to the "industrial problem"; for what lies behind his conviction that "the mass of people oughtn't even to try to think" but should be "alive and frisky, and acknowledge the great god Pan" is his own problem in this very respect: "I'm sure you're sick of all this," he tells Connie. "But I don't want to harp on myself, and I've nothing happening to me. I don't like to think too much about you, in my head, that only makes a mess of us both. But of course, what I live for now is for you and me to live together" (*LCL* 371–73).

To the very extent that Mellors is "hopeful" about the future, therefore, so much is he Christian rather than pagan in his orientation, and emphasizing this point further is not merely the "preachiness" of his letter but also the "religious" diction and biblical metaphors to which he resorts: "It's my Pentecost, the forked flame between me and you. . . . My soul softly flaps in the little pentecost flame with you, like the peace of fucking"; Clifford, he tells Connie, "will want to get rid of you at last, to cast you out. . . . In the end he will want to spew you out as the abominable thing" (*LCL* 373–75). The attitude toward adultery reflected in the latter comment is not merely "Christian" however; it was also in such terms that Hephaestus castigated Aphrodite when he found her in the arms of Ares. And with this observation we begin to see why Clifford is presented as a "Christ" figure in his "rebirth" as an industrialist, and why he identifies with Plato, that precursor of Christian attitudes. In turn, we also see the tragic significance of the change in Mellors from a man of passion to a man of peace, from a pagan who speaks the language of the body to a Christian who sends a wordy epistle about chastity to his "brothers in love"—in short, from a man who *incarnated* the qualities of Ares/Mars to a man who *likens* himself to Hephaestus/Vulcan: all of these changes are forms of the triumph of mind over body that is described in the myth.

If *Lady Chatterley's Lover* seems to qualify as a genuinely "mythic work" by reason of the way in which the Ares/Aphrodite/Hephaestus complex *inheres* within its plot and texture, the genesis of the novel presents a very different situation, points indeed to an anti-mythic attitude. For the crippling of Clifford—the thing that distinguishes this myth from others concerned with adultery—was something Lawrence personally disliked: "It made it so much more vulgar of [Connie] to leave him." As for why he nevertheless went against his personal feelings, Lawrence's explanation was that "the story came as it did, by itself, so I left it alone" and that "in the sense of its happening" the crippling of Clifford was "inevitable" (*Phoenix II* 514).

A better description of the driven artist—of the artist who does not set out to write a mythic work—would be hard to find, and when one realizes that the story that "came" to Lawrence was that of Ares/ Aphrodite/Hephaestus, then his argument that Clifford had to be paralyzed because the story demanded it does not sound at all like question begging. It can also be demonstrated that Lawrence was not speaking loosely when he attributed the plot and symbolism of *Lady Chatterley's Lover* to a surrender to "inevitability." For the genesis of *Lady Chatterley's Lover* has a long history, and Lawrence's willingness to "let the story alone" really represents the climax of an almost lifelong resistance to the myth—a resistance, significantly, which roughly coincided with the war and which initially took the form of a critique of inorganic mythic literature.

In a November 1916 letter to Lady Cynthia Asquith he begins by criticizing her husband's poetry for not being true to "his own realities" and by arguing that "it needs the death of an old world in him, and the inception of a new. Not Ares, not Aphrodite—these two are old hat, and not *real* in us." But he then contradicts himself when he observes that "the war is and continues because of the lust for hate and war"—in short, because of the "worship of Ares and Aphrodite— ('But a bitter goddess was born of blood and the salt sea foam')—both gods of destruction and burning down." Nevertheless, he stubbornly concludes that "Ares and Aphrodite have ceased to be gods. We want something else: it is fulfilled in us, this Ares-Aphrodite business" (*CL* 486–87).

A similar latent admission and conscious rejection characterizes his handling of the Ares/Aphrodite motif in the novel he was writing at the time, *Women in Love.* On the one hand, there is a positive evocation of the birth of the goddess of love in the description of the bride—"a sudden foaming rush . . . like a sudden surf-rush, floating all white"—but, on the other hand, there is Birkin's denunciation of her as "the flowering mystery of the death-process. . . . Aphrodite is born in the first spasm of universal dissolution." To the same effect, but conversely, when Birkin attempts to enunciate the "star equilibrium" theory, Ursula retorts: "There you are—a star in its orbit! A satellite—a satellite of Mars—that's what she is to be! . . . You want a satellite, Mars and his satellite."[6]

This same recourse to mockery as a mode of resistance also characterizes a novel that Lawrence began in 1920 but never completed, a novel that in many ways anticipates the central situation of *Lady Chatterley's Lover*. Entitled *Mr. Noon*, the novel is concerned with "the tripod footing" of the universe, as Lawrence mockingly describes the "eternal triangle" (*Phoenix II* 190). Actually, there are two triangles, with the titular hero as the link between them, and with the first—which involves his sexual entanglement with an engaged girl— serving to prevent one from taking the second as seriously as its dramatization seems to warrant. This second plot focuses upon the relationship between the hero and a frustrated married woman, a relationship that is sparked by his account of Mars: "Mars, its canals, and its inhabitants . . . ah, how wonderful it was! And how wonderful was Mr. Noon, with his rough bass voice, roughly and laconically and yet with such magic and power landing her on another planet" (*Phoenix II* 115). The effect of their relationship is her emergence as "a new Aphrodite from the stiff dark sea of middle-aged matronliness . . . ivory-white and soft, woman still, leaving the sea of all her past . . . Aphrodite, mistress, mother of all the worlds of unknown knowledge" (*Phoenix II* 141–44).[7]

Putting *Mr. Noon* aside, Lawrence turned his attention to explicating his theory of the dynamics of the unconscious, and in the process once again found himself tangling with the Aphrodite material. In attempting to define the relationship between man's daytime self and the night-self, for example, he explained in *Fantasia* that "you must start every single day fresh from the source. You must rise every day afresh out of the dark sea of the blood. . . . The self which rises naked every morning out of the dark sleep of the passionate, hoarsely-calling blood: this is the unit for the next society. . . . This is under the spell of the moon, of sea-born Aphrodite, mother and bitter goddess."[8] Later, when he goes on to suggest how Christianity blocks this renewal, Hephaestus is also brought into the picture: "We bruise the serpent's head. . . . But his revenge of bruising our heel is a good one. . . . The serpent has bruised our heel till we limp. The lame gods, the enslaved gods, the toiling limpers moaning for the woman" (*FU* 216). At the conclusion of *Fantasia,* furthermore, the third member of the triangle is also introduced in terms of Lawrence's critique of a recent scientific thesis, which argued that "It is almost as certain that there's life on the moon as it is certain there is life on Mars" (*FU* 224). But if he ridicules this scientist for reducing the symbolic significance of these planets by attempting to make them familiar—"All I can say is: 'Pray come in, Mr. Moony. And how is your cousin Signor Martian?' " (*FU* 225)—he himself ridicules Aphrodite by presenting the Statue of Liberty as her avatar, emerging from the waters of New York harbor still clutching in her raised hand the severed phallos of Uranus.

Lawrence's next strategy involved an attempt simply to ignore Aphrodite—in the political novels of the so-called leadership period. But, in the last of these, *The Plumed Serpent,* he also deliberately tried to announce her demise by having Kate, in her sexual relationship with Cipriano, realize "the death in her of the Aphrodite of the foam: the seething, frictional, ecstatic Aphrodite. . . . [H]e, in his dark, hot silence, would bring her back to the new, soft, heavy, hot flow, when she was like a fountain gushing noiseless and with urgent softness from the volcanic deeps."[9] But in rejecting one aspect of the Aphrodite complex, Lawrence is betrayed into drawing attention to another; for the volcanic imagery is as central to the myth as the foam, evoking as it does Aphrodite's "Roman" husband, Vulcan. Similarly, the more Lawrence succeeds in substituting the religion of Quetzalcoatl for Christian beliefs, the more he evokes the cult of Aphrodite; for if the "Morning Star" is the symbol of Quetzalcoatl, astrologically the morning star is Venus.

Where one finds evidence of his final capitulation, in turn, is significantly in two of his "philosophical" works which are most concerned with defining the true nature of myth and mythic consciousness.

In *Apocalypse*, for example, he observes that "our idea of time as a continuity in an eternal straight line has crippled our consciousness cruelly," and he traces our loss of an organic relationship to the mythic past to the early explicators' tendency to "fix" the meaning of symbolism (A 87, 97). And even more pointedly, in *Etruscan Places*—which he wrote, one should recall, in the interval between the second and the final versions of *Lady Chatterley's Lover*—Lawrence argues that the old religious sense of man's essential harmony with nature "changed with the Greeks and Romans into a desire to resist nature, to produce a mental cunning and a mechanical force that would outwit Nature and chain her down completely, completely, till at last there should be nothing free in nature at all, all should be controlled, domesticated, put to man's meaner uses."[10]

If the complete history of *Lady Chatterley's Lover* thus takes the form of a reluctant surrender to the myth, so too is its immediate genesis characterized by overcoming resistance. Though the first and the last drafts of the novel structurally have the same plot, the first version is less a story of exposed lovers than it is an exposé of what goes on behind the scenes in upper-class society. Similarly, instead of leaving the story alone in the second version, Lawrence makes it the vehicle for social criticism, and attempts to deflect its mythic direction by introducing a series of literary analogues: *Romeo and Juliet, Wuthering Heights, Jane Eyre,* and *Ulysses.*[11] The overcoming of resistance, in turn, can be charted in the changes that serve to bring the myth to the foreground and into clearer focus. Thus one of the essential differences between the gamekeeper in the first and the final versions is Lawrence's characterization of Mellors as a military man, a change that makes Connie's attraction to him more that of Aphrodite for Ares and less that of a sexually deprived woman willing to sacrifice decorum for a virile male.[12] A second major change was to make Clifford not merely an industrialist but also a writer,[13] a change which again is required if Clifford is to reflect not merely the smithy side of Hephaestus but also his mental cunning and his basically spiteful nature; and again Lawrence draws attention to the significance of the change by describing Clifford's stories as "curious, very personal. . . . Clever, rather spiteful" and by emphasizing their similarity to Hephaestus's contrivance: "A display! a display! a display!" (*LCL* 50, 90).

A third change, seemingly minor but important if one is to appreciate the contemporary relevance of Hephaestus's attitude toward adultery, involved the renaming of a key site. In *John Thomas and Lady Jane*, there is mentioned in passing a spring, called "Robin Hood's Well," in the vicinity of the gamekeeper's hut. In *Lady Chatterley's Lover*, the site is called "John's Well": it is there that Connie rests before her first encounter alone with Mellors; it is there that he gives her the key to his hut; it is there that they drink in anticipation of their first night together. From being initially dry, furthermore, the spring becomes active, as the love between Connie and Mellors develops. Easily overlooked by those unfamiliar with the biblical story of Jesus' encounter with the adulterous Samaritan woman at Jacob's Well, as told by "John" (4: 6–26), the name change draws attention to the fact that the morality of Hephaestus finds its counterpart in the Christian view that only the man to whom one is legally married can be called one's "husband."

This is not to suggest, however, that even in the final version of *Lady Chatterley's Lover* all traces of resistance have vanished; on the contrary, the last draft is best described as a recapitulation of Lawrence's earlier struggles and as his only gradual capitulation to the myth. The opening of the novel, for example, is about as unmythic as could be, consisting not only of glib generalizations but also of a parody of the Isis/Osiris myth—Clifford is shipped home to Connie "more or less in bits" with Connie searching for the missing piece, as "the bits seemed to grow together again" (*LCL* 37). In Connie's affair with the bounderish Michaelis, one has a direct parody of the adulterous Ares/Aphrodite relationship, just as the discussion of proper sexual relations on the part of Clifford's cronies—a discussion that begins with the key refrain, "Blest be the tie that binds"—may be seen as an ironic portrayal of the gods' discussion when Hephaestus summoned them to witness the adulterous lovers and to uphold his legal rights.

Nor, finally, are the concluding chapters of the novel without their component of mockery of the myth, although indicative of Lawrence's own changed attitude is the fact that his ridicule is now presented through Clifford and as an aspect of the Hephaestus mentality. Thus in his letter to Connie detailing the return of Bertha Coutts to Mellors's hut, Clifford writes: "Unable to evict the somewhat man-handled Venus from his couch, he beat a retreat and retired, it is said, to his mother's house in Tevershall. Meanwhile the Venus of Stacks Gate is established in the cottage, which she claims is her home, and Apollo, apparently, is domiciled in Tevershall" (*LCL* 328). Clifford's contempt for mythology, in short, is matched only by his ignorance of the myth he is in, and to criticize him even further on this account Lawrence has Mrs. Bolton express her scorn of Clifford in terms that clearly recall Hephaestus's recourse to a trick rather than direct confrontation when he learns of his wife's infidelity: "If he would have admitted it, and prepared himself for it; or if he would have admitted it, and actively struggled with his wife against it: that would have been acting like a man"; and she concludes by evoking an image of Hephaestus caught in his own net: "he's like a mummy tangled in its own bandages" (*LCL* 360).

Similarly, Lawrence presents Mrs. Bolton's attempts to "comfort" Clifford as an ironic version of the "Aphrodite calming the tempestuous Ares" motif: "And she drew him to her, and held her arms round his great shoulders, while he laid his face on her bosom and sobbed, shaking and hulking his huge shoulders, whilst she softly stroked his dusky-blond hair." Though there is an "Oedipal" aspect to this relationship, Lawrence makes clear that this is not the myth in question when he describes this "perverted child-man" as otherwise being "impervious as a bit of steel" with "an almost uncanny shrewdness, hardness," and when he has Mrs. Bolton express her reaction in terms suggestive of the degrading objective of the Hephaestean net: "It was so ridiculous! It was so awful! such a come-down! so shameful!" (*LCL* 361–63).

Where the importance of an Oedipal echo in *Lady Chatterley's Lover* does lie is in drawing our attention to Lawrence's first attempt to give mythic articulation to the crippling nature of modern trends, for in so doing it emphasizes the fact that the mythic artist is compelled to keep going over the same material until he truly gives voice to the myth that truly informs his culture. *Sons and Lovers* was inadequate on both accounts: first, Lawrence was too close to his subject matter to "leave the story alone" or to realize its wider implications; second, the

Oedipus myth does not concern itself with two of the primary features of modern culture—its technological orientation and its puritanical and legalistic morality. As a result, the real value of Lawrence's articulation of the Oedipus myth in *Sons and Lovers* was that it enabled him to come to terms with his own psychological problem—a necessary first stage, since until the artist has contended with his personal unconscious he is incapable of becoming the spokesman of the collective unconscious.

This is not, of course, to suggest that an artist should be remote from the myth of his times. On the contrary, it could be argued that Lawrence's initial resistance to the Ares/Aphrodite/Hephaestus complex derived from a lack of personal identification, and conversely that his ultimate capitulation had to do with the adulterous triangle— he, Frieda, and Ravagli—in which he found himself at the time of writing *Lady Chatterley's Lover*. The relevance of this experience to *Lady Chatterley's Lover* has been discussed elsewhere,[14] however, and for the present what is important is simply to point out that such biographical considerations are not alien to a mythic reading of Lawrence's novel. For by way of conclusion, we want to address two related misconceptions about myth criticism and the nature of myth in *Lady Chatterley's Lover*.

One is the complaint that mythic interpretations accommodate only a part of Lawrence's novels and as a result end up distorting their full meaning;[15] the other is that the "symbolic" and the "naturalistic" dimensions of *Lady Chatterley's Lover* are not well-integrated.[16] From our discussion, however, it should be clear that a mythic approach can accommodate the complete range of *Lady Chatterley's Lover* and that to see the mythic as existing in contrast to the realistic is to have misidentified the novel's informing myth. For the Ares/Aphrodite/Hephaestus complex has within it both an "idyllic" and a "social consciousness" side: it is as much concerned with industrialism as with love; with marriage and divorce as with the rightness of passion; with a puritanical as with a pagan morality. To provide a discussion of how this myth informs the novel, therefore, does not involve ignoring the world outside the "sacred wood" or rejecting the later part of the novel as anticlimactic.

Nor, finally, does such a reading interpose between the text and the reader's emotional response. Rather its effect is a kind of "unconsciousness raising," an awakening not to new insights but to forgotten knowledge. Of course there will always be those who resist, but in doing so they will be providing a related kind of evidence of the reality of eternal recurrence: they will simply be registering the same Modernist reaction to myth that characterized the genesis of *Lady Chatterley's Lover* itself.

NOTES

1. The distinction is Leslie Fiedler's, although he phrases it as the difference between "archetypal literature" and "literature about archetypes." See "Archetype and Signature," in *Art and Psychoanalysis*, ed. William Phillips (Cleveland and New York: Meridian Books, 1963), pp. 454–72.

2. Schopenhauer, "On History," in *The Works of Schopenhauer*, ed. Will Durant (New York: Frederick Ungar Publishing Co., 1955), p. 327.

3. For a discussion of the composite character of Mars and the confusion in iconography, see Jean Seznec, *The Survival of the Pagan Gods*, trans. Barbara F. Sessions (New York: Harper and Row, 1961), pp. 190–94.

4. Robert Graves, *The Greek Myths*, vol. 1 (Harmondsworth, Middlesex: Penguin, 1975), p. 68.

5. D. H. Lawrence, *Apocalypse* (New York: Viking, 1966), p. 47; hereafter cited in the text as A.

6. D. H. Lawrence, *Women in Love*, ed. Charles L. Ross (New York: Viking, 1982), pp. 66, 239, 213.

7. Although another essay would be required to do full justice to the topic, of more than passing interest here is Mr. Noon as a portrait of H. G. Wells, legendary for the triangular configurations of his sexual relationships and an author with whom Lawrence shared a common background and with whom he felt a degree of competitiveness. It can be conjectured that, despite Lawrence's remark to Blanche Jennings that Wells's *The War of the Worlds* was "not worth reading" (*CL* 54), his description of the sexual triangle as a "tripod" recalls for us the mechanical tripods of the Martians in that novel which enable them to overcome earth's stronger gravity and *almost* conquer England. More to our purpose, however, is that after their defeat on Earth the Martians apparently succeeded in invading Venus, leaving the narrator to conclude: "It may be that in the larger design of the universe this invasion from Mars is not without its ultimate benefit for men; it has robbed us of that serene confidence in the future which is the most fruitful source of decadence." (See *The War of the Worlds* [New York: Lancer Books, 1967], p. 251).

8. D. H. Lawrence, *Fantasia of the Unconscious*, in *"Psychoanalysis and the Uncon-*

scious" and "Fantasia of the Unconscious" (New York: Viking, 1960), pp. 210–12; hereafter cited in the text as *FU*.

9. D. H. Lawrence, *The Plumed Serpent* (New York: Vintage Books, 1959), p. 463.

10. D. H. Lawrence, *Etruscan Places* (New York: Viking, 1957), p. 123.

11. For a detailed discussion of the essential generic differences between the three versions, see Evelyn J. Hinz, "Pornography, Novel, Mythic Narrative: The Three Versions of *Lady Chatterley's Lover*," *Modernist Studies* 3, no. 2 (1979): 35–47.

12. Our attention was drawn to this specific change by Michael Squires, who, however, argues for an autobiographical explanation of its significance. See "New Light on the Gamekeeper in *Lady Chatterley's Lover*," *D. H. Lawrence Review* 11, no. 3 (Fall 1978): 234–45.

13. Oriented toward "proletarian" fiction, Kingsley Widmer finds this change "morally" well-taken but lacking in "plausibility." See "The Pertinence of Modern Pastoral: The Three Versions of *Lady Chatterley's Lover*," *Studies in the Novel* 5 (Fall 1973): 302.

14. See Mark Spilka, "Lawrence Versus Peeperkorn on Abdication; or, *What Happens to a Pagan Vitalist When the Juice Runs Out*," in *D. H. Lawrence: The Man Who Lived*, ed. Robert B. Partlow, Jr., and Harry T. Moore (Carbondale: Southern Illinois University Press, 1980), pp. 105–20, 274–76. Spilka's approach is not mythic, however, but Freudian.

15. For a provocative discussion of how critics who adopt the "fertility myth" approach distort the meaning of many of Lawrence's works, see Charles Rossman, "Myth and Misunderstanding D. H. Lawrence," in *Twentieth-Century Poetry, Fiction, and Theory*, ed. Harry R. Garvin (Lewisburg, Pa.: Bucknell University Press, 1977), pp. 81–101.

16. See Keith Sagar, *The Art of D. H. Lawrence* (Cambridge: Cambridge University Press, 1966), pp. 193–96.

Lady Chatterley in London:
The Secret Third Edition

In an appendix to his *Bibliography of D. H. Lawrence,* Warren Roberts lists as a piracy or forgery a very rare edition of *Lady Chatterley's Lover.*[1] Dated 1929, this edition bears the same imprint as the genuine 1928 first edition: "Florence—Printed by the Tipografia Giuntina." It was, however, not printed in Italy, nor was it published in 1929. Identified as the "Third edition / limited to 500 copies," this "forgery" could not have appeared in 1929 because, as Roberts points out, it includes as frontispiece a photograph of Jo Davidson's clay bust of Lawrence, which was sculpted a few days before the writer's death on 2 March 1930. Despite having all the hallmarks of yet another *Lady Chatterley* forgery, this edition may in fact have been a genuine "third edition," following the two earlier ones printed in Florence and Paris. There is enough evidence to suggest that the plan had been approved by Lawrence, although the secret printing in London did not take place until about the middle of 1930, a few months after Lawrence's death, and he had no part in preparing the text for publication.

Those responsible for organizing this mysterious edition were the bookseller Charles Lahr and an Australian writer and publisher, P. R. Stephensen (1901–1965). A former Rhodes Scholar, "Inky" Stephensen had been threatened with expulsion from Oxford for his Communist Party activities there, but had faded out of politics to join Jack Lindsay in the Fanfrolico Press in 1927.[2] Based at Bloomsbury Square, this energetic private press published sumptuous limited editions and issued the literary magazine *London Aphrodite* (1928–29). Charles Lahr had been involved with another similar magazine, *The New Coterie* (1925–27), which had been published from his "progressive bookshop" in Red Lion Street, Holborn. Lawrence's story "Sun" had appeared in the autumn 1926 number of *New Coterie,* and Lahr had issued the story separately as a pamphlet. Lahr was something of an eccentric, as well as being the center of a small literary coterie. He spoke with a slight German accent and had been interned during the First World War as an enemy alien. Lahr's bookshop on the fringe of Bloomsbury specialized in the work of contemporary and experimental writers. He printed cards and occasional catalogues himself on a hand press that had belonged to William Morris, and used the name Blue Moon Press on some of his small productions.[3]

In the semi-bohemian milieu of the late 1920s, Stephensen and Lahr became well acquainted with each other, and with Lawrence. Lahr, in particular, was one of Lawrence's surreptitious London distributors for *Lady Chatterley's Lover* in the stormy period following its publication, and Lahr corresponded regularly with the exiled novelist throughout 1929. Stephensen first met Lawrence a few days before Christmas 1928, visiting him at the Hotel Beau Rivage in Bandol. Stephensen was on a business trip to the South of France, and traveled down by train from Nice with his friend the writer Rhys Davies to see Lawrence. From their subsequent correspondence, it is apparent that Stephensen and Lawrence found each other stimulating, and their discussions and arguments covered publishing, politics, literature, and art.[4]

In December 1928, Stephensen also wanted to discuss with Lawrence the publication of his paintings, an idea Jack Lindsay had casually suggested in October to Pino Orioli. It was Orioli who had helped Lawrence arrange the first edition of *Lady Chatterley's Lover* in Florence during the spring of 1928. Lawrence was excited about the possibility of having his paintings reproduced in book form, and took a keen interest in Stephensen's plans for the Mandrake Press, a new small press Stephensen was starting with Edward Goldston's backing. The Lawrence paintings would be Mandrake's first publication. The Fanfrolico Press was not doing the book because Jack Lindsay was concerned about police action. "Inky" Stephensen, on the other hand, was quite willing to run the risk of prosecution, and he had become something of a crusader against England's repressive and antiquated censorship laws. He had written, and published in pamphlet form, a number of lampoons attacking James Douglas, editor of the

Sunday Express, and Sir William Joynson-Hicks, the Home Secretary, who had been the leaders of the puritanical campaign during 1928 to suppress not only *Lady Chatterley's Lover* but also Radclyffe Hall's lesbian novel *The Well of Loneliness.* Stephensen's Mandrake Press became for a while Lawrence's favored alternative publisher, and Lawrence arranged for Mandrake to handle two translations by his friend S. S. Koteliansky.

In late 1928 and early into the new year, Lawrence was still preoccupied with the distribution and further printing of *Lady Chatterley's Lover.* Although the first Florence edition of a thousand copies had sold out, he was now dispatching copies of the cheap paper-covered issue of two hundred, and planning a larger edition to be printed with paper covers in Paris. He was also furious over pirated editions of his novel which were appearing at a remarkable rate in America. The first of these had been on sale within weeks of the arrival of the genuine copies, and by April 1929 no less than five pirated editions were available in the United States.[5] The Paris edition, with a prefatory essay by Lawrence, appeared in May, but the piracies continued to proliferate.

With his knowledge of the bookselling trade, Charles Lahr helped keep Lawrence informed of the latest *Lady Chatterley* piracies, and in January he suggested to Lawrence a plan for a German edition of the novel. Like the Paris edition in May, this German edition was an attempt to compete with the pirates. With Joynson-Hicks as Home Secretary, any English edition of *Lady Chatterley* would have been quickly suppressed. In January alone, the English authorities seized in the post various Lawrence manuscripts and confiscated half a dozen copies of *Lady Chatterley's Lover.* While all this was happening, Stephensen returned to England, slipping nonchalantly through customs at Folkestone with three of Lawrence's new paintings in his suitcase. Stephensen planned to print five hundred copies of the *Paintings of D. H. Lawrence* at ten guineas each, with ten signed copies on vellum at £52/10/- each, publication to coincide with the exhibition of Lawrence's paintings at the Warren Gallery.

In February, Stephensen sent Lawrence a copy of the latest number of the *London Aphrodite,* which included Stephensen's polemical poem "Barrel-Organ Rhapsody" praising unemployed workers as the new "bulldog breed." Lawrence replied sharply that he was against the worker as much as he was against the bourgeois; both were part of industrial civilization, which sought to destroy "real humanness." "I *hate* our civilisation, our ideals, our money, our machines, our intellectuals, our upper classes," he railed, but it was the upper classes that attracted his special attention. The chauffeur, Lawrence said, was now a lady's "favorite fucker," but he stayed where he was—as a *"machine à plaisir"*—and the lady stayed where she was. To reinforce his argument, Lawrence cited *Lady Chatterley's Lover:* "If Mellors had never *found out* the upper classes, by being one of them, Connie would just have had him and put him down again—elle m'a planté là!—No, it's all much more difficult than you imagine. The working man is not much of a British Bulldog any more—he's rather a shivering cur—one has to try slowly to rouse the old spirit in him—and *definitely* disillusion him about the 'upperness.' "[6]

Early in 1929, Stephensen and Lahr must have discussed their mutual friend Lawrence and the distribution of *Lady Chatterley's Lover.* Lahr had now changed his mind from a German to an English edition, and he conveyed this bold plan to Lawrence, who replied on 18 April: "I don't mind a bit if your friend does 500 of Our Lady. He can give me 15% on his selling price, that being the usual. Let me know" (CL 1143). In the same letter Lawrence authorized Lahr to print a small unexpurgated edition of *Pansies,* which appeared a few months later bearing Stephensen's name as publisher. It is likely therefore that Lahr's friend who was going to organize an English edition of *Lady Chatterley's Lover* was Stephensen. The young Australian had contacts with many London printers, and relished just such anti-censorship activism.

On 9 May Lawrence wrote to Pino Orioli about this secret project: "A man in London talks of doing an edition of 500 [of *Lady Chatterley's Lover*] there—printing it himself in London, right under Jix's [Joynson-Hicks's] nose. Don't know if this will come off."[7] Then, a month later from Mallorca, Lawrence wrote to Lahr inquiring about the progress of the London edition: "How's the man getting on with Our Lady?" (CL 1161). Stephensen's name was never mentioned in this correspondence, possibly to protect his identity in the same way that Lawrence referred to *Lady Chatterley's Lover* as "Our Lady." Stephensen had been under surveillance by MI5 (the British secret service) since his days as a communist agitator at Oxford, and had learned the value of discretion in letters. There was no mention at all of the secret publishing project in the continuing correspondence between Lawrence and Stephensen, which was throughout 1929 more concerned with the proofs and other arrangements for the volume of paintings.

While Lahr and Stephensen were trying to find a printer to handle the dangerous job of a London edition of *Lady Chatterley*, Lawrence again became the cause of a public sensation after police raided the exhibition of his paintings at the Warren Gallery in July. Some copies of the Mandrake edition of the *Paintings of D. H. Lawrence* were seized, as well as thirteen of the paintings themselves. This action ensured that any remaining stock of the book quickly sold out, bringing in a gross return of £4,000 for the Mandrake Press.[8] Frieda Lawrence had come to England for the exhibition, staying for a few days with Stephensen at his weekend cottage in Kent.

Lawrence, and his friends like Lahr and Stephensen, were too preoccupied with the court prosecutions that had been instigated over the paintings to worry about the London plan for *Lady Chatterley's Lover*. The seizure of his paintings had raised again in Lawrence's mind the awful specter of a public burning, and this, combined with ill health and his continuing frustration over *Lady Chatterley* pirates, meant his fighting spirit was much weakened. For the time being, Lawrence was concentrating on the unexpurgated edition of *Pansies*, which Lahr was then preparing with Stephensen's name as publisher. This definitive edition of *Pansies* was not actually ready till August, though it bore the specific date "June 1929," no doubt as a further snub to Secker's fainthearted edition that had already appeared. To Lawrence, Stephensen wrote in July that it was an honor to have his name as publisher on the defiantly complete edition of *Pansies*. It was a risk as well, and Stephensen was already facing possible court action over the confiscated copies of the *Paintings of D. H. Lawrence*. However, he assured Lawrence that in the event of trouble over *Pansies*, "I'm ready for 'em, without either heroics or hysteria. This fight for free expression has to be fought all over again since those blackguardly little police pimps and spies have goose-stepped into action" (Stephensen to Lawrence, 21 July 1929).

As it happened, no action was taken over *Pansies,* and it was Lawrence's paintings that continued to outrage the guardians of public morality in England. The case against the paintings, under the anti-quated Obscene Publications Act of 1857, was heard by an eighty-two-year-old magistrate, and the prosecutor was Herbert G. Muskett, who had appeared for the police in the action against Lawrence's novel *The Rainbow* in 1915. Muskett fired off the charge that Lawrence's paintings were "gross, coarse, hideous, unlovely, and obscene."[9] Lawrence had instructed his lawyers to compromise, and when the hearing resumed in August, the magistrate agreed to the return of the paintings provided they were not further exhibited, although he ordered that the seized Mandrake books be destroyed, including one of the expensive vellum copies. The victory was still with the Home Secretary, and any printer contemplating a London edition of *Lady Chatterley's Lover,* no matter how secretly arranged, would have been warned by these events that his reputation and his livelihood could be seriously affected.

Nothing further appears to have happened in 1929 regarding the Lahr/Stephensen plan for an English *Lady Chatterley.* Between July and October, Stephensen was busy with new titles at the Mandrake Press, and he had also become entangled with Aleister Crowley. A practicing magician and author of numerous privately printed volumes of verse, Crowley was a rogue and an adventurer who had been vilified by the English press for his "sex magic" and drug taking. About the time of the publication of Lawrence's paintings, Crowley latched on to the Mandrake Press, setting up house near Stephensen in Kent. Stephensen failed to take Crowley's magic seriously, being amused rather than frightened by his antics, but Crowley eventually sucked the remaining lifeblood from the Mandrake Press. Considering Crowley, like Lawrence, to have been the subject of unfair and vicious newspaper attacks, Stephensen agreed to publish a number of the magician's works, including his projected six-volume *Confessions of Aleister Crowley.* Toward the end of 1929 there were even a couple of half-hearted attempts to stage an exhibition of Crowley's gruesome paintings, to repeat the *succès de scandale* of the Lawrence exhibition. But where Lawrence and his book of paintings had made a small fortune for the Mandrake Press, Crowley was a disaster in every way, and

Stephensen's business partner Goldston refused to continue with the press, closing it down temporarily. Lawrence too had been concerned that Mandrake was carrying Crowley at "such heavy tonnage" (Lawrence to Stephensen, 5 September 1929), and he was right, for the press eventually sank under the weight of its albatross, Aleister Crowley.

During January 1930, while an attempt was being made to reconstruct the Mandrake Press, Stephensen contracted to publish Lawrence's *A Propos of "Lady Chatterley's Lover,"* an expanded version of "My Skirmish with Jolly Roger," which had prefaced the Paris edition of *Lady Chatterley.*[10] Rather inexplicably, Lawrence tried to withdraw from the contract only a week after signing it, apparently not satisfied with the new version of the essay. "I just feel I don't want to publish it as it stands," he wrote to his agent Laurence Pollinger (*CL* 1237). When Mandrake refused his request, Lawrence commented: "Oh, that Mandrake—vegetable of ill omen!" (*CL* 1244). This was a reference to Crowley's bad magic rather than a reflection on Mandrake itself, though the death of the press and the death of Lawrence himself were not far off.

In the letters currently available, there was no further discussion of the plan for a London *Lady Chatterley's Lover* before Lawrence's death, but neither is there any evidence that Lawrence had specifically forbidden Lahr to proceed with the secret edition. Lawrence's relations with Lahr and Stephensen remained reasonably cordial to the end. In the six months before his death, Lawrence was writing regularly to Lahr, and during the early autumn of 1929 he had enthusiastically encouraged Lahr to start a satirical magazine, to be called *Squib.* Lawrence also wanted Lahr to do an English edition of *The Escaped Cock,* which was first published by the Black Sun Press in Paris in September 1929. In late October, however, Lawrence still had not received the final accounting for Lahr's unexpurgated *Pansies,* and he began to have second thoughts about Lahr. Lawrence told Koteliansky that Lahr was "perfectly honest—but not calm enough."[11] By February 1930, Lawrence was still prepared to allow Lahr to publish *The Escaped Cock* in England, but only after a final settlement of accounts for *Pansies.*

Lawrence's erratic behavior in late 1929 and early 1930 can be partly explained by his deteriorating state of health. The sculptor Jo Davidson modeled his head in clay a few days before his death on Sunday, 2 March. Lawrence's death may have renewed Lahr's interest in an English edition of *Lady Chatterley's Lover,* because by about April, Stephensen had located a printer willing to take on the edition. The firm was that of W. Graves, who worked with his sons in a basement at the corner of Stanhope and Drummond streets in London.[12] Bearing a false date and place of publication, and also the telltale evidence of the frontispiece photograph of Davidson's bust, the edition was hurriedly put together about the middle of 1930. Graves also printed *A Propos of "Lady Chatterley's Lover"* for the Mandrake Press in June 1930, but this bore the printer's correct name and address. The London *Lady Chatterley's Lover,* on the other hand, remains shrouded in mystery. It is not clear how many copies were printed, and how many of these were distributed. The title page closely resembles that of the Florence first edition, though the text has been reset, not photographically reproduced as with so many piracies.

Uncharacteristically, Stephensen remained silent about the edition for thirty years. He returned to Australia in the 1930s and became involved with an extreme right-wing group, spending most of the Second World War in an internment camp. As a struggling literary agent in Sydney in the 1950s, he renewed contact with Laurence Pollinger. During the celebrated trial of the Penguin *Lady Chatterley's Lover* in 1960, Stephensen wrote to Pollinger describing what he claimed was the first authorized English edition: "My recollection is that Charles Lahr came to me and asked if I could find a printer who would do it. He stated that Lawrence wanted it done and that all profits from the publication would go to Lawrence. Lahr was trembling and sweating with fear and insisted on complete secrecy." Lahr told Stephensen: "Lawrence does not want Pollinger to be in any way implicated in a criminal prosecution."[13]

Replying a few days later from London, just before the verdict was given in the Penguin case, Pollinger said he had known of Lahr's plan and had been firmly against it. Pollinger denied that Lawrence had wanted it done (though Lawrence's own letters refute this claim), and Pollinger also maintained that no profits had reached Lawrence. In a handwritten postscript he added that Lahr was a "crook" (Pollinger to

P. R. Stephensen in 1929.

Stephensen, 28 October 1960). Stephensen's response was to concede that he may have been fooled by Lahr and "a few other booksellers, including Davis (of Davis and Orioli)," who were concerned with making money out of the edition. Stephensen stressed his innocence of any charge of piracy, and said he was saddened to think his youthful idealism might have been exploited by the syndicate of booksellers backing the edition (Stephensen to Pollinger, 3 November 1960).

Stephensen, however, had hardly been a naive idealist at the time. Though still in his twenties, he was then an experienced publisher and a former communist agitator. Stephensen also had a curious failure of memory about the date of his *Lady Chatterley* edition. When he wrote to Pollinger in October 1960, he gave the printing date as 1931, but when he wrote an account of the edition a few weeks later for the Sydney *Observer*, under the title "Lady Chatterley's Secret," he changed the date back to 1929. He had probably dug out his copy of the edition in the meantime and accepted the 1929 imprint. Working from memory, he also may have foreshortened the events of 1929–30 when he came to describe them in the *Observer* of 26 November 1960:

> A bookseller, whom I had better name, even now, only as "Charlie" [Lahr], came to me, in November 1929, sweating and trembling with fear, and asked me if I could arrange the printing and binding, in London, of a full and unexpurgated edition of the novel, *Lady Chatterley's Lover*. This, he said, was to be done at Lawrence's request. He and other booksellers would pay the printer and binder, and would sell the book surreptitiously. All profits would go to Lawrence.
>
> Being young, foolish and Quixotic, I felt that I had a duty to Lawrence and to Literature to make this gesture, regardless of Legality. I found the printer, and for a fortnight worked every evening with him and his son in their basement workshop, helping to print and bind the book, in an edition of 1,000 copies. The printer insisted on putting on it a false imprint, "Printed in Italy," as a red herring.

Stephensen cannot have checked his own copy very carefully because the imprint listed Florence and the original printer's name, and the book itself specified only 500 copies, not 1,000. Stephensen reiterated, in his *Observer* article, that he "had no part in the financial transaction of this surreptitious and illegal edition." All he had ever received from it was satisfaction and a single copy of the book.

This copy is now in the Stephensen Papers, Mitchell Library, Sydney, and, as might be expected of an early or proof copy, it is unnumbered. However, the copy examined by Warren Roberts was also unnumbered, and the scarcity of this "third edition" suggests that Lahr and the other booksellers associated with it may have distributed only a few copies. Although Lawrence had certainly authorized the London edition, he was dead several months before it was printed, so Stephensen's claim of altruism—"All profits would go to Lawrence"— looks less convincing. The false Florence imprint may indeed have been designed to protect Graves the printer, but, along with the misleading publication date, it would also have increased the value of the stock.

The false imprint has always suggested that the edition was a piracy, and it was regarded as such by Frieda Lawrence. On a visit to London in January 1931, a year after her husband's death, she discovered Lahr was behind the rare edition of *Lady Chatterley's Lover*. She wrote to Edward Titus, who had printed the 1929 Paris edition of the novel: "I want to tell you quickly that that pirated edition of *our* Lady you sent me with the photograph of Davidson's bust in it was done *here*—We know by whom; Orioli is *so* angry that on the first page it says 'Printed in Florence etc'—We just found out this minute—We can stop them though—I won't take any money for it, but only stop them. . . . '"[14] This suggests that Frieda had already been offered money, possibly by Lahr, for the edition. Someone later informed Titus that Frieda had in fact been paid off by the "pirates," a charge she vehemently denied. A year afterward, she was still writing to Titus: "I wonder if Lahr or whoever published it, started the lie."[15] Frieda even threatened to expose the incident in her autobiography, but forgot or omitted it when preparing *Not I, But the Wind* for publication.

Lady Chatterley's Lover, beyond its status as a novel, is the most notorious example of literary censorship in the twentieth century, and the novel's strange and fascinating history still holds many secrets. The timidity of Lawrence's regular publishers meant he had to arrange the publication of *Lady Chatterley's Lover* himself, printing and distributing it in a clandestine way. The novel was, however, still exposed to wide publicity and to numerous piracies. In the last year of his life, Lawrence planned not only the controversial publication of his paintings and his poems *Pansies,* but, most secretive of all, the London edition of "Our Lady," as he facetiously nicknamed his novel. This London edition would be printed, he told Orioli with considerable relish, right under the Home Secretary's nose. The novel had appeared in Italy and been printed in Paris also with Lawrence's blessing. So the planned "third edition" in England would be quite a coup for him. But Lawrence's death subtly altered this genuine, if surreptitious, English edition into a seeming piracy. Those ultimately responsible, Lahr and Stephensen, had been Lawrence's friends, and Stephensen's interest in the novel, at least, was polemical rather than financial. He knew the value of Lawrence material, but he had taken many risks already for Lawrence in the cause of freedom of expression.

All that can safely be said from this distance is that up until the time of its appearance, the Lahr/Stephensen edition of *Lady Chatterley's Lover* was an authorized third edition, but when it was finally printed in London in 1930 it masqueraded under a false date and place of publication, and its author was unable to defend it. Authentic in spirit, this rare and still intriguing edition of *Lady Chatterley* went forth clothed as an impostor.

NOTES

1. Warren Roberts, *A Bibliography of D. H. Lawrence* (Cambridge: Cambridge University Press, 1982), p. 563. See also p. 111.

2. For a more detailed history of the Fanfrolico Press, see: Jack Lindsay, *Fanfrolico and After* (London: Bodley Head, 1962); Harry F. Chaplin, *The Fanfrolico Press* (Sydney: Wentworth Press, 1976); Anthony Adams, "The Fanfrolico Press," *American Book Collector* 9, no. 8 (April 1959): 9–14; and Craig Munro, "Two Boys from Queensland: P. R. Stephensen and Jack Lindsay," in *Culture and History*, ed. Bernard Smith (Sydney: Hale and Iremonger, 1984).

3. Details about Lahr from Roberts, *Bibliography of D. H. Lawrence*, pp. 91, 142, 149; and from an interview with London bookseller Robert Cris (November 1980, author). The name "Blue Moon Press" may have been Lahr's lighthearted riposte to the Black Sun Press in Paris.

4. There are more than twenty letters from Lawrence to Stephensen, covering the period December 1928 to October 1929. Until recently these were in a private collection in Australia, and quotations from this correspondence are from photocopies

held by the author. They are reproduced with the kind permission of Laurence Pollinger Ltd. and the Estate of Frieda Lawrence Ravagli.

5. Lawrence to D. V. Lederhandler, 5 April 1929, in *The Letters of D. H. Lawrence*, ed. Aldous Huxley (New York: Viking, 1932), p. 800.

6. Lawrence to Stephensen, 15 February 1929, copy in the author's possession.

7. Lawrence to Orioli [9 May 1929], in Harry T. Moore, *The Priest of Love* (Carbondale and Edwardsville: Southern Illinois University Press, 1974), p. 470.

8. The book of paintings was published in June 1929, and the 500 ten-guinea copies sold out quickly, although Stephensen "sacrificed" 150 of them at half price to an American dealer visiting London (Stephensen to Lawrence, [? 21 July 1929], copy in the author's possession). The ten vellum copies were all subscribed before publication. There is also some question as to whether all the royalties from the book reached Lawrence. He had earlier received an advance fee of £250 from Stephensen, but on 2 December 1929 Laurence Pollinger wrote to Stephensen (copy in the author's possession) complaining that neither the 10 percent royalty on the vellum copies nor the 5 percent royalty on the ten-guinea edition had been received. Lawrence may, however, have received some more money from Stephensen's partner Goldston via Charles Lahr (see *CL* 1220).

9. D. H. Lawrence, *Sex, Literature, and Censorship*, ed. Harry T. Moore (New York: Viking, 1971), p. 21. See also the *London Times* report of the hearing, 9 August 1929.

10. A copy of the *A Propos* contract, dated 22 January 1930, is in the Stephensen Papers, Box K164728, Mitchell Library, Sydney. The number of copies was not specified, but a quick printing was clearly envisaged as the Mandrake Press agreed to publish the book "before the middle of February 1930."

11. Lawrence to Koteliansky, 25 October 1929, in *The Quest for Rananim: D. H. Lawrence's Letters to S. S. Koteliansky, 1914 to 1930*, ed. George J. Zytaruk (Montreal and London: McGill-Queen's University Press, 1970), p. 391.

12. Arthur Freeman, of Stirling Press Ltd., London, around May 1930 charged Stephensen a special fee for placing "the job" with Graves (Stephensen Papers, Box Y2120, Mitchell Library, Sydney). That Graves was in fact the printer of the secret London edition of *Lady Chatterley's Lover* was confirmed by Stephensen's sister, who, in an interview with the author (June 1981), remembered visiting Graves's basement printery, which was the place, she was told, where the novel was printed. By 1933 the firm had become Messrs. Graves & Sons (details supplied by the British Telecom Museum from a 1933 Trade and Commercial Directory).

All the evidence for Stephensen's London edition of *Lady Chatterley's Lover* is corroborated by the appearance in R. A. Gekoski's *Modern First Editions* catalogue of the printer's copy Stephensen must have used for the "third edition." It consists of a set of sheets of the Florence "second edition" (Roberts, *Bibliography*, entry A42b) which have been corrected in pencil, but not by Lawrence. From an examination of this set of sheets (which was bound up later in the same cloth used for the rest of the London "third edition"), the corrections are most probably Stephensen's. All but one were incorporated in the London secret edition. See R. A. Gekoski, *Modern First Editions*, catalogue 1 (Warwickshire, England: R. A. Gekoski, 1982), item 109.

13. Stephensen to Pollinger, 23 October 1960, Stephensen Papers, Box K164728, Mitchell Library, Sydney.

14. Frieda Lawrence to Edward Titus, [? 18 January 1931], in *Frieda Lawrence and Her Circle: Letters from, to and about Frieda Lawrence*, ed. Harry T. Moore and Dale B. Montague (London: Macmillan, 1981), p. 28.

15. Ibid., p. 36.

GERALD J. POLLINGER

Lady Chatterley's Lover: A View from Lawrence's Literary Executor

This is not the whole story. I expect that only one person could really fill in the gaps in regard to the publication of *Lady Chatterley's Lover.* My father Laurence E. Pollinger, who died several years ago, never would put pen to paper nor would he be interviewed on the subject of any of his authors. I am sure he was right, protecting their privacy much in the same manner as does a lawyer or a doctor. But from time to time he would let the odd anecdote slip out in conversation.

There was the lady, Enid Hopkin, I believe, who smuggled copies of the first edition into London in her bloomers. There was Caresse Crosby (who, like Helen Corke, still managed the several flights of stairs up to our office in London to the end of her days), who also "smuggled" in a few forbidden copies. There was Charles Lahr, the bookseller about whom much has been said and written, though not for publication, who distributed copies.

My contribution to the present collection of essays must necessarily be concerned with personal recollection, and since I do not have the gift of perfect recall claimed by others, I stand open to correction on reminiscence.

I remember, for example, a luncheon early in 1960 at Quaglino's in St. James's, my father's favorite watering hole, when Allen Lane and his brilliant brother Richard (who shortly afterwards emigrated to Australia) discussed with my father and myself the possibility of Penguin Books issuing eight more titles by D. H. Lawrence in paperback and what they might be. They had successfully printed up to fifteen thousand copies of each of fifteen titles and thought they should issue another batch. One of these was to be *Lady Chatterley's Lover,* and the question of which edited version was to be used came up.

My father and Martin Secker had each censored the original version, privately printed by the Tipografia Giuntina in 1928, changing words like "heart" to "senses," and my father, in fact, deleted the last sentence, which, as everyone now knows, reads: "John Thomas says good-night to lady Jane, a little droopingly, but with a hopeful heart" (*LCL* 375).

At the D. H. Lawrence Festival in Nottingham in 1980, the autographed copy of the Orioli version I still hold was on display side by side with the unique, specially pulled bound copy which Martin and my father amended. This is inscribed in Secker's own hand in the words: "To L. E. Pollinger—this melancholy relic, in commemoration of the 'authorised British edition'—with the affectionate regards of Martin Secker." This volume has no title page, prelims, or anything other than the title in gilt on the brown cloth spine. Throughout the text their deletions or amendments are to be seen in pencil and red or blue crayon. This copy formed the basis of the first edition published by Martin Secker in 1932.

The Lanes decided it would only be right and proper to publish the unexpurgated edition, and at that time no thought entered the minds of anyone present other than to print the same number of copies as for the other titles in the series. Much later the sky was to fall in when the Beaverbrook Press, if memory serves, decided to castigate Penguin for issuing "a dirty book."

The trial that followed is history and has been much chronicled. It should have been clear from the outset that the twain would never meet, for the prosecution was intent on upholding a law that had been on the statute books for years, and the defense was fighting, in a way, for the freedom of speech and the right to publish.

The indirect result of the trial has been to release the pent-up flood of pornography which sadly adorns our bookshelves and cinemas, and which it is not my place to comment upon. But one overlooked item is that neither counsel involved really wished to call my father to the witness stand, for they knew he would have to answer one question in the negative, which both of them were bound to have to pose. And that question was: "Did Lawrence want this book to be published in England?" We all know the answer to that and the reasons therefor. But to have that question put and answered would have cut short the trial in a matter of seconds, and at the time neither Counsel wanted that to happen.

The Press paid scant attention to us once they had ascertained that *Lady Chatterley's Lover* was just one of a number of D. H. Lawrence titles being issued by Penguin Books and that the contract had been drawn on that basis. If they could have shown it was a special case and that vast profits were expected, they could have had a field day.

The result for Allen Lane was remarkable in one or two ways. On the wall of my office I keep the first two royalty statements. These show that the sales from publication on 10 November 1960 to 31 December 1960 were 1,986,121, and for the next six months, 1,240,435.

To provide these copies for the voracious public, fed by the column inches of sensational reporting by the newspapers, Penguin had to use all the printers they could engage. This meant putting back the proposed reprinting of lots of other worthy titles with a resultant loss in sales and profits a couple of years later, for by then these reprints were not required by the public who had requested them.

The figures I have quoted above were a salutary indicator to all paperback publishers, as they showed the maximum sales over a short period of time that anyone could achieve. The financial reward en-abled Penguin Books to "go public" and to place their shares on the Stock Exchange for purchase.

The Press are not always bad to agents, despite their exaggerations to make a story interesting to the general public, who think publishing is still an occupation for gentlemen or emigrés who give parties. One useful report was that certain libraries intended to bind Penguin paper-back copies in hard covers. This would have been illegal. Years earlier my father had arranged for his friends Charles Evans and Alexander Frere at Heinemann to take over the hardcover volume rights of Lawrence from Martin Secker and one or two others (Duckworth, for instance, published *The Trespasser*). Aspiring authors' agents should note my phraseology here, for my father retained all the paperback rights, and did not grant what are now deemed full volume rights. Shrewd he was.

So, rapidly I devised a sentence which, with minor modifications, has appeared in nearly every paperback book printed in England since it first appeared in *Lady Chatterley's Lover.* The sentence reads:

> Except in the United States of America, this book is sold subject to the condition that it shall not, by way of trade or otherwise, be lent, re-sold, hired out or otherwise circulated without the publisher's prior consent in any form of binding or cover other than that in which it is published and without a similar condition including this condition being imposed on the subsequent purchaser.

And yes, several legal actions have been brought and won against transgressors.

Since the unexpurgated edition of *Lady Chatterley's Lover* was first published by Penguin in 1960, the copyright therein in the British Commonwealth and Empire (to use the traditional publishers' phrase) subsists from that date. William Heinemann published their first hardcover edition in 1961, and the book has since appeared in the Omnibus Collection (codenamed "Pickles" after one of its inventors, Charles Pick) issued by Heinemann and Octopus jointly. And there have been several book-club editions.

In America, where *Lady Chatterley's Lover* was not copyrighted (although the famed lawyer Morris Ernst indicated in correspondence that it could have been, retroactively), Grove Press published an unauthorized edition which was also the subject of a trial and a successful outcome for the publisher. Grove's Barney Rosset and his lawyer visited my father and me shortly after, and although terms were agreed, Rosset changed his mind and never signed a contract. To this day the only authorized and unexpurgated edition published in the United States is that issued by New American Library of World Literature, Inc., whose farsighted pioneers, Kurt Enoch and Victor Weybright, early on made proper approaches to my father. And, to get ahead of myself for a moment, when the definitive edition is available, New American Library will issue it.

I needs must refer to an unknown story about something which happened at the time of the trial. In our home my father had an excellent collection of books by authors with whom he was associated; I tried to read, without much success, the copy of the limited edition of *Ulysses* by James Joyce which he had arranged to be published at a high price to avoid "censorship," on the grounds that a rude volume was already available. There were copies of all the books by Hendrik Van Loon, Theodore Dreiser, and Upton Sinclair, and of course the first crossword puzzle books, a pastime which he had introduced to England. Such a varied library was not available to many, and his three sons thrived on a diet of A. A. Milne, Dorothy L. Sayers, Howard Spring, and H. E. Bates. When the brouhaha started, I remembered that there was on a shelf in our house in the country a typescript (yes, I still have it) of what I thought was *Lady Chatterley's Lover,* and I believed it might be relevant.

I telephoned my farmer brother, Russell, who located it, put it in an envelope, and gave it to the conductor on the next train to London, together with half-a-crown (half-a-dollar we used to call it). I met the train, collected the envelope, gave the carrier another half-a-crown and departed the terminus. In the taxi back to the office I leafed through the pages and my brow furrowed. This was not *Lady Chatterley's Lover.* I gave it to my brother Murray; before joining the firm he had spent several years with Heinemann and was familiar with Lawrence. (He now has his own successful agency.) Shortly he declared we had an unpublished version; and so it was, for this was *John Thomas and Lady Jane.* So we arranged that Heinemann should publish it and also *The First Lady Chatterley,* which had never been published in England but had been issued by the Dial Press in the United States. I commend to your attention the Publisher's Note to these volumes by Roland Gant, then Editorial Director of Heinemann.

Heinemann, and later the Viking Press in the United States, issued both of these volumes, which are of course still in copyright. I had always hoped Heinemann would issue all three in like format, but they never did. The only publisher to issue all three in one volume was Mondadori in Italy (in 1954). I suppose I should add that there are translations and editions all over the world, and new arrangements are constantly being made for publication. The most recent in Britain was the appearance in newspaper form in the Complete Bestsellers series of the edition originally published in Germany by the Odyssey Press.

The important and definitive edition of *Lady Chatterley's Lover* will be issued by Cambridge University Press in cloth and paperback editions, complete with textual apparatus, edited by Michael Squires. Granada will then issue the book in cloth and paperback without the apparatus and footnotes. To prepare this edition involves a considerable amount of work because of the many extant versions—some edited, some expurgated, some bowdlerized—but the result will be a milestone in the Lawrence canon.

And to set the record straight, I shall touch briefly on other media. In France the motion picture of *Lady Chatterley's Lover* was made by Daniel Angel Productions, starring Leo Genn and Danielle Darrieux, and the rights were later assigned to M.G.M. The proposed N.B.C. television version (was Joanne Woodward cast?) did not proceed because of copyright problems. The second version, *John Thomas and Lady Jane,* has not been produced as yet. *The First Lady Chatterley,* starring Sylvia Kristel, was made recently by Cannon Films, who incorrectly titled it *Lady Chatterley's Lover;* the producers announced it before discussing an offer, then agreed terms, but have not yet signed the contract, even though the film has been released. An unrelated soft-porn film called *The Young Lady Chatterley* also appeared some years ago, for which M.G.M. supplied the opticals.

The production of the novel itself appeared in some detail in *Priest of Love* (the film based on Harry T. Moore's biography of Lawrence), and the producer/director, Christopher Miles, undertook a great deal of research and trouble to check the type of paper, binding, and the like so that the film would be authentic. The next time it will be featured is in *Frieda,* Richard Bates's production of Frieda Lawrence's *Not I, But the Wind.* . . .

May I leave you with a smile? Our dramatic associates, Margery Vosper, Ltd., were recently approached by a Japanese impresario who wanted to produce a musical version of *Lady Chatterley's Lover* on ice! But as I said at the beginning, this is not the whole story . . .

Contributors

T. H. ADAMOWSKI is a professor of English at Erindale College, University of Toronto. His essays on Lawrence, Faulkner, Sartre, and other authors have been published in the *D. H. Lawrence Review, Critical Inquiry, University of Toronto Quarterly, Dalhousie Review, Mosaic, Canadian Review of American Studies,* and other journals.

GAVRIEL BEN-EPHRAIM is a lecturer in English at the Hebrew University of Jerusalem. Author of *The Moon's Dominion: Narrative Dichotomy and Female Dominance in Lawrence's Earlier Novels,* he has also written on Dickens, Forster, Sophocles, and others. He is now working on a study of the destructive imagination in romantic literature.

LYDIA BLANCHARD is on the faculty of the Department of English at Southwest Texas State University. Her essays on Lawrence have appeared in *Mosaic, Modern Fiction Studies,* the *D. H. Lawrence Review,* and in the collections *D. H. Lawrence: The Man Who Lived* and *Lawrence and Women.* She has also published on women and literature in such journals as *Studies in the Novel, Literary Review,* and *Style.*

ZACK BOWEN is chairman of the department and a professor of English at the University of Delaware. He is the author of *Mary Lavin, Musical Allusions in the Works of James Joyce,* and *Padraic Colum;* the general editor of the *Irish Renaissance Annual;* and the author of more than forty articles on James Joyce and other modern writers.

JAMES C. COWAN is the founding editor (1968–1984) of the *D. H. Lawrence Review,* author of *D. H. Lawrence's American Journey: A Study in Literature and Myth,* editor of *D. H. Lawrence: An Annotated Bibliography of Writings About Him,* and author of numerous articles on Lawrence and other writers. He is Research Professor in the Department of Social and Administrative Medicine, University of North Carolina School of Medicine, Chapel Hill.

KEITH CUSHMAN is a professor of English at the University of North Carolina at Greensboro. He is the author of *D. H. Lawrence at Work* and, with E. Claire Healey, he is editing the correspondence between Lawrence and Amy Lowell. His many published essays include studies of Lawrence, Joyce, Kafka, Beckett, Fitzgerald, Larkin, Ted Hughes, Bellow, Philip Roth, Anaïs Nin, Hardy, Trollope, and Dowson.

EVELYN J. HINZ is a professor of English at the University of Manitoba. Official biographer of Anaïs Nin, her publications include a critical study (*The Mirror and the Garden*), an edition of scholarly essays (*The World of Anaïs Nin*), and an edition of Nin's interviews and lectures (*A Woman Speaks*). She has edited *Mosaic* since 1979. Among her scholarly articles is a discussion of marriage as an index of genre, which was awarded the William Riley Parker Prize for an outstanding essay published in *PMLA*.

DENNIS JACKSON is an associate professor of English at the University of Delaware and the editor of the *D. H. Lawrence Review*. He is managing editor of the *Irish Renaissance Annual*, editor of "Newspaper Writing as Art" (special issue, *Style*), associate editor of *D. H. Lawrence: An Annotated Bibliography of Writings About Him*, and compiler of a bibliography that formed a chapter of A *D. H. Lawrence Handbook*. His articles on Lawrence and other subjects have appeared in the *D. H. Lawrence Review, British Book News, Etc., Style,* and elsewhere.

FREDERICK P. W. McDOWELL, professor of English at the University of Iowa, is the author of *E. M. Forster* and the editor of *E. M. Forster: An Annotated Bibliography of Writings About Him*. In addition to essays on Forster and other authors, he has published books on Ellen Glasgow, Elizabeth Madox Roberts, and Caroline Gordon.

CRAIG MUNRO is head of the Editorial Department at the University of Queensland Press. He edited the anthology *New Australian Stories* and is the author of *Wild Man of Letters,* a biography of the writer and publisher P. R. Stephensen.

GERALD J. POLLINGER is the managing director of Laurence Pollinger Limited, Authors' Agents, London, and the literary executor of the Estate of Frieda Lawrence Ravagli. He is also the author or coauthor of a number of standard books on the identification of aircraft, having devised the recognition system adopted by NATO. In addition, he has written several books on model railroads, on which he is an authority.

SCOTT R. SANDERS is a professor of English at Indiana University. Among his critical writings are studies in the sociology of literature, essays on speculative fiction, and a book on Lawrence, *D. H. Lawrence: The World of the Five Major Novels.* His books of fiction include *Wilderness Plots, Fetching the Dead,* and a forthcoming novel about John James Audubon.

MICHAEL SQUIRES, professor of English at the Virginia Polytechnic Institute and State University, has published *The Pastoral Novel: Studies in George Eliot, Thomas Hardy, and D. H. Lawrence,* and *The Creation of "Lady Chatterley's Lover."* He is editing the third version of *Lady Chatterley's Lover,* which will be published by Cambridge University Press.

JOHN J. TEUNISSEN is a professor of English and acting head of the department at the University of Manitoba. He has coedited Roger Williams's *A Key into the Language of America* and Henry Miller's *The World of Lawrence,* and has edited *Other Worlds: Fantasy and Science Fiction Since 1939.* Author or coauthor of numerous essays on American, British, and Canadian literature, he edits the *Canadian Review of American Studies.*

Index

250